AF703865

'Focusing on Great Britain, Rosenblatt offers the first empirical results on this subject, making it a must-read for anybody who is interested in the relationship between Restorative Justice and Communities. It should be on the bookshelf of any serious scholar in this area. The future lies in works like this.'

Elmar G.M. Weitekamp, *Ph.D., University of Tübingen, Germany*

'In *The Role of Community in Restorative Justice*, Rosenblatt confronts the mythology of government programs that claim to be "restorative" by exploring the concept of community more closely and examining how it is employed. She provides an excellent assessment and critique of how youth justice panels in the United Kingdom fall far short of meaningful community involvement. Her work will inspire others to scrutinize the implementation of restorative justice initiatives to ensure fidelity to its fundamental premises.'

Ted Wachtel, *President, IIRP Graduate School, USA*

'This book represents an important contribution to restorative justice scholarship by providing theoretically-informed and empirically-rich insights into the role of community in restorative practices. Rosenblatt gives us a nuanced and balanced appraisal of the restorative pretentions of youth offender panels in theory and in practice, as well as the benefits and challenges of engaging community members in such processes. The book will be of considerable interest and value to all those – academics, policymakers and practitioners, both in the UK and beyond – who are seeking to advance community involvement in dispute resolution and justice systems more generally.'

Adam Crawford, *Professor of Criminology and Criminal Justice, University of Leeds, UK*

The Role of Community in Restorative Justice

Although restorative justice is probably one of the most talked about topics in contemporary criminology, little has been written about how community involvement in restorative justice translates into practice. While advocates have presented the community as an essential pillar of restorative justice, the rationale for why and how this is the case remains underdeveloped and largely unchallenged. This book offers an empirical and theoretical explanation of what 'community involvement' means and what work it does in restorative justice.

Drawing on an empirical case study and the wider sociological literature, *The Role of Community in Restorative Justice* examines the involvement of the community in one selected practice of restorative justice, and also considers the implications of the English and Welsh experience for development of a more coherent framework for operationalising community involvement in restorative justice practices. It is argued that restorative justice programmes need to start from a more concrete and up-to-date notion of community. While operationalising community involvement, they need to acknowledge, all at once: the importance of place; the importance of family links, friendship and other social ties; and the importance of similar social traits and identities.

This book is essential reading for students, researchers and academics in the fields of criminology, criminal justice, sociology, community studies, policy studies, social policy and socio-legal studies. It will also be valuable reading for a variety of practitioners and policymakers, particularly working with restorative justice and youth justice.

Fernanda Fonseca Rosenblatt is an Assistant Professor in Law at the Catholic University of Pernambuco (UNICAP), Brazil, where she teaches Criminal Law and Criminal Procedure. Fernanda completed her DPhil in Criminology at the Centre for Criminology, University of Oxford, in January 2014. In 2005 she was awarded a Master's degree from the Catholic University of Leuven, Belgium. Fernanda is currently a member of the Executive Committee of the World Society of Victimology. She is also a member of the Asa Branca Research Group of Criminology (UNICAP, Brazil). Her areas of expertise are: Restorative Justice, Community (Justice), Youth Justice and Street Children.

Routledge Frontiers of Criminal Justice

1. Sex Offenders: Punish, Help, Change or Control?
Theory, policy and practice explored
Edited by Jo Brayford, Francis Cowe and John Deering

2. Building Justice in Post-Transition Europe
Processes of criminalisation within Central and Eastern European societies
Edited by Kay Goodall, Margaret Malloch and Bill Munro

3. Technocrime, Policing and Surveillance
Edited by Stéphane Leman-Langlois

4. Youth Justice in Context
Community, compliance and young people
Mairead Seymour

5. Women, Punishment and Social Justice
Human rights and penal practices
Margaret Malloch and Gill McIvor

6. Handbook of Policing, Ethics and Professional Standards
Edited by Allyson MacVean, Peter Spindler and Charlotte Solf

7. Contrasts in Punishment
An explanation of Anglophone excess and Nordic exceptionalism
John Pratt and Anna Eriksson

8. Victims of Environmental Harm
Rights, recognition and redress under National and International
Matthew Hall

9. Doing Probation Work
Identity in a criminal justice occupation
Rob C. Mawby and Anne Worrall

10. Justice Reinvestment
Can the criminal justice system deliver more for less?
Chris Fox, Kevin Albertson and Kevin Wong

11. Epidemiological Criminology
Theory to practice
Edited by Eve Waltermaurer and Timothy A. Akers

12. Policing cities
Urban securitization and regulation in a 21st century world
Edited by Randy K. Lippert and Kevin Walby

13. Restorative Justice in Transition
Kerry Clamp

14. International perspectives on police education and training
Edited by Perry Stanislas

15. Understanding Penal Practice
Edited by Ioan Durnescu and Fergus McNeill

16. Perceptions of Criminal Justice
Vicky De Mesmaecker

17. Transforming Criminal Justice?
Problem-solving and court specialization
Jane Donoghue

18. Policing in Taiwan
From authoritarianism to democracy
Liqun Cao, Lanying Huang and Ivan Y. Sun

19. Reparation for Victims of Crimes against Humanity
The healing role of reparation
Edited by Jo-Anne M. Wemmers

20. Victims of Violence and Restorative Practices
Finding a Voice
Tinneke Van Camp

21. Long-Term Imprisonment and Human Rights
Edited by Kirstin Drenkhahn, Manuela Dudeck and Frieder Dünkel

22. Working within the Forensic Paradigm
Cross-discipline approaches for policy and practice
Edited by Rosemary Sheehan and James Ogloff

23. Positive Criminology
Edited by Natti Ronel and Dana Segev

24. Inmates' Narratives and Discursive Discipline in Prison
Rewriting personal histories through cognitive behavioral programs in prison
Jennifer A. Schlosser

25. Municipal Corporate Security in International Context
Kevin Walby and Randy K. Lippert

26. Victims and Restorative Justice
Edited by Ivo Aertsen, Inge Vanfraechem and Daniela Bolivar

27. The Role of Community in Restorative Justice
Fernanda Fonseca Ronseblatt

The Role of Community in Restorative Justice

Fernanda Fonseca Rosenblatt

Routledge
Taylor & Francis Group
LONDON AND NEW YORK

First published 2015
by Routledge
2 Park Square, Milton Park, Abingdon, Oxfordshire OX14 4RN

and by Routledge
711 Third Avenue, New York, NY 10017

First issued in paperback 2016

Routledge is an imprint of the Taylor & Francis Group, an informa business

© 2015 Fernanda Fonseca Rosenblatt

The right of Fernanda Fonseca Rosenblatt to be identified as author of this work has been asserted by her in accordance with sections 77 and 78 of the Copyright, Designs and Patents Act 1988.

All rights reserved. No part of this book may be reprinted or reproduced or utilised in any form or by any electronic, mechanical, or other means, now known or hereafter invented, including photocopying and recording, or in any information storage or retrieval system, without permission in writing from the publishers.

Trademark notice: Product or corporate names may be trademarks or registered trademarks, and are used only for identification and explanation without intent to infringe.

Simultaneously published in the USA and Canada

British Library Cataloguing in Publication Data
A catalogue record for this book is available from the British Library

Library of Congress Cataloging in Publication Data
Rosenblatt, Fernanda Fonseca.
The role of community in restorative justice / Fernanda Fonseca Rosenblatt. – First Edition.
pages cm. – (Routledge frontiers of criminal justice ; 27)
Includes bibliographical references.
1. Restorative justice. 2. Communities. I. Title.
HV8688.R667 2015
364.6'8–dc23
2014049172

ISBN 13: 978-1-138-28870-6 (pbk)

ISBN 13: 978-1-138-85895-4 (hbk)

Typeset in Times New Roman
by Taylor & Francis Books

Contents

	List of illustrations	x
	List of statutes	xi
	Foreword	xii
	Acknowledgement	xiv
	Abbreviations	xvi
	Introduction	1
1	The restorative justice 'spirit'	5
2	Restorative justice's problematic appeals to community	41
3	Selecting a case study of community involvement in restorative justice	66
4	Notes on an empirical study	83
5	Youth offender panels: A play in three acts	90
6	The role of community in youth offender panels	128
7	Towards a coherent framework for operationalising community involvement in restorative justice programmes	175
	Conclusions	207
	Index	218

List of illustrations

Figures

6.1 The socio-demographics of community panel members in YOT11 141
6.2 The socio-demographics of community panel members in a London YOT 142

Tables

5.1 The Scaled Approach and supervision levels 97
5.2 Panel attendance (offender's family members and supporters) 103
5.3 Guide to the hours of community reparation 109
5.4 Report vs. contract 111

List of statutes

Crime and Courts Act 2013
Crime and Disorder Act 1998
Criminal Justice and Immigration Act 2008
Legal Aid, Sentencing and Punishment of Offenders Act 2012
Powers of Criminal Courts (Sentencing) Act 2000
Rehabilitation of Offenders Act 1974
Youth Justice and Criminal Evidence Act 1999

Foreword

Over the past decade there has been more ink spilled and academic attention devoted to restorative justice than almost all other criminological topics, and all the time, practice on the ground has been rather thin. Why then do we need a further monograph on restorative justice? The answer has to be that we do not need more of the same, but that what we do hunger for is good scholarship on the role of community in restorative interventions.

Until now, this topic – unlike other areas of restorative justice – has been under-researched, both empirically and theoretically. Hence, this book provides a useful and important contribution to the restorative canon. It is innovative in that it develops an original theoretical analysis of what 'community involvement' means and how it works in restorative justice. Thorough empirical research is conducted in youth offending teams observing youth offender panels and interviewing participants, and the author makes recommendations for how 'community' might be understood and operationalised in restorative justice programmes. Given the lacuna in the literature on 'community' in restorative justice, this book is a welcome addition to our libraries and may well emerge as a 'classic' in this somewhat barren field.

While this monograph does not try to present an analysis of broader notions of community involvement in the official responses to crime, or of notions of community beyond criminal justice, it does draw on the wider sociological literature on community; for example, on critiques of communitarianism and the criticisms that came to dominate the informal justice literature in the 1980s. When exploring the 'whys' of community involvement in criminal justice practices, the author brings to the fore discussions on the role of community in other 'non-restorative justice' movements or initiatives, ranging from Neighbourhood Watch to volunteer involvement in community service orders. In other words, the book brings together thorough empirical and theoretical research to provide a valuable in-depth study of the role of community in restorative justice.

This book is based on rigorous empirical research, with meticulous attention to detail. The rather brief methods chapter contained herein does not do justice to the laborious and careful data collection process that resulted in the powerful material presented in the following chapters. Fonseca Rosenblatt travelled across England and Wales visiting the offices of many Youth Offending Teams, interviewing staff and observing panel meetings, followed by further interviews with panel participants. She got to know the length and breadth of this initially foreign country and, in that time, the very many colloquial expressions of its citizens, helping her to communicate with those who may initially have been surprised by her Brazilian accent. Her commitment to the empirical endeavour was most impressive and was rewarded by a rich, thick database of material.

One of the problems of collecting and presenting empirical research is that in the absence of a comparative approach that explicitly draws on material from across various jurisdictions, the data will always, inevitably, be particular to the country where it is collected. This, of course, begs the question of what there is within these covers for those interested in restorative justice and community beyond the shores of England and Wales. The answer lies in the critical approach of the author. Readers from other jurisdictions will be able to turn her critical lens on their own criminal justice systems, and indeed in Chapter 7 the author explicitly considers the implications of the English and Welsh experience for development of a more coherent framework for operationalising community involvement in restorative justice practices in general. That is, she reflects on what other countries could learn from the English and Welsh experience, and in other chapters contrasts these empirical data with previous findings of community involvement in restorative justice initiatives elsewhere (for example, family group conferencing in New Zealand, sentencing circles in Canada, and reparative boards in the USA). Hence, while not an explicitly comparative approach, this book presents an English case study within an international context of research on community involvement in restorative justice. Furthermore, it is fair to say, youth offender panels – of the type described here – have much in common with other initiatives across the world (they are very similar, for example, to the reparative boards in Vermont). Hence, the findings should have international appeal. Fonseca Rosenblatt's theatrical metaphor for the presentation of the empirical data is particularly persuasive, and something with which those from overseas will no doubt identify.

When Fernanda Fonseca Rosenblatt arrived in the UK to start her PhD, her written English was good, but imperfect. A diligent and tenacious academic, she was determined to learn to write so that her ideas could be shared by people around the world. The proof of her success is within this book.

Professor Carolyn Hoyle
December 2014, Oxford

Acknowledgement

This book is based on doctoral research I conducted while in the Centre for Criminology at the University of Oxford. First and foremost, I am grateful to my supervisor, Professor Carolyn Hoyle, for her 'restorative' approach to supervision. Our meetings always felt like restorative encounters: after each one, I felt empowered to do more and to do better. Moreover, this book is far stronger for the comments, corrections and constructive criticism that I have received from her. Of course, any limitations and shortcomings remain entirely my own. Thank you, Professor Hoyle. One could not wish for a better supervisor!

Assurances of anonymity mean that I cannot do so by name, but I would also like to thank those individuals who agreed to be interviewed and/or observed for this research, or who helped me in the process of gaining and sustaining access to my research sites and participants. A special thank you to the community panel members. By giving up their time to help other people in trouble, they have taught me that I can become a better person. I hope they understand that this book criticises the process of youth offender panels, not them.

For transcribing over 50 hours of audio into written interviews, I thank Kate Hillier and Liz Almond. I am also indebted to them for proofreading the thesis on which this book is based – and for 'controlling' my Brazilian style of writing.

This study has been supported by funding from CAPES, an agency under the Brazilian Ministry of Education. I have also received an Oxford University Law Faculty Travel Grant, a Worcester College Travel Grant, a Travel Grant from the Dutch Ministry of Foreign Affairs, and a Travel Grant from the International Institute for Restorative Practices, all of which have allowed me to attend and present papers at several conferences, providing me with additional opportunities for constructive feedback. I am very grateful to all of these institutions for the funding they provided and for having faith in me and in the value of this research.

Thanks also to John Wiley & Sons, Bloomsbury, the American Society of Criminology and Taylor and Francis for their kind permission to reproduce previously published materials in this book.

For helpful comments and advice throughout the process – including the opportunity to go to Belgium to present my research aims – I would like to thank my 'Leuven family'. A special thank you to Ivo Aertsen, Lode Walgrave and Stephan Parmentier, whose support has opened professional doors for me which otherwise would have remained closed. For their encouragement and trust in my potential as a researcher, I would like to thank Dawn Rothe, Ester Kosovki, Jorge Zaverucha, Martin Wright, Mary Bosworth, Robert Peacock and Ted Wachtel. A special thank you to Martin Wright for reading and commenting on earlier drafts of this book in its various forms. For making my DPhil life less lonely, I am deeply thankful to my Centre for Criminology friends: Angela Sherwood, Daniel Alati, Daniel Pascoe, Harry Annison, George Mawhinney, Marie Manikis, Marion Vannier and Rudina Jasini, among many others. I am also deeply indebted to Elmar Weitekamp and Rachel Condry, who were my examiners; their constructive criticism of my DPhil thesis was invaluable to me in preparing this book. I also wish to thank the anonymous reviewers selected by Routledge for their thought-provoking comments on my manuscript.

I am enormously grateful for the encouragement of numerous Brazilian friends and colleagues throughout the process of turning my thesis into this book. In particular, I would like to thank my fellow members of the *Asa Branca* Research Group of Criminology (at Universidade Católica de Pernambuco), Marilia Mello, Carolina Salazar, Erica Babini, Helena Castro and Manuela Abath, whose support greatly eased my 'reintegration' into the Brazilian academic world.

Finally, completing this work would have been impossible were it not for the support and encouragement of my 'community of care'. Thank you to my parents-in-law, Izaias and Aronita Rosenblatt, for their kindness and endless encouragement. Thank you to my brother, Lúcio Fonseca, for being one of my true believers and for gifting me with the best nephew (Bernardo Fonseca) that I could have hoped for. Thank you to my mother, Lucimar Fonseca, for being a part of me, a constant source of inspiration, and the safe harbour that I can turn to at any time. Thank you to my father, Fernando Fonseca, who after a childhood of poverty, earned a doctoral degree (at the University of Kent) and developed a successful academic career. You, *Painho*, have been my biggest source of inspiration since I was of the age to understand what I wanted to be when I grew up. Last, but not least, thank you to my loving husband, Paulo Rosenblatt, for his support and patience during the duration of this research and final write-up of this book. As he mentions in the acknowledgements of his book, pursuing a doctoral degree abroad was the topic of our first date. I am so glad that we did this, and I would never have been able to do it without him.

Fernanda Fonseca Rosenblatt
December 2014, Recife

Abbreviations

AOPM	Association of Panel Members
ASBO	Anti-Social Behaviour Order
ASSET	Young Offender Assessment Profile
CJS	Criminal Justice System
CPD	Australian Centre for Policy Development
CPM	community panel member
CRB	Criminal Records Bureau
CV	curriculum vitae
GCSE	General Certificate of Secondary Education
NACRO	National Association for the Care and Resettlement of Offenders
RJ	restorative justice
RJC	Restorative Justice Council
RJCF	Restorative Justice Conference Facilitation (training)
RSQM	Restorative Justice Quality Mark
UNODC	United Nations Office on Drugs and Crime
YCS	Youth Conferencing Service (Northern Ireland)
YJB	Youth Justice Board for England and Wales
YJILS	Youth Justice Interactive Learning Space
YOS	Youth Offending Service
YOT	Youth Offending Team
YP	young person
YRO	Youth Rehabilitation Order

Introduction

The question of *whether* the community should be involved in modern criminal justice practice is an outdated one; the institutions of the jury and the lay magistracy in England and Wales, for example, show that participatory democracy has long been at the heart of criminal justice systems (Crawford 2004). Although we can see that both institutions (the jury and the lay magistracy) periodically come under threat – particularly the jury for trials of complicated serious offences, such as certain corporate crimes or fraud – this has not stopped governments from promoting the idea of citizens as 'partners against crime' (Crawford 2003). In fact, in times of 'late modernity' it has become increasingly common to emphasise that government agencies (or, indeed, the state) cannot do business alone; they 'must devolve power and share the work of social [and crime] control with local organizations and communities' (Garland 2001: 205). Restorative justice's appeals to community, thus, sit within a wider 'late modern' criminal justice landscape where the limitations of the state's capacity to control crime have become ever more apparent.

What still remain highly controversial, though, are the issues of *why*, precisely, and *how* community involvement should occur. In this context, the restorative justice literature has made some interesting contributions to the debate. On the one hand, it has drawn attention to the fact that current forms of community participation in criminal justice practice are too superficial to enable meaningful outcomes – *so we need to find more meaningful ways of involving the community.* On the other hand, restorativists have revisited the reasons why the community should be involved in criminal justice practice but added new (restorative) goals – *so now we have 'all the reasons we need' to pursue more meaningful community participation.*

This all sounds very good and worthwhile, and hard to argue against. As Bauman (2001) reflected, 'community' is one of those words that has a good feeling rather than just a meaning, so the idea of community involvement in criminal/restorative justice practices 'feels' good. However, as will be further explored throughout this study, one should bear in mind that in order to justify community participation in restorative justice practices, scholars have often relied on assumptions that have not yet been empirically verified. The work undertaken in this book is aimed at confronting such assumptions. Indeed, motivated by the questions of *why* (that is, *for what purposes*) and *how* (that is, *within what limits and under which conditions*) the community should be involved in restorative justice practices, the aim of this study is to advance our empirical and theoretical understanding of what 'community involvement' *means* and *what work it does* in restorative justice.

In this way, in the first part of the book (Chapters 1–2), I draw mainly on the restorative justice literature to identify and explore the theoretical justifications for community participation in restorative processes, and to problematise the role of community in restorative justice. Because restorative justice advocates do not all have precisely the same thing in mind when they speak of restorative justice, Chapter 1 begins by giving a clear view of what I have in mind when I refer to it – providing, in turn, a brief overview of restorative justice's main attributes. Chapter 2 sets out the problem that this study aims to address and reviews existing studies that have touched upon the issue. In this vein, it is aimed at answering three basic questions. First, *why do restorativists promote the involvement of the community in restorative justice practices?* Second, *how has the community typically been involved in restorative justice programmes?* Third, *what remains unclear about the role of community in restorative justice?* It is against this theoretical background that I shall later consider my empirical findings.

The second part of the book (Chapters 3–6) is devoted to empirically exploring *why* and *how* the community has been involved in one selected practice of restorative justice, namely youth offender panels in England and Wales.[1] The reasons why a case study design was chosen, along with the motives for selecting youth offender panels as a case study, are detailed in Chapter 3. Chapter 4 offers an outline of the research process. It describes the methods of data collection and analysis employed, providing justification for their use and an explanation of the various steps involved. In Chapter 5, I begin presenting my empirical findings by providing a detailed narrative description of how youth offender panels operate on the ground. Drawing on the findings presented in Chapter 5 and on further empirical data, Chapter 6 sets out the key themes that emerged from the data, and discusses these themes in relation to the literature.

Finally, pulling the previous chapters together, and drawing on the wider theoretical literature on 'community' from outside the field of restorative justice, I consider the implications of the English and Welsh experience for development of a more coherent framework for operationalising community involvement in restorative justice practices. In this vein, Chapter 7 first reflects on the restorativeness of youth offender panels, particularly on issues related to community involvement. It then draws on the wider sociological literature – for example, on critiques of communitarianism (e.g. Bauman 2001; Young 1999), and the criticisms that came to dominate the informal justice literature in the 1980s (e.g. Abel 1982; Santos 1982) – so as to revisit restorative justice's problematic appeals to community. By doing so, I shall arrive at an answer to the question of what lessons can be learned from the English and Welsh experience – in other words, it is in Chapter 7 that I reflect on how the outputs arising from an English and Welsh case study on youth offender panels might be of interest to restorative justice academics and practitioners from other countries. The concluding chapter (Conclusions) then summarises the analysis provided in the previous chapters, highlights the achievements and limitations of this study, and provides suggestions on which directions future research might take.

It is important to note that while there has been considerable academic focus on other themes, such as the potential of restorative justice to satisfy victims, little has been written about how 'community involvement' translates into practice (Ashworth 2001; Bolivar 2012; Crawford 2002; Dzur and Olson 2004; Hudson 1998; McCold 1996, 2004; Pavlich 2001, 2004; Vanfraechem 2007; Walgrave 2002; Weisberg 2003; Zehr 2002). On the other hand, there has been no up-to-date study of the restorative component of referral orders, and certainly not on the role of community in youth offender panels. Indeed, the evaluation of the pilot areas (Newburn *et al.* 2002), which was conducted over 10 years ago, is still today the most comprehensive study on referral orders and youth offender panels. This book therefore contributes to the restorative justice literature by confronting the assumptions underlying restorative justice's appeals to community, but it also provides a current analysis of referral orders and youth offender panels in times when the UK government is to invest 'at least £29 million to help deliver restorative justice over the coming three years'.[2] The hope, overall, is for this book to contribute to the growing body of critical scholarship on restorative justice.

Notes

1 The United Kingdom does not have a unified legal system – England and Wales have one system, while Scotland and Northern Ireland each have their own system. The present study covers one jurisdiction, thus – that of England and Wales.

2 In late 2013, then Justice Minister Damian Green announced that millions of pounds would be made available over the next three years for restorative justice. For more details, see www.standard.co.uk/panewsfeeds/29m-for-restorative-justice-scheme-8947979.html.

References

Abel, R.L. (1982) 'The Contradictions of Informal Justice', in R.L. Abel (ed.), *The Politics of Informal Justice*, New York: Academic Press.

Ashworth, A. (2001) 'Is Restorative Justice the Way Forward for Criminal Justice?', *Current Legal Problems*, 54(1): 347–376.

Bauman, Z. (2001) *Community: Seeking Safety in an Insecure World*, Cambridge: Polity.

Bolivar, D. (2012) 'Community of Care from a victim-perspective: A Qualitative Study', *Contemporary Justice Review*, 15(1): 17–37.

Crawford, A. (2002) 'The State, Community and Restorative Justice: Heresy, Nostalgia and Butterfly Collecting', in L. Walgrave (ed.), *Restorative Justice and the Law*, Cullompton: Willan Publishing.

Crawford, A. (2003) 'In the Hands of the Public?', in G. Johnstone (ed.), *A Restorative Justice Reader: Texts, Sources, Context*, Cullompton: Willan Publishing.

Crawford, A. (2004) 'Involving Lay People in Criminal Justice', *Criminology & Public Policy*, 3(4): 693–702.

Dzur, A.W. and Olson, S.M. (2004) 'The Value of Community Participation in Restorative Justice', *Journal of Social Philosophy*, 35(1): 91–107.

Garland, D. (2001) *The Culture of Control: Crime and Social Order in Contemporary Society*, Oxford: Oxford University Press.

Hudson, B. (1998) 'Restorative Justice: The Challenge of Sexual and Racial Violence', *Journal of Law and Society*, 25(2): 237–256.

McCold, P. (1996) 'Restorative Justice and the Role of Community', in B. Galaway and J. Hudson (eds), *Restorative Justice: International Perspectives*, Monsey, NY: Criminal Justice Press.

McCold, P. (2004) 'What is the Role of Community in Restorative Justice Theory and Practice?', in H. Zehr and B. Toews (eds), *Critical Issues in Restorative Justice*, Monsey, NY: Criminal Justice Press.

Newburn, T., Crawford, A., Earle, R., Goldie, S., Hale, C., Hallam, A., Masters, G., Netten, A., Saunders, R., Sharpe, K. and Uglow, S. (2002) *The Introduction of Referral Orders into the Youth Justice System: Final Report*, Home Office Research Study 242, London: Home Office.

Pavlich, G. (2001) 'The Force of Community', in J. Braithwaite and H. Strang (eds), *Restorative Justice and Civil Society*, Cambridge: Cambridge University Press.

Pavlich, G. (2004) 'What are the Dangers as Well as the Promise of Community Involvement?', in H. Zehr and B. Toews (eds), *Critical Issues in Restorative Justice*, Monsey, NY: Criminal Justice Press.

Santos, B.d.S. (1982) 'Law and Community: The Changing Nature of State Power in Later Capitalism', in R. Abel (ed.), *The Politics of Informal Justice*, New York: Academic Press.

Vanfraechem, I. (2007) 'Community, Society and State in Restorative Justice: Some Reflections', in R. Mackay, M. Bosjnak, J. Deklerck, C. Pelikan, B.V. Stokkom and M. Wright (eds), *Images of Restorative Justice Theory*, Frankfurt am Main: Verlag fur Polizei und Wissenschaft.

Walgrave, L. (2002) 'From Community to Dominion: In Search of Social Values for Restorative Justice', in E.G.M. Weitekamp and H.-J. Kerner (eds), *Restorative Justice: Theoretical Foundations*, Cullompton: Willan Publishing.

Weisberg, R. (2003) 'Restorative Justice and the Danger of "Community"', *Utah Law Review*: 343–374.

Young, J. (1999) *The Exclusive Society*, London: SAGE Publications.

Zehr, H. (2002) *Fundamental Principles of Restorative Justice*, Intercourse, PA: Good Books.

1 The restorative justice 'spirit'

Restorative justice is probably one of the most talked about topics in contemporary criminology. In fact, 'it is now the rare professional conference, journal, or textbook dealing with criminal justice that does not make room for restorative justice topics' (Dzur and Olson 2004: 92).[1] There has also been a considerable development in academic courses devoted to the field – to the point that there now exists a graduate school entirely devoted to restorative practices.[2] Restorative justice has also achieved a great deal of recognition outside the academy. Indeed, governments are increasingly incorporating 'restorative justice language' into their laws and political discourses and, while not without problems, restorative justice is drawing support from both liberal and conservative policymakers (Levrant *et al.* 1999). Also, criminal justice systems increasingly proclaim themselves to be embracing the 'restorative justice philosophy' through a variety of practices adopted at different stages of the criminal process, and performed by people who are allegedly trained to think and act more 'restoratively' (Johnstone 2011).

In this context, some commentators claim that restorative justice has been 'one of the most significant developments in criminal justice and criminological practice and thinking over the past two decades' (Crawford and Newburn 2003: 19; see also Walgrave *et al.* 2013). Others suggest that 'no movement in recent memory has captured the imagination of those interested in crime, society, and governance in the way that restorative justice has' (Wheeldon 2009: 91). Be that as it may, restorative justice 'is now not only an ideal proposed by a small group of progressive criminologists and criminal justice practitioners' (Hudson 2005: 64). The campaign for restorative justice has moved far beyond that.

How far? Well, probably further than Howard Zehr would have imagined when he wrote his classic *Changing Lenses* (1990) to propose a 'restorative model' of thinking about crime and justice. Indeed, while some authors (e.g. Walgrave 2008) remain faithful to a more restricted notion of restorative justice wherein the focus is invariably on crime, or suggest a theoretically conservative model of restorative justice where only a few practices can be considered restorative or 'fully' restorative (e.g. McCold 2000), others now have a broader focus on the potential of restorative justice for 'social transformation' (e.g. Woolford 2009). Caught by such enthusiasm, campaigns have gone so far as to promote the creation of 'restorative cities', or even 'restorative counties'.[3]

The campaign for restorative justice has not only expanded in terms of focus, but also geographically. Indeed, restorative justice debates are now taking place in countries all over the world and on every continent,[4] and resonating even at the supra-national level (see Roberts 2003), whereas 30 years ago it was 'a largely white, North American and European vision to fundamentally change [their] juvenile and criminal justice systems' (Umbreit and Armour 2011: ix). Today, initiatives under the label of 'restorative justice' are flourishing all over the world to deal with criminalisable matters and non-criminal quarrels (e.g. in schools), to cases of interpersonal violence and of mass victimisation (e.g. cases of genocide in societies in transition), to adults and young people; covering a range of different practices provided by criminal justice agencies and third sector organisations; and being promoted by victim-led as well as offender-led initiatives (Cunneen and Hoyle 2010; Johnstone 2011; Wachtel 2013; Weitekamp *et al.* 2006).

Not surprisingly, it follows that restorative justice advocates do not all have precisely the same thing in mind when they speak of restorative justice (McCold 1998). In fact, restorative justice is a difficult concept to grasp, let alone to summarise. Having said that, this chapter hopes to achieve the following aims: first, to give a rounded view of what I have in mind when I refer to restorative justice; and second, to provide a brief overview of restorative justice's main attributes – which will inevitably reflect my own personal vision of restorative justice. Whilst I hope that this book will make a significant contribution to the literature on restorative justice, the present chapter will not provide new theories or concepts for those who are already familiar with the topic. It was designed to provide information on the basic concepts necessary for understanding the more specific and in-depth discussions of the later chapters.

1.1 Restorative justice as a response to crime

Could restorative justice be a model of substantive and/or procedural justice? A philosophy of conflict resolution? An alternative *to* punishment? An alternative form of punishment? A modality of governance? A form of responsive regulation? A political project? A transformative social movement? A lifestyle? There are many possible starting points for a definition of restorative justice, and authors often slip from one premise to another over time or even throughout the same piece of writing. The truth is that restorative justice still means 'different things to different people' (Fattah 1998b: 393; see also Peters and Aertsen 2000), and it has become quite difficult to be clear about what, precisely, it means to whom. It is probably the case that 'when people now talk about restorative justice, we should not assume that they have in mind an organised activity which occurs at a specific time in a specific place'

(Johnstone 2011: 155). Such blurred visions of restorative justice, though, are 'detrimental for the development of restorative justice in practice, the quality of restorative research and for the credibility of restorative justice in policy' (Walgrave 2012: 35). Therefore, without claiming to tell 'the real story' (Daly 2002), I shall make clear from the outset what I have in mind when I refer to restorative justice.

Until about a decade ago, the predominant focus of restorative justice advocates was on crime and on the ways in which the aftermath of a criminal act should be handled. The feasibility (and/or desirability) of restorative justice to deal with non-criminal matters – in schools, in the workplace, or in residential care, for example – is markedly *not* discussed in the literature of the 1990s. So although the meaning of restorative justice has never been entirely clear, while the focus was on crime, 'it was possible to form a fairly clear impression of what people had in mind when they referred to "restorative justice"' (Johnstone 2011: 154). In general, they meant a (new) way of dealing with crime. Accordingly, restorative justice debates were largely over the principles – or values – upon which criminal (or youth) justice systems could be reformed, or even replaced, so as to become 'restorative' (see, for example, Bazemore 1996; Bazemore and Walgrave 1999; Fattah 1998a, 1998b; Walgrave 1995, 1998; Weitekamp 1992; Wright 1996b; Zehr 1990).

Nevertheless, as previously mentioned, the focus of the campaign for restorative justice has changed significantly over recent years. Indeed, there has been a fairly widespread view among campaigners that restorative justice has the potential to be part of 'something bigger', as Johnstone (2011: 144) states:

> [...] the focus of the campaign can be understood as having expanded 'downwards' from crime towards more everyday problems of disruptive behaviour and underperformance in schools and workplaces and harmful conduct in everyday life, and 'upwards' from crime towards problems such as political violence, gross violations of human rights, genocide and large-scale historical injustices.

Not everyone shares such ambitions though. Again, according to Johnstone (2011: 157), there is a continuum of minimalist and maximalist thinking about how extensive the views of restorative justice should be:

> At the minimalist end [restorative justice is] seen as applicable to the way we think about and handle crime. Towards the middle, [it is] seen as applicable also to an array of social and political problems and professional tasks. At the maximalist end, [it is] seen as applicable to the way we approach any situation and live our everyday lives.

Within this continuum, scholars such as Walgrave and Vanfraechem, for example, would stand at the 'minimalist' end. They do acknowledge that other deliberative practices (for example, aimed at resolving conflicts in schools) may share much in common with restorative justice, but draw attention to how intrinsically different criminalisable matters are from other injustices and conflicts (Vanfraechem and Walgrave 2009; Walgrave 2008). Moreover, for them, the restorative justice notion 'has been so filled up with meanings, that it risks becoming empty of significance' (Vanfraechem and Walgrave 2009: 2). Therefore, in the name of clarity, the aforementioned authors insist that only practices aimed at dealing with the aftermath of crime should fall under the restorative justice umbrella.

At the other, 'maximalist', end of the continuum stand Hopkins and Wright, for example, according to whom restorative justice should be about 'responding restoratively to all forms of harmful or criminal behaviour in communities, schools, commercial organisations and other contexts' (Hopkins and Wright 2009: 3). Also Roche (2006: 234), for whom restorative justice 'is not just a criminal justice policy, but also a policy for regulating child welfare, schools, corporations, civil litigants, and authoritarian regimes that abuse human rights'. Probably also Braithwaite, who once stated that restorative justice 'is not simply a way of reforming the criminal justice system, it is a way of transforming the entire legal system, our family lives, our conduct in the workplace, our practice of politics' (Braithwaite 2003: 1).

Although at first glance didactic, Johnstone's 'taxonomy' is probably not the most enlightening nor practical of its kind. Unless one clearly expresses an opinion for or against a wider vision of restorative justice, it is nearly impossible to figure out where most scholars stand in this continuum. For example, those in the field of criminology, as a matter of course, tend to talk of restorative justice as a method for dealing with crime – not necessarily because they have a restricted view of restorative justice, but probably to remain within their (and their readers') areas of interest and expertise. Even an abolitionist such as Fattah, for whom there is no qualitative difference between criminal and non-criminal behaviour (Fattah 1997), has consistently referred to restorative justice as a reaction to crime (see Fattah 1998a, 1998b, 2012).

According to Johnstone (2011: 144), '[i]t is probably not an exaggeration to say that Walgrave and others who prefer to focus only on crime no longer represent the mainstream of the campaign for restorative justice'. For me, the bulk of restorative justice literature has been generated from a criminal justice context and it is probably not an exaggeration to say that the mainstream restorative justice literature still tends to focus its attention on criminalisable matters without even reflecting on the possibility of widening the concept of restorative justice. This does not necessarily mean that the majority of restorative justice proponents would not include deliberative practices in social welfare or education within their notions of restorative justice, but it certainly should not lead one to think that the number of 'maximalists' is outpacing the number of 'minimalists'. Even Roche (2006), for example, who explicitly makes the case for a broader definition of restorative justice, acknowledges that what for him are 'restorative justice' initiatives in schools, feature only peripherally in the restorative justice literature.

So, where do I stand on this continuum? Nowhere. I shall explain why. According to McCold (1998: 19), '[o]ne's understanding of restorative justice partly depends upon the early sources of information about the concept and partly from the practices which one first associates with the term'. He is probably right. I am a lawyer whose research interests have always been in the fields of criminal justice and criminology. Also, I had the privilege to be introduced to restorative justice by Professor Walgrave, back in 2004, when I was his student. Further, my 'conversion' (Walgrave 1998) to restorative justice happened whilst I was searching for that 'something better' (than retribution or rehabilitation) in the response to crime, particularly youth crime. Unsurprisingly, I have always seen restorative justice from a criminal justice/criminological standpoint, and I have always believed that extending the notion of restorative justice to include non-criminal matters (which can be stretched to including 'everything') would blur its meaning and make research in the field impracticable (or 'unscientific').

That said, I must admit that, at times, I do feel tempted to agree with those standing at the 'maximalist' end of Johnstone's continuum. During fieldwork conducted for the present study, for example, I have come across several referral order cases involving offences that happened in school, or that involved young people from the same school, or that involved young people who had been (or were about to be) excluded from school due to the school system's traditional punitive approach to discipline. What if restorative justice principles and practices were indeed implemented in schools? Would it not be easier to get the 'victim' (in criminal justice jargon) involved in the process? Would it not be more relevant to include the 'school community' – and not 'detached members' of a 'general community' – in the process? Would the outcome reached in school have the potential of being more 'restorative' than, for instance, some several hours of litter-picking at a graveyard as 'contracted' with the youth offender panel? Ultimately, would it not be more restorative if cases of this sort were dealt with in school?

Probably the answer to all of these questions is 'yes'.[5] Maybe Wright (2010) is correct when he states that the 'philosophy of restorative justice' begins in schools. But why do I choose to remain focused on criminal matters? First, because I believe that a restricted view of restorative justice has nothing to do with the issue of youth (or criminal) justice systems dealing with problems that should be (and were in fact once) dealt with by teachers (or family members, or neighbours, or parochial groups, etc.); the problem of ever expanding criminal and youth justice systems has to do with the complexities embedded in our current 'culture of control' (Garland 2001) which cannot be unravelled by an extended conception of restorative justice. In fact, as Greene (2013: 378) notes, by concentrating on low-level crime or other non-criminal quarrels, 'conflict that may not have been absolutely criminalized (e.g. fights at school, motorists arguing, petty vandalism) is being labelled as more serious so as to "experiment" with it'. That is, by 'using' restorative justice to deal with both criminalisable *and non-criminalisable matters* (such as misbehaviour or antisocial behaviour in school), we may well run the risk of criminalising extra-legal conflicts, and thus of expanding the network of penal control.

Second, I remain focused on criminal matters because although I hope for a world where conflicts of all sorts will be dealt with restoratively, I do not believe in a one-size-fits-all theory of restorative justice. If I am to keep this study under 'methodological control' (Walgrave 2008: 3), I have to be clear about what I have in mind when I refer to restorative justice. I cannot make any sense of this 'something big' applicable to the way we deal with crime and any other problematic situation in any other non-criminal context such as in schools or even at home. The idea of an omnipresent and omnipotent 'restorative justice', for me, is just incompatible with the domain of scientific research.

No one can deny that there is an ongoing – and very welcome – wider social or ideological movement that, guided and inspired by the same participatory and peace-promoting philosophy of restorative justice (and not necessarily resulting from it), is aimed at promoting better socio-ethical attitudes in schools and in other non-criminal contexts. However, to say that restorative justice is part of 'something bigger' is not the same as to say that this 'something bigger' is restorative justice. Walgrave (2008: 17) offers an important distinction here:

> Values are not restorative justice in the strict sense of the word. They are socio-ethical and/or ideological beliefs, over which restorative justice does not have the monopoly. The same values and visions drive and inspire many other movements in social policy and political engagement.

Hence, promoting in schools (or in any other non-criminal context) the same moral values underlying restorative justice (such as mutual respect, solidarity, inclusiveness, apology, forgiveness, healing, reparation, reconciliation, etc.) is not the same as implanting a 'restorative justice system' in schools. The term 'justice' is not even seen as appropriate for a school setting – in fact, those working with or in school environments suggest terms such as 'restorative *practices*' (see Costello *et al.* 2009, 2010), or 'restorative *approaches*' (see Hopkins 2004).[6] Surely those working in criminal (and particularly youth) justice settings have much to learn from 'restorative approaches' developed in schools, and vice versa; and, therefore, the communication between 'restorativists' of all kinds should be encouraged and celebrated. Nevertheless, when one compares criminalisable and non-criminalisable matters we are still talking about 'different matters, in different contexts, with different actors and sometimes even different purposes' (Walgrave 2008: 17), and such differences should not be overlooked.

The challenges that come with putting school practices and criminal (or youth) justice practices all under the same 'restorative justice' label have become more and more apparent. It has reached a stage where at the 2012 Annual General Meeting of the European Forum for Restorative Justice, Belinda Hopkins – an enthusiastic and influential 'maximalist', under Johnstone's taxonomy – announced that the forum's working group on restorative approaches in schools had decided to leave the European Forum to start their own forum which would focus exclusively on schools, and not on crime. According to Hopkins, the European Forum's goals are to reform the criminal justice system, whereas the goals of those in schools are to reform the disciplinary systems in schools (and then, by extension, the nature of adult–child relationships and the fundamental question of what schools are for).[7] She pointed out the difficulties in reconciling these two completely different focuses, and the priority that has been given to the forum's focus on crime when applications for funding were sought, which among other issues had led them to want to leave. Her speech, or more importantly, the establishment of this new forum,[8] might mark a moment when the promotion of restorative approaches in schools will move from the periphery of the restorative justice literature to become the focal point of a completely independent field of research and practice – in my opinion, as it is meant to be.

So, for me, restorative *justice* is a set of values, principles and practices to be used in response to crime, but when I say crime, which types of crime do I mean? This is another critical issue in the field of restorative justice, with which one needs to contend before getting to restorative justice's actual attributes. It is probably at this point of the discussion that I fall outside Johnstone's continuum, and diverge from Walgrave's views.

Restorative justice processes are still largely confined to low-level crime (Greene 2013), although the feasibility and desirability of extending the restorative paradigm to serious forms of offending is increasingly promoted in the literature (Daly 2006; Hudson 2002; Miller 2011; Pelikan 2010; Umbreit 1999; Weitekamp *et al.* 2006). The application of restorative justice to power-based offences such as sexual assaults and domestic violence has drawn perhaps the strongest reactions. Critics warn of the risk of secondary victimisation, risks to victim safety, the potential manipulation of the process by the offender, and so on (Stubbs 2007). It should be noted, however, that the 'heated debate' over the application of restorative justice to these types of offences 'is largely fuelled by the fact that they remain under-researched, which means that a great deal of speculation informs arguments on both sides, rather than empirical evidence' (Clamp 2013: 18). In fact, if anything, increasing empirical evidence suggests that restorative justice *should* move into cases of serious offending. For example, in their recent systematic review of conferencing, Strang *et al.* (2013: 48) concluded that:

> [...] banishing RJC [restorative justice conference] to low-seriousness crimes is a wasted opportunity. If governments wish to fund Restorative

> Justice at all, this evidence suggests that the best return on investment will be with violent crimes, and with offenders convicted after long prior histories of convictions.

Those who are sceptical about the use of restorative justice for more serious crimes also often argue that restorative justice practices minimalise or trivialise serious criminal offences by returning them to the status of a 'private' matter (Morris 2002). That is, restorative justice, for the critics, would not be enough of a response (or 'tough' enough as a response) to serious crimes. A strong argument against this is that crime is trivialised by processes in which the victims have no role to play and offenders are just passive observers. This is not so in the case of restorative justice which 'focuses on the consequences of the offence for victims and attempts to address these and to find meaningful ways of holding offenders accountable' (Morris 2002: 603).[9]

Moreover, '[i]f restorative justice is thought to be unable to denounce or punish serious crimes, it may exist mainly as an add-on to the existing system and one that may produce a real risk of net-widening' (Roberts and Roach 2003: 252). In fact, as introduced above, there has been a growing argument that by focusing on low-level crime, restorative justice initiatives tend to widen the net of social control and result in minor offenders being given harsher punishment than they would otherwise receive (see Boyes-Watson 1999; Griffin 2007; Polk 1994; Woolford 2009; Young 2001).

In this context, one can turn to another concept of maximalist thinking in restorative justice – this time to the original concept, as proposed by Walgrave in 1997, at the first international conference of the International Network for Research on Restorative Justice (see Walgrave 1998). For Walgrave, the 'maximalist' adjective has nothing to do with the extended focus on non-criminal matters. In effect, for Walgrave (1998, 2008, 2012), 'maximalists' are those who advocate for the replacement of the current 'punitive apriorism' in criminal justice by a 'restorative apriorism', and therefore, in the longer term, for the emergence of a 'restorative justice system' in place of a criminal (penal) justice system. Such a vision entails *making the case for the use of restorative justice even for the most serious cases*, conceding the use of coercion in restorative justice processes where cooperation and voluntariness is not possible, and adding restorative justice practices completely into a legal framework to ensure they comport with due process. If these things are not done, maximalists argue, restorative justice will never be a feasible or desirable plan for the future of criminal justice. Walgrave, thus, is actually a 'maximalist', and so am I.[10]

Nevertheless, I see restorative justice as a response to any crime – even to mass victimisation and gross human rights violations (in a similar vein, see Aertsen *et al.* 2008; Clamp 2013; Sullivan and Tifft 2006; Varona 2014; Weitekamp *et al.* 2006). This is my point of divergence from Walgrave, according to whom truth commissions and peace committees – such as the Truth and Reconciliation Commissions of South Africa and Rwanda, set up to deal with genocide, mass torture, and rape – should not be included in the term 'restorative justice' (Walgrave 2008). Here I also fall outside Johnstone's continuum – indeed, my notion of restorative justice is not extended so as to include 'any situation in life' (the 'maximalist' end) or 'professional tasks' ('towards the middle'), but it is also not limited to 'ordinary' crimes (the 'minimalist' end).

There is yet another important discussion surrounding restorative justice's basic theoretical foundations, with which I would like to contend before focusing on the exploration of restorative justice's main attributes: the relationship between restorative justice and the current criminal justice system. When the (modern) concept of restorative justice was being introduced – and probably in order to better 'sell' the idea of restorative justice – it was very common that 'advocates [...] painted a dichotomous, oppositional picture of different justice forms, with restorative justice trumping retributive justice as the superior one' (Daly 2002: 72). In turn, restorative justice is often referred to as a completely new criminal justice paradigm capable of standing alone and replacing the current one (e.g. Zehr 1990). Only more recently have some advocates found 'the need to combine [restorative justice's] values and practices with existing traditions of criminal practice and philosophy', such as the right to a fair trial, sentencing proportionality, etc. (Gavrielides 2007: 39; see also Daly 2000; Daly and Immarigeon 1998; Dzur and Wertheimer 2002; Green *et al.* 2013) – and I think this is what we should be aiming at. Indeed, I stand with Gavrielides (2011), who rejects the idea that restorative justice can only be approached as an abolitionist concept, and with Weitekamp (2002: 326), according to whom:

> Even if we could come close to achieving [a restorative justice system], the important question remains whether we still need parts of the current system in order to guarantee the rights of offenders, and in particular the rights of victims who do not want to participate in programs of restorative justice. [...] We will have also to face offenders for whom the restorative justice approach will not work and who have to be incarcerated in order to protect citizens, communities and societies.

In a similar vein, Nils Christie, who has been widely referred to as one of the founders of penal abolitionism,[11] has once stated that:

> There are limits to my abolitionistic urge. Some people might be absolutely impossible to prevent from burning Mosques or Synagogues or Churches, or from beating their wives or parents. If we have tried all, from conversation to mediation, we might as a last resort be forced to use physical restrictions.
>
> (Feest and Paul 2007, as cited in Pali and Pelikan 2014: 144)

In line with the abovementioned considerations, Braithwaite (2002: 30) proposes a useful 'regulatory pyramid' with restorative justice for the majority of cases, and punishment where restorative justice is not applicable or does not work:

> The idea of the pyramid is that our presumption should always be to start at the base of the pyramid, then escalate to somewhat punitive approaches only reluctantly and only when dialogue fails, and then escalate to even more punitive approaches only when the more modest forms of punishment fail.

This, it seems to me, makes sense. I embrace the idea of restorative justice as an alternative *to* punishment (Walgrave 2013b), and I would argue that restorative justice practices have the potential of replacing incarceration in many cases that are deemed serious. Nevertheless, whenever this proves impossible or undesirable – and, like Weitekamp (2002), I believe sometimes it will – we should still seek the application of the restorative justice 'philosophy' at all levels of criminal justice, even in the 'naturally non-restorative' environment of the prison system. Even when incarceration proves necessary, there may well be ways to start healing and reparative processes between offenders, victims and the communities in which they live or to which they feel attached (see Dhami *et al.* 2009; Fox 2012; Gavrielides 2011; Hagemann 2003; Johnstone 2007; Robert and Peters 2003; Umbreit *et al.* 2003). In fact, if restorative justice programmes are to become the rule rather than the exception, we should be finding ways of making current criminal justice practices that have traditionally been directed towards treatment or public safety more restorative (Bazemore 2000). This is not a cry for a piecemeal reform of the criminal justice system; reflecting on how criminal justice practices could shift their thinking towards reparation 'implies a reformulation of a great deal of the principles of criminal justice' (Walgrave 2000: 424).

The overall thrust here is *not* to say that the abolitionist 'roots' (or, indeed, 'impetus') of restorative justice should be overlooked or disregarded. Quite the contrary, I do see the restorative justice agenda as a move away from the so-called 'punitive turn' in criminal justice (Garland 2001) and, thus, from incarceration. What I want to suggest, though, is that restorative justice programmes need to 'dialogue' with criminal justice practices as they currently exist. That is, perhaps, for the time being, more important than deciding whether restorative justice practices should 'replace, be woven into, or operate alongside our current justice system' (Greene 2013: 380), we should be asking 'under what conditions it [restorative justice] can cooperate with the CJS [Criminal Justice System] while retaining its unique character and defining principles' (Pali and Pelikan 2014: 143).

Having said that, I take as my starting points the following:

1 Restorative justice may well *be part of* a bigger 'project' aimed at 'creating social arrangements that foster human dignity, mutual respect, and equal well-being from the outset' (Sullivan and Tifft 2004: 388). And it is certainly true that despite any arguments against it, 'the name restorative justice is the one that has travelled the world' (Liebmann 2007: 25) to refer to many entirely different practices carried out in completely different contexts. Nevertheless, here I consider restorative justice as a response to *crime*.
2 I would argue that restorative justice could be used for lesser and more serious crimes – even for cases of domestic violence, or cases of genocide and other gross human rights violations. Nevertheless, my (empirical) focus will inevitably be on rather less serious crimes – those that do not lead young people, in England and Wales, to custody but to the referral order sentencing process.
3 Borrowing from Christie's vocabulary (see quotation above), 'there are limits to my abolitionistic urge'. As such, I believe restorative justice can (and should) be used at any stage of the criminal process (even in prison). However, my focus here is on restorative justice as a diversion from 'normal' court-based criminal justice, and that will become particularly evident when I begin to consider my empirical findings.
4 Finally, I am convinced that restorative justice is a feasible option (and is equally challenging) for both adults and young people, but my focus will be on the use of restorative justice with young offenders, particularly when I begin to consider my empirical experience.

1.2 The 'spirit' of restorative justice

Having established the premises of this research, I shall now present a brief overview of restorative justice's main attributes. It is worth noting that although all efforts will be made to provide an unbiased summary of the theoretical discourses of restorative justice, all my reference points inevitably will be influenced by how I see restorative justice – as a response to any crime, not through abolitionist lenses, and so on. As mentioned above, my intention is not to tell the 'real story' of restorative justice, but to make clear how I read this story.

Authors often start their exposition of restorative justice by listing and challenging its 'top ranked' working definitions, which emphasise different aspects of restorative justice's theoretical appeals. It is apparently expected that readers will absolutely understand what restorative justice is by going through all of the possible criticisms of each of the imperfect working definitions available 'in the market'. Then, as odd as it may sound, the commentators often conclude their reasoning by suggesting a 'brand new' working definition to add to the list of (already unsatisfactory) definitions. The 'new' definition then prompts well-founded objections and, again, readers are presented with a new set of critical views by the next commentator.

As a restorative justice 'reader' myself (Johnstone 2003), I remain unconvinced that this is the best way to contend with the question of what restorative justice is. Indeed, when one gets to the explanations of specific working definitions, the truth is that they all begin to look very much alike.[12] The explanations of restorative justice's main attributes have helped me to understand it far better than the rough-and-ready working definitions. Furthermore, I believe that the coining of a consensual definition is not the answer to the ambiguities around restorative justice (Gavrielides 2007; Zehr and Mika 1998). In fact, because restorative justice is both 'a scholarly field and [...] a practice field' (Pali and Pelikan 2014: 143), and since new and unforeseen developments can affect the way we use the concept of restorative justice, this should remain an 'open concept that continues to develop with experience' (Johnstone and Van Ness 2007: 8). Therefore, as opposed to confronting the available definitions, criticising them all, and then coming up with my own definition of restorative justice, I shall attempt to identify the least opposed characteristic features of restorative justice. That is, I shall explore what sorts of reasoning would prompt restorativists to say, 'Well done! That's the (restorative justice) spirit!' As broad as this may sound – and as inappropriate as the word 'spirit' may be for a field too often tied to spiritual or religious traditions (Bender and Armour 2007; Wheeldon 2009) – the overview of restorative justice's key principles and theoretical claims should be enough to make the case later (in Chapter 3) for the restorative justice 'spirit' of referral orders and youth offender panels, and then to discuss (in Chapter 7) the 'restorativeness' of youth offender panels on the ground.[13]

Restorative justice involves returning the conflict to those most affected by crime

Criminal law and criminal justice practices are conventionally presented as being aimed at penalising 'those forms of wrongdoing which [...] touch public rather than merely private interests' (Ashworth 1992, as cited in Cavadino and Dignan 1997: 237). So crime, rather than an offence against individuals, is traditionally (and very abstractly) conceived of as an offence against the state (Dzur and Olson 2004; Morris and Young 2000). In turn, it is the professionals who, representing the state, make the decisions about how a particular criminal case should be dealt with (Morris 2002). The next logical step is that the emphasis is placed on the detached ideals of punishment and retribution, rather than on the more intimate or personal endeavours of reparation and reconciliation.

Decades ago, in 1977, in his seminal piece 'Conflicts as Property', Christie argued that lawyers and other professionals had stolen the conflicts from the parties directly involved, and that these should be given back to whom they belong: the victims, the perpetrators and the community (Christie 1977). In other words, advancing the idea that crime is personal, 'Christie advocated the "de-professionalisation" of responses to crime, so that responsibility for resolving conflicts associated with crime should be returned to those with a personal stake in such matters' (Shapland *et al.* 2011: 6).

On a perhaps overly optimistic note, Walgrave (1998: 12) suggests that citizens have now become more self-conscious, and 'do not accept any more that government or formal social institutions take over the crime conflicts and settle it in a formalized way, pushing aside the interests of those who are directly involved'. We might not quite be there yet, but the fact is that, drawing from Christie's notion of conflicts as property, one of restorative justice's main attributes is that it sees crime as a violation against 'real' people rather than a violation against the abstract interests of the state or against abstract legal rules (Morris and Young 2000; Pavlich 2005). In turn, within a restorative justice approach to crime, 'the State no longer has a monopoly over decisionmaking' and 'the principal decision makers are the parties themselves' (Morris and Young 2000: 14). That is, conflicts are returned to those to whom they belong (victims, offenders and community), and the logic of justice is converted from repression against the enemy (the offender) to the more collectively meaningful outcomes of reparation (of the harms caused by crime) and, whenever possible, reconciliation (of the conflicting parties).

Although writing in the 1970s Christie did not mention the term 'restorative justice',[14] not even *en passant*, his 'Conflicts as Property' became the basis of much of restorative justice's theoretical constructions. As will become apparent, many of the characteristic features of restorative justice stem from this notion that the decision on how to deal with the aftermath of crime should be put in the hands of the direct stakeholders.

Restorative justice processes are inclusive, informal and empowering

Some scholars have preferred 'process-focused' definitions of restorative justice (e.g. Marshall 1996), whereas others have sought to generate 'outcome-focused' definitions that emphasise restorative justice products and, sometimes, by-products (e.g. Bazemore and Walgrave 1999). Along with most restorativists, I am persuaded that restorative justice is both a process and an outcome (see, for example, Braithwaite and Strang 2001; and Dignan 2005).[15]

As a process, restorative justice is supposed to be inclusive, with the active participation of all parties encouraged and facilitated. Restorative justice's call for inclusiveness (or inclusion) arises directly from the idea that conflicts should be handed back to the parties most directly affected, or, putting it the other way round, the idea of handing conflicts back to their owners can only go ahead if the process of restorative justice is indeed inclusive. Thus, ideally, restorative justice should happen through engaging processes whereby all participants help to define the harm and develop a plan to repair it. The more inclusive the better – that is, the more the relevant people are involved, the earlier they are involved, and the more each of them actively participates in the process, the more restorative the process is likely to be. Mainly for that reason, an ideal or 'purist' (McCold 2000) model of restorative justice is that in which dialogue and deliberation happen through face-to-face encounters. That is, on the ground, restorative justice practices should ideally involve a 'live' meeting between all parties with a stake in a particular offence – victims, offenders, and members of the (affected) community – so that chances are given to all of them to express their feelings and to share their ideas on how the aftermath of a particular offence should be dealt with (Van Ness 2002).

The ideal of inclusiveness is highly central to restorative justice's attributes as it ties in with the elements of procedural justice identified by Tyler (1990). Tyler (1990: 7) suggests that 'where people feel they have control over decisions they believe that the procedure is fair', and accordingly, people who feel fairly treated by the justice system are more likely to obey the law in the future. Regardless of whether they focus on the process or on the outcome, restorativists often turn to Tyler's ideas in promoting the 'restorative justice way' of conducting criminal processes (Bazemore 2000; Vanfraechem 2007; Walgrave 1995).

Another value often enthusiastically related to restorative justice processes is informality (see McCold 2000). In fact, the ideal of inclusion as it is described above – that is, as a means by which effective communication between the direct stakeholders is enabled and encouraged – relies greatly on the idea of an informal process whereby participants will feel comfortable and able to speak for themselves (Morris and Young 2000). The main rationale underpinning informality, thus, is to create the 'ideal' atmosphere for the active involvement of all stakeholders; or said differently, to enable a non-threatening and non-stigmatising environment whereby all participants can feel free to 'talk things out' (Van Ness and Strong 2010). Hence, restorative justice practices usually take place in non-courtroom settings (ideally in community venues such as community centres), with participants sitting in a circle, with no one wearing wigs or gowns, and with tea and coffee being served (often at the end of the restorative meeting). Ultimately, it has been suggested, the informality of restorative justice processes leads to more 'personalised' outcomes that take into consideration the specific needs of the affected parties, whereas more formalised ways of doing justice would rely on the more 'one-size-fits-all' or 'blanket responses' to crime (McCold 2000).

Nevertheless, whilst it has got something to do with greater flexibility or adaptability, informality 'does not mean that there are no rules which must be adhered to or that there are no rights which must be protected' (Morris and Young 2000: 15). That is, although it might sound intuitively appealing to many, the ideal of a 'de-formalised' restorative justice process is one that ought to be bounded by clear norms and expectations. A basic question regarding a restorative justice response to crime then is how to combine the informalities of restorative justice with those formalities of criminal justice that are 'necessary to maintain the balances demanded by the principles of a democratic state' (Walgrave 2006: 561). More specifically, how to combine informality and due process standards. The truth is that when restorative justice practices are situated within criminal justice, they cannot be characterised as completely informal (Shapland *et al.* 2006). As argued by Walgrave (2000: 421):

> Formalized proceedings are indispensable to achieve the strict and controllable conditions in which citizens can be deprived of their liberty. [Formalization] rightly is a key characteristic to the justice system, because it offers the clues for necessary control of legal safeguards.

Besides, the power imbalances between offenders and victims may well proliferate within completely informal processes, leading to situations of revictimisation (Shapland *et al.* 2006; Strang 2002). All in all, restorative justice processes, particularly those running within criminal justice, should be as informal *as possible* rather than completely informal.

The inclusiveness and informality of restorative justice processes are often associated with the values of cooperativeness and voluntariness – and here, again, one needs to clear some of the controversy surrounding restorative justice. For some proponents, everyone present at a restorative justice meeting, or participating in a restorative justice process, should be there voluntarily if the practice is to be included under the 'restorative justice' tent or to be considered 'fully restorative' – that is, such proponents do not see a role for coercion in the restorative justice framework (see, for example, McCold 2000). Others have claimed that a certain level of coercion is necessary 'when voluntariness is not achieved and when it is deemed necessary to respond to the offence' (Walgrave 2000: 422), and ultimately, to avoid restorative justice practices remaining at the margins of the criminal justice system, as a diversionary tactic incapable of challenging the 'punitive apriorism' of formal responses to crime (Walgrave 1999, 2000, 2008). I agree that, given its ideals of being as informal and collaborative as possible, the preference tends to be for restorative justice to respond to crime with the maximum amount of voluntary cooperation and the minimum amount of coercion. Nevertheless, just as *minimal* formality is not the same as *no* formality, *minimal* coercion is not the same as *no* coercion.

In fact, restorative justice processes can only be fully informal and voluntary if they operate outside the criminal justice system – but, as such, they 'would not affect the fundamentally punitive and unsatisfying manner in which societies now deal with most crimes' (Bazemore and Walgrave 1999: 52). Instead, they would remain a form of diversion limited to minor offences. Moreover, if on the one side operating at the margins of any justice system would allow for an unmatched degree of informality and voluntariness, on the other side restorative justice would not have any impact on the coercion that is used by current criminal justice systems to enforce punishment and treatment (Bazemore and Walgrave 1999). This, indeed, would mean the 'same laws, same process, same coercion and the same goals' (McCold 2000: 396).

Furthermore, I am not sure how genuinely voluntary are processes whereby offenders know that non-participation will lead to 'sanctions imposed by the court that are more severe than if they agree to participate [in the restorative justice process]' (Boyes-Watson 2000: 444; see also Mesmaecker 2013).

In 1977, Christie had already suggested that there is a role for coercion even within a system primarily directed towards voluntariness. Whilst describing his model of neighbourhood courts – which has very much in common with what we would now describe as restorative justice – Christie (1977: 9) warned:

> But let me add that I think we should do it quite independently of his [the offender's] wishes. It is not health-control we are discussing. It is crime control. If criminals are shocked by the initial thought of close confrontation with the victim, preferably a confrontation in the very local neighbourhood of one of the parties, what then?

The bottom line is that, as mentioned previously, I do not see restorative justice through abolitionist lenses, nor do I believe in the feasibility or desirability of a new criminal justice system that looks nothing like the current one. I agree with Bazemore and Walgrave (1999: 47) when they say that restorative justice interventions should preferably occur in informal settings as a voluntary meeting between victims, offenders and their relevant communities, but that 'it is also possible to imagine a transformation of the formal system to make it operate in a more restorative manner as well'. In turn, I would argue that harm can be repaired even if the offender is compelled into repairing the harm (e.g. through court-imposed victim restitution). Furthermore, I would argue that offenders who are mandated to participate in restorative processes may in the longer term understand the 'restorative sanction' in a constructive way (Walgrave 2000; see also Hoyle, in Cunneen and Hoyle 2010). Indeed, I am persuaded that healing in relationships and new learning, although cooperative processes (see Claassen 1995, cited in McCold 2000), may be reached through restorative processes that start without the full cooperation of the offender. This is not to say that court-imposed 'restorative sanctions' (such as victim restitution or community service) should substitute collaborative and voluntary processes, but rather that coercion should remain a possibility when stakeholders are unwilling to (or unable to) 'own' their conflict. Finally, one should bear in mind that whereas the use of coercion might not fit into an 'encounter conception' (Umbreit and Armour 2011) of restorative justice (since forcing people to meet may well present risks of further victimisation and/or pointless retaliation), it makes sense within the idea that restorative justice is not limited to a process whereby the parties should meet, but open instead to a process directed towards reparation.[16]

Last, but not least, restorative justice as a process 'is designed to empower victims, offenders and communities to redress the material, psychological and relational harms generated by crime' (Pavlich 2005: 2). That is, restorative justice is idealised as an empowering process. To combat a mindset that thinks conflicts are better dealt with by professionals, victims need empowerment to 'own their conflict'; they should be empowered to have a say on how they think their own case should be resolved. On the other hand, in order to overcome a long-standing tradition of passively 'taking' punishment, offenders should be empowered to 'own' their behaviour, to face the consequences of their actions by making amends to individuals and relationships, and to seek reintegration into their communities by taking every opportunity they can to demonstrate trustworthiness. Finally, community members should be empowered to inquire into the local sources of crime, to resolve a community's own conflicts, and to help determine a plan of action through which repentant offenders are reaccepted into their community (McCold 2000). If the empowerment 'good' of restorative practices does not stem directly from the inclusiveness of the whole restorative justice process, it is certainly interconnected with such value. In fact, the parties can only feel empowered within a process in which they are given a sense of inclusion (Morris 2002). Said differently, to be empowering, restorative justice processes depend on the active engagement of the parties (McCold 2000).

At the end of the day, restorative justice is a process of 'talking things out', and of 'increasing awareness of self and others' (Sullivan and Tifft 2004: 387). It is a process where the preference is for deliberation over adjudication, for informality and voluntariness over formality and coercion. Finally, it is a process with a collective ethos where all participants are empowered to take collective responsibility for the crime that has been committed and the repair of its effects (Morris and Young 2000). In this context, restorative conferences (e.g. family group conferences) and restorative circles (e.g. sentencing circles) are most probably the best practical manifestations of restorative justice – if not by default, definitely by design (McCold 2001; Zinsstag 2012). Indeed, both conferences and circles are designed as inclusive processes that encourage dialogue and mutual agreement through a cooperative structure. They are supposed to take the form of a meeting whereby before a collaborative decision is reached as to what should be done to repair the harm caused by crime, the victim is given the opportunity to ask questions, express their feelings and describe directly to the offender the full consequences of the offence. The non-threatening and non-stigmatising atmosphere of the meeting then allows for offenders to explain their side of things, to demonstrate understanding of the full consequences of their actions, and to be part of the solution. Finally, immediate and sometimes extended family members have the opportunity to support the offender or the victim whilst being reassured that what happened was not their fault. The main difference between conferences and circles is that the latter model further extends the range of actors involved in the process to include members of the wider (affected) community, giving these the opportunity to express the impact of the offending behaviour in that particular neighbourhood or setting. In both models professionals act as facilitators and/or resource/information providers rather than directors (McCold 2001; Morris and Maxwell 2000, 2001; Shapland 2012; Umbreit and Stacey 1996; Vanfraechem *et al.* 2010; Zinsstag 2012).

Having said that, restorative justice should not be limited to its 'pure' forms. Even 'purists' recognise that sometimes non-pure restorative justice is 'all that is possible (e.g. in cases of victimless or irreparable crimes) or reasonable (e.g. in cases of minor misbehaviour)' (McCold 2000: 405). In fact, whilst in some circumstances the 'full restorative stakeholder production' might not be possible, in others it 'might be quite an overreaction' (Braithwaite 2000: 436). Thus, as a matter of coherence, although I agree that restorative encounters such as family group conferences and sentencing circles include the complete potentialities of the restorative paradigm, and that all restorative justice programmes should *allow for* meetings between stakeholders to occur, I do not see the value of limiting restorative justice processes to an encounter. Conferences and circles are by no means the only practical manifestation of restorative justice; they are currently the ideal form of restorative justice processes, but they cannot always be realised, and they may well be overruled by other programmes yet to be invented which may provide evidence of more capable ways of achieving restorative outcomes.

Restorative justice is aimed at reparation

Restorative justice cannot be limited to a process: justice should be restorative in its means, intentions and ends. As summarised by Braithwaite (2000: 435):

> If we have a conference in which all of the parties with a stake in the offence participate actively and it is decided to boil the offender in oil and criticize the victim for bringing the trouble on herself, for outcome reasons we would not want to say the conference was restorative. Conversely, if a judge makes a non-punitive order to help both an offender and a victim to get their lives back together but refuses to hear submissions from them that this is not the kind of help they want, for process reasons we would be reluctant to call this restorative.[17]

Braithwaite's anecdotal example is useful, particularly to illustrate the shortcomings of thinking that a good process is enough of an outcome. The truth is that an 'ideal' process that does not lead to any outcomes or obligations, or that – as described above – leads to a purely punitive response, should not be incorporated within the concept of restorative justice (Bazemore and Walgrave 1999; Walgrave 2008). Moreover, by not including any criteria for outcomes or intentions, a process-based understanding of restorative justice may well endorse already overly procedural criminal justice systems. More precisely, limiting restorative justice to a process entails a commitment to certain programmes or techniques (e.g. conferences and circles), when we should actually be committing to the principles underpinning restorative processes, outcomes and objectives as a means of effectively challenging existing structures of justice (Bazemore 2000; Braithwaite and Strang 2001; Morris and Maxwell 2001). Hence, as much as it is important to discuss the value commitments of restorative justice processes, it is equally important to examine what sorts of outcomes should be aimed at (and accepted) by such processes.

In this context, 'unless repairing harm is at the core of the definition of restorative justice, [...] stakeholders and [criminal justice] staff will often slip into the traditional and comfortable mode of simply trying to help or hurt the offender' (Bazemore 2000: 464). To avoid such a throwback, Bazemore and Walgrave (1999: 48) have suggested definitions of restorative justice where its 'primary distinguishing feature [...] is an effort to repair the harm crime causes', and where principles, not programmes, are used to distinguish between what is and what is not restorative justice.

These are important points made by Bazemore and Walgrave. One should bear in mind that a basic principle of restorative justice is that crime causes harm to people and communities, and that offenders should accept responsibility for doing such harm. The next logical step 'is to try to put things right, as far as possible' (Liebmann 2007: 26). Indeed, the 'restorative intuition' is that 'because crime hurts, justice should heal' (Braithwaite 2005: 296). This is the core idea espoused in what is probably the first systematic writing on restorative justice: Howard Zehr's 1990 book *Changing Lenses*. According to Zehr (1990), the 'grandfather' of restorative justice (Van Ness and Strong 2010: 24), if crime is to be seen as an act that causes harms to people and communities (as opposed to a mere violation of criminal law), the primary goal of restorative justice should be to repair such harms by addressing the real needs of all parties involved in the aftermath of crime. One of restorative justice's main attributes thus – if not the most important amongst them all – is that it is aimed at changing the criminal justice system's normative orientation from (punitive) retribution to restoration (Hudson 1998).[18] As such, its most representative outcome is restoration (alias reparation). On the ground, though, what types of action can be considered reparation?

An offender making financial restitution to the victim is the most obvious and concrete form of direct reparation to victims, but direct reparation can also take the form of practical work (material reparation) or apology (symbolic reparation). The offender can, for example, fix the victim's fence that she has broken (material reparation), or write a letter of apology (symbolic reparation). The reparation to victims can also be indirect – for example, the offender can carry out unpaid work at a charity chosen by the victim. Reparation to the 'victimised community' is usually achieved symbolically through community service. That is, to compensate for the harm they have caused to the community, offenders are often required to complete a period of unpaid work for the benefit of the community or its institutions, such as cleaning and repairing trails in a city park. In such cases it is believed that the 'community itself is restored through the material results of the service rendered and through the peace-restoring gesture of the offender' (Walgrave 1999: 139).[19]

Because conflict should be returned to its owners, the nature of reparation should be determined, as much as possible, by those affected by crime. When the direct stakeholders are given the opportunity to decide what should be done by way of reparation, specific restorative solutions (or 'personalised' outcomes) will become the rule, and (imposed) generic solutions will become the exception. Nevertheless, as argued earlier, there will always be times when stakeholders will not be ready or able to collaborate in the process, and in such instances it should be possible for criminal justice agencies to assume responsibility for determining reparative obligations (Bazemore 2000; Walgrave 2000). This is not to say that professionals are entitled to 'steal the conflict back' (Christie 1977) from the directly affected parties, but rather to say that criminal justice agencies should not remain inert when a reaction to crime is considered necessary and informal community processes are proving unworkable. Indeed, '[h]aving judges order reparation will almost never have the same restorative impact as having victims, offenders, and communities work out these obligations, ideally in face-to-face encounters' (Bazemore 2000: 471), but if that is all that is left to do, courts should still be able to operate within a restorative justice framework whilst imposing sanctions in view of reparation.

As has become clear, restorative justice seeks 'to produce some form of mutually satisfactory resolution to a harm or conflict' (Dzur and Olson 2004: 92). As such, and through a process that allows for offenders to recognise and accept responsibility for the harm they have caused, offenders' reintegration into their communities is also an expected outcome of restorative justice practices. It is often argued that the assembling of people who care about and respect the offender 'provide one possible gateway to engage community support for offender reintegration at a time when this is a very difficult political enterprise' (Bazemore 1998: 795).[20]

Restorative justice also encourages other outcomes, including remorse, forgiveness and reconciliation. However, these would be better described as possible 'by-products' of restorative justice processes, rather than the primary outcome that they hope to achieve. Indeed, it is not always possible to reach such reconciliatory outcomes – offenders and victims 'are not equally disposed to be restorative toward each other' (Daly 2003: 49), 'victims may remain angry or bitter; offenders may remain unmoved and untouched' (Morris 2002: 599). Nevertheless, even when the process fails to reconcile the affected parties, provided that some sort of reparation has occurred (e.g. through agreed community service hours), the process can still be called restorative. A restorative justice process that reaches all the aforementioned 'changes of heart' or 'internal transformations' (Boyes-Watson 2000) deserves to be called 'fully restorative' (McCold 2000), but there are no reasons to limit restorative justice to such degrees of 'perfection'.

The focus on restorative justice's 'by-products', though, has at times been so prominent that one may run the risk of blurring the line between what is (very) *welcome* and what is *crucial* in restorative justice. For example, it has become quite common to elaborate on the connections between fully restorative processes and the goal of wider social change (see Woolford 2009). Some advocates have sought to explain why restorative justice could also be a 'way out' of structural harms (e.g. poor education, community disintegration, poverty, abuse, etc.), or a 'transformative' model of justice capable of transforming the economic and social injustices correlated with violent and other crimes (see, for example, Pranis 2001). It should be said that such 'transformative conceptions' of restorative justice have only added to the already too high expectations surrounding restorative justice, many of which have not yet been met by the outcomes of empirical research (Daly 2003). The enthusiasm for restorative justice's possible by-products may further explain why some advocates still insist on excluding coercion from restorative justice thinking. Authorities cannot compel remorse, forgiveness or reconciliation as they can compel restitution, but what should remain clear is that although remorse, forgiveness, reconciliation and, of course, 'social transformation' are all very welcome, they are not crucial outcomes of restorative justice.

Perhaps because the idea of restorative justice needs to appeal to government (the 'funding providers'), restorative justice has also been promoted as a potentially more effective way of reducing reoffending (see Ahmed *et al.* 2001; Hayes and Daly 2004; Latimer *et al.* 2005; Moore *et al.* 1995; Pollard 2001; Sherman *et al.* 1998; Sherman *et al.* 2000; Strang *et al.* 1999; Zehr 2002). However true this may be, '[w]hile reoffending is not the first concern of restorative justice, the bottom line is that restorative justice interventions should not provoke more reoffending than traditional interventions' (Walgrave 2012: 34). Henceforth, to argue that restorative justice has the potential for the reduction of recidivism, restorative justice advocates (explicitly or implicitly) draw upon Braithwaite's theory of reintegrative shaming.

According to Braithwaite (1989), shaming is key to crime control, provided that the right kind of shame is used. He argues that current criminal justice practices create shame that is stigmatising, when they should be creating reintegrative shaming where opportunity is given for offenders to truly express remorse for their criminal behaviour, apologise to their victims and repair the harm caused by their crime. His central argument is that informal crime control methods involving the offender's 'significant others' are more effective in reducing reoffending. Braithwaite's theory has been in many ways influential in providing a rationale for restorative justice theorising and practice, but its explicit focus on the reduction of reoffending is definitely among its most influential aspects.[21] Although it has proven very difficult to confirm empirically such theoretical presuppositions, a recent evaluation of a number of restorative pilots in England and Wales has found that they were more effective than the control groups (that is, non-restorative interventions) in reducing *the frequency* of reoffending (Shapland 2012; Shapland *et al.* 2011). Even more recently, in their systematic review of 10 different experiments of restorative justice, Strang *et al.* (2013) found that '[a]mong the kinds of cases in which both offenders and victims are willing to meet, RJCs seem likely to reduce future crime'. Also recently, a study by the New Zealand Ministry of Justice, examining reoffending rates and frequency of reoffending over the period from 2008 to 2011, found that 'restorative justice has increased the number of offenders who did not reoffend in the year following their conference (as opposed to a control group), and reduced the frequency of reoffending by nearly a quarter' (Ministry of Justice (New Zealand) 2014: 1).

All in all, ideally, restorative justice should lead to personal forms of reparation through informal, inclusive and empowering processes where the parties are allowed to voice their specific needs and actively participate in the decision over how to put things right. In non-ideal circumstances (e.g. when stakeholders choose not to be involved in the justice process), restorative justice processes and outcomes are still possible within a mindset directed towards reparation as opposed to retaliation or 'punitive retributivism' (Walgrave 2013a).

Restorative justice is victim aware, not necessarily victim centred

As it starts to become clearer, whilst restorative justice may lack an explicit theoretical foundation (Wheeldon 2009), it has been associated with many different criminological traditions, justice philosophies, and political, social and cultural movements. The examples of Christie's (1977) notion of conflicts as property, Tyler's (1990) theory of procedural justice and Braithwaite's (1989) reintegrative shaming theory have all been of great influence to restorative justice theorising (and, to be frank, to restorative justice practice in general), and there has been a further attempt to locate restorative justice within theories of social disorganisation, social learning and moral development (Wheeldon 2009). Also, restorative justice has been influenced by many different tendencies or groups such as feminist movements, decarceration movements, indigenous peoples' emancipation movements, among others (Walgrave 2008). Yet, probably the most influential among all restorative justice's influences are the so-called communitarianism, the victims' rights movements and critical criminology (Walgrave 2008). Whilst attempting to explain the 'restorative justice spirit', I have already elaborated on how some of the aforementioned theories and movements link with restorative justice (and I shall eventually come back to others that remain unexplored), but for now I would like to draw attention to the last two influences: victims' rights movements and critical criminology.

Because crime is traditionally defined as an offence against the state, 'it is not surprising that victims are so consistently left out of the [criminal justice] process and that their needs and wishes are so little heeded' (Zehr 1990: 82). In fact, current criminal justice systems, based on a punishment-oriented mentality where emphasis is placed on exacting a just measure of pain upon the offender, tend to neglect 'the more complex nonretributive needs of victims' (Dzur and Olson 2004: 91). All attention in 'courtroom justice' (Strang and Sherman 2003) tends to be drawn to 'the battle between the prosecutor and the defendant' (Groenhuijsen 2004: 65), whilst the victim, besides possibly witnessing court proceedings, tends to be an outsider to his/her own case or a 'non-person in a Kafka play' (Christie 1977: 8). The situation is no better in the context of youth justice systems, which are characterised by obsessive tensions over whether to adopt notions of welfare or punishment.

Unsurprisingly, surveys have repeatedly found that victims are unhappy with the criminal justice system, not so much as a result of lenient sentencing, but more significantly due to the lack of information about the progress of their own cases, the lack of recognition of the emotional and material harms they have experienced, and the lack of opportunities for them to become actively involved in their own justice process (Hoyle 2012; Strang 2002; Walters and Hoyle 2012). Accordingly, research has revealed what crime victims generally want from the criminal justice system in the aftermath of crime: more information on 'their' case, greater opportunities to take an active role in 'their' process, more attention paid to the emotional and psychological harms associated with their experience of victimisation, and so on (Strang and Sherman 2003). Research also suggests that victims need answers as to why they were victimised, as well as the opportunity to express their emotions to the offender in a more informal process where they have a true chance to be heard (Dzur and Olson 2004; McCold 2000).

Over the past two or three decades, the growing strength of victims' rights movements has impacted on modern criminal justice systems, resulting in most countries having introduced some piecemeal reforms on behalf of crime victims. For example, in many jurisdictions victims now have the right to be provided with information on 'their' cases, the right to make personal impact statements that are taken into account in sentencing, the right to compensation from the state, and so forth (Hoyle 2012). Nevertheless, despite this now long-standing tradition of victims' rights movements, victims remain widely neglected parties in criminal and youth justice processes (Dignan 2005; Groenhuijsen 2004; Strang and Sherman 2003). Besides the more clichéd argument of poor implementation of such rights, some commentators have proposed that 'it seems unlikely that the needs and preferences of victims will be well met by piecemeal reforms' (Strang and Sherman 2003: 25). This is where victims' rights movements and the restorative justice 'movement' begin to intertwine.

On the one hand, it is argued that the needs of crime victims can only be met by a new paradigm of justice that includes victims as stakeholders, and where the focus has been shifted from retribution to reparation (Strang and Sherman 2003; Wright 1996a). On the other hand, whilst placing emphasis on the harm caused by crime, restorative justice 'holds the promise of restoring victims' material and emotional loss, safety, damaged relationships, dignity and self respect' (Hoyle 2002: 101), and 'purports to take [the abovementioned piecemeal reforms] one step further – to one of [active] victim *participation* in the system' (Miers 2004: 24, emphasis in the original). In fact, proponents of restorative justice argue that there are strong reasons to believe that the restorative justice approach to crime is more beneficial to victims than criminal justice's long-standing traditions of punishment and retribution. For them, increasing empirical evidence suggests that: restorative justice interventions provide a much greater opportunity for victims to know about the progress of their cases since they are actively involved in the process; restorative justice processes allow for the active participation of victims as they are given the opportunity to voice their suffering and opinions on how the offence should be dealt with; restorative justice initiatives provide ample opportunity for emotional reparation to occur while face-to-face meetings between victims and offenders enhance the likelihood of repentance and of a genuine apology being offered; restorative justice encounters allow for a sense of closure for victims that is unmatched by traditional court proceedings, most probably due to the chance they are given to ask offenders the 'why me?' question and to explain how they have been affected by the offence. Ultimately, restorative justice's focus on the (material, psychological and relational) harms caused by crime, and then on the need to repair such harms, is deemed of obvious benefit to victims.[22]

Restorative justice, however, should not be seen as simply part of a victims' movement, but rather as an independent and complex movement in itself aimed at providing constructive outcomes for both victims and offenders (Hudson 2003). Actually, one of restorative justice's impulses is to move away from the 'zero-sum game assumption' – quite typical of (early) victims' movements (Bazemore 1998; Garland 2001) – where any enhancement in the rights or interests of the offenders is assumed to be at the expense of the victims (Hoyle 2012; Hudson 2003; Strang 2002). Indeed, the 'theoretical position of restorative justice is that [the] win/lose [dichotomy] can be avoided and transformed to win/win' (Strang and Sherman 2003: 36). Or, as summarised by Hudson (2003: 178), restorative justice 'is envisaged as a way of dealing constructively with both victims and offenders, jumping off rather than on to the populist bandwagon, which believes that what *helps* the victim must necessarily *hurt* the offender'.

In this context, it should be highlighted that critical criminological thinking has also been of great influence to restorative justice theorising. Hence, one of the ideas behind restorative justice is undoubtedly to provide less severe and more humane sanctions for the offender (Weitekamp 1992) – or even to forgo punishment (Walgrave 2013b; Wright 2013b). Furthermore, besides helping to improve the handling of victims in criminal justice systems, restorative justice should also 'offer (as a minimum) no fewer opportunities for offender reintegration and rehabilitation than systems grounded in individual treatment assumptions' (Bazemore and Walgrave 1999: 363–64). The concept that offenders are as much stakeholders as any other stakeholder intertwines harmoniously with Christie's notion of conflicts as property (Christie 1977). One should bear in mind that although current criminal justice systems are often accused of being offender focused, what happens in fact is that, 'like victims, offenders are largely bystanders in their own cases' (Dzur and Olson 2004: 92). Restorative justice cannot be centred solely on victims because returning conflict back to *all* parties with a stake in a particular offence necessarily entails being aware of, and responsive to, offenders as much as victims. In fact, crime ought to be considered as a conflict involving 'real' people, and real people do not resemble abstract and polarised litigating parties. On the contrary, regardless of being labelled as victims or offenders, 'real' people very often have the same needs and have done similar deeds. Therefore, although the restorative justice model is not based on meeting offenders' needs, the direct confrontation between victims and offenders offers great opportunities for the synergy of emotions and, therefore, meeting offenders' needs can be part of the process (Wright 1996b).

By centring on victims, restorative justice could risk (re)creating a model where offenders are still 'taking punishment', instead of taking responsibility for what they have done (Liebmann 2007). While holding offenders accountable for their offences in meaningful ways, restorative justice is 'naturally' (or intrinsically) victim aware. Indeed, when the victim is reintroduced in the case, serious attention will inevitably be placed on the victim's losses and on how these can be alleviated or repaired (Christie 1977). However, being victim aware is not the same as being victim centred (Llewellyn 2006). Even when victims do not wish to participate in programmes of restorative justice, or in cases of 'victimless crime' (such as environmental crimes), offenders should still be empowered to understand the consequences of their actions on the wider community, encouraged to repair the (in)direct harm caused by their behaviour and, in turn, be given the opportunity to take part in a reforming process from which they will ultimately benefit. That is, restorative justice processes should happen even when direct victims choose not to take part, or when there is no direct victim, because in such cases there will still be harms to be repaired and lessons to be learned.

One should also bear in mind that the meanings we attach to the label of victim are socially constructed – no one is a victim in a natural sense (Woolford 2009). In fact, the victim is a heavily politicised figure, so much so that there were periods in our history when:

> Husbands and fathers were assumed to rule over their households, and therefore women and children who were subject to 'moderate correction' at the hands of husbands/fathers were not considered victims of injustices, but rather the subject of a legitimate form of political control.
>
> (Woolford 2009: 91)

This is not to say that restorative justice has managed (or will manage) to avoid the victim–offender labels, but it is a reminder of how contingent our notions of victimhood are, and of just how blurred the line might be between the person harmed and the person who has caused that harm. In fact, because restorative justice is ideally an informal process whereby the parties are allowed to 'talk things out', it allows for the exploration of the ripple effect of criminal harm (Van Ness and Strong 2010). Or, as Hoyle reminds us (in Cunneen and Hoyle 2010: 10), restorative justice processes allow us to move beyond the victim–offender labels whilst they move 'towards exploring the multiple layers of harms done by the offending behaviour, including harms to offenders and their supporters'. All in all, the aim that restorative justice sets itself to achieve is much more difficult and meaningful than that of being victim-*centred*: restorative justice processes are aimed at being truly victim *aware*.

1.3 Concluding comments

This chapter was not meant as a comprehensive review of the vast literature on restorative justice. That would require a book on its own. In fact, since restorative justice still means 'different things to different people', and because the work undertaken in this study is aimed at confronting *restorative justice's* appeals to community, I wanted to start by providing a clear idea of what I have in mind when I refer to restorative justice: that it is a response to crime; that it is a process as well as an outcome; that as a process, it should be inclusive, informal and empowering; that as an outcome, it should be directed towards reparation; and so on. Now that the basics of restorative justice are explained, I will turn to one of the weakest points of the restorative justice formulations, the one motivating this study: the question of what role community plays in restorative justice processes.

Notes

1 At the time of this research, for example, a new international journal entirely dedicated to the field of restorative justice was launched (see www.hartjournals.co.uk/rj/index.html).

2 Here I am referring to the International Institute for Restorative Practices (www.iirp.edu), based in Bethlehem (Pennsylvania, USA), and founded by a well-known restorative justice advocate called Ted Wachtel. However, it should also be noted that an increasing number of universities now offer degrees in restorative justice. For example, nowadays one can obtain a 'Masters Degree (MA) in Restorative Justice' at the University of Hull (UK). In Canada, the Department of Justice Studies at the University of Regina and the Centre for Restorative Justice at Simon Fraser University also have degrees focused on this area (Tomporowski 2014). Not to mention the innumerable broader degrees, such as master's degrees (MSc or MA) in 'Criminology' and/or 'Criminal Justice', all over the world, which comprise restorative justice courses.

3 Hull (in the UK) was the first city to embark on such a project where the goal is for everyone who works with youth to employ restorative practices (Mirsky 2009). According to Green *et al.* (2013: 447), the aim, ultimately, 'has been to generate a common restorative language through which all children and young people experience education, criminal justice, social services, and so on'. Nowadays, one

can easily search online for a list of other cities willing to become 'restorative', such as Swansea (UK), Santa Cruz (USA), Oakland (USA), Rochester (USA) and Cardiff (UK). There are also examples like Norfolk (UK) which aims to become a 'restorative county'.

4 Updated estimates would probably indicate over 100 countries in which restorative justice is used as a response to crime (see Van Ness 2005).

5 In fact, the International Institute for Restorative Practices has published some compelling evidence to this effect (see, for example, Wachtel 2013; Wachtel and Mirsky 2008; Wachtel *et al.* 2010).

6 Christie (2013) has recently argued that the 'worst part' of the term 'restorative justice' is the word 'justice'. According to him, instead of allowing for a radical alternative approach to conflict, this word has brought restorative justice closer to the (traditional) criminal justice system. Of course, 'behind the language-centred argument, and between the lines of Christie's reflection, we can read Christie's worry – that of the co-option of RJ [restorative justice] into the CJS [Criminal Justice System]' (Pali and Pelikan 2014: 146). Nevertheless, like others (e.g. Braithwaite 2013; Maxwell 2013; Walgrave 2013b), I think that 'the term [restorative justice] has indeed stuck to the field, and the moment for changing it has passed' (Pali and Pelikan 2014: 151).

7 I was present at this meeting and afterwards exchanged emails with Dr Hopkins to check the accuracy of this information.

8 By the time I finished this study, the new forum had been launched under the name 'European Circle of Restorative Educators' (more details can be found here: europeancircleofrestorativeeducators.com/content/who-are-we).

9 For practical examples of how restorative justice can be used for the most serious offences, including homicide and rape, see Wright 2013a.

10 The use of coercion and the need to keep restorative justice within due process standards will be explored later; for now, I shall keep focused on the feasibility and desirability of restorative justice for serious crimes.

11 Although he has been reluctant to call himself an abolitionist (see, for example, Pali and Pelikan 2014).

12 For example, see how close 'purists' and 'maximalists' get to one another when they begin to compare and debate the differences in their views (McCold 2000; Walgrave 2000), or when a third author critically compares these two different approaches (Braithwaite 2000).

13 Others have also used the phrase 'the spirit of restorative justice' to refer to the basic principles and values of restorative justice (see, for example, Raye and Roberts 2007: 217).

14 According to Denscombe (2010: 62), the term 'restorative justice' appeared in a 1977 article written by Albert Eglash and entitled 'Beyond Restitution: Creative Restitution'.

15 For me, this is where Walgrave actually stands in his more recent thinking (see his current maximalist version of restorative justice in Walgrave 2008).

16 These arguments will be further strengthened in the next section of this chapter.

17 Braithwaite, J. (2000) 'Decomposing a Holistic Vision of Restorative Justice', published in *Contemporary Justice Review*, 3(4): 433–440, reproduced here by permission of Taylor & Francis Ltd, www.tandfonline.com

18 Or, in Walgrave's terms, 'Restorative justice does not add more hurt, but tries to take hurt away by inversing *punitive retributivism* into *constructive restorative retributivism*' (Walgrave 2013a: 365, emphasis added).

19 For a comprehensive discussion on what constitutes reparation, see Strang and Sherman 2003.

20 This theme is returned to in more detail in later chapters, particularly when I begin to consider my empirical findings.

21 For an interesting critique of Braithwaite's reintegrative shaming theory, see Nussbaum 2004.

22 For a comprehensive list of potential benefits to victims, see Aertsen *et al.* 2015 (forthcoming); Dignan 2005; Shapland *et al.* 2011; Van Camp and Wemmers 2013; and Wachtel 2013.

References

Aertsen, I., Arsovska, J., Rohne, H.-C., Valinas, M. and Vanspauwen, K. (2008) *Restoring Justice after Large-Scale Violent Conflicts*, Cullompton: Willan.

Aertsen, I., Vanfraechem, I. and Fernández, D.B. (2015, forthcoming), *Victims and Restorative Justice*, Abingdon: Routledge.

Ahmed, E., Harris, N., Braithwaite, J. and Braithwaite, V. (2001) *Shame Management through Reintegration*, Cambridge: Cambridge University Press.

Ashworth, A. (1992) 'What Victims of Crime Deserve', *Paper presented to the Fulbright Colloquium on Penal Theory and Penal Practice*, University of Stirling.

Bazemore, G. (1996) 'Three Paradigms for Juvenile Justice', in B. Galaway and J. Hudson (eds), *Restorative Justice: International Perspectives*, Monsey, NY: Criminal Justice Press.

Bazemore, G. (1998) 'Restorative Justice and Earned Redemption: Communities, Victims, and Offender Reintegration', *American Behavioral Scientist*, 41(6): 768–813.

Bazemore, G. (2000) 'Rock and Roll, Restorative Justice, and the Continuum of the Real World: A Response to "purism" in Operationalizing Restorative Justice', *Contemporary Justice Review*, 3(4): 459–477.

Bazemore, G. and Walgrave, L. (1999) 'Restorative Juvenile Justice: In Search of Fundamentals and an Outline for Systemic Reform', in G. Bazemore and L. Walgrave (eds), *Restorative Juvenile Justice: Repairing the Harm of Youth Crime*, Monsey, NY: Criminal Justice Press.

Bender, K. and Armour, M. (2007) 'The Spiritual Components of Restorative Justice', *Victims & Offenders*, 2(3): 251–267.

Boyes-Watson, C. (1999) 'In the Belly of the Beast? Exploring the Dilemmas of State-Sponsored Restorative Justice', *Contemporary Justice Review*, 2(3): 261–281.

Boyes-Watson, C. (2000) 'Reflections on the Purist and Maximalist Models of Restorative Justice', *Contemporary Justice Review*, 3(4): 441–450.

Braithwaite, J. (1989) *Crime, Shame, and Reintegration*, Cambridge: Cambridge University Press.

Braithwaite, J. (2000) 'Decomposing a Holistic Vision of Restorative Justice', *Contemporary Justice Review*, 3(4): 433–440.

Braithwaite, J. (2002) *Restorative Justice and Response Regulation*, Oxford: Oxford University Press.

Braithwaite, J. (2003) 'Principles of Restorative Justice', in A.V. Hirsch, J.V. Roberts, A.E. Bottoms, K. Roach and M. Schiff (eds), *Restorative Justice and Criminal Justice: Competing or Reconcilable Paradigms?* Oxford: Hart Publishing.

Braithwaite, J. (2005) 'Between Proportionality & Impunity: Confrontation => Truth => Prevention', *Criminology*, 43(2): 283–306.

Braithwaite, J. (2013) 'Western Words', *Restorative Justice: An International Journal*, 1 (1): 20–23.

Braithwaite, J. and Strang, H. (2001) 'Introduction: Restorative Justice and Civil Society', in H. Strang and J. Braithwaite (eds), *Restorative Justice and Civil Society*, Cambridge: Cambridge University Press.

Cavadino, M. and Dignan, J. (1997) 'Reparation, Retribution and Rights', *International Review of Victimology*, 4(3): 233–253.

Christie, N. (1977) 'Conflicts as Property', *British Journal of Criminology*, 17(1): 1–15.

Christie, N. (2013) 'Words on Words', *Restorative Justice: An International Journal*, 1 (1): 15–19.

Claassen, R. (1995) 'Restorative Justice: Fundamental Principles', *Paper presented at the National Center for Peacemaking and Conflict Resolution*, Fresno, CA.

Clamp, K. (2013) *Restorative Justice in Transition*, Abingdon: Routledge.

Costello, B., Wachtel, J. and Wachtel, T. (2009) *The Restorative Practices Handbook for Teachers, Disciplinarians and Administrators*, Bethlehem, PA: International Institute for Restorative Practices.

Costello, B., Wachtel, J. and Wachtel, T. (2010) *Restorative Circles in Schools: Building Community and Enhancing Learning*, Bethlehem, PA: International Institute for Restorative Practices.

Crawford, A. and Newburn, T. (2003) *Youth Offending and Restorative Justice: Implementing Reform in Youth Justice*, Cullompton: Willan Publishing.

Cunneen, C. and Hoyle, C. (2010) *Debating Restorative Justice*, Oxford: Hart Publishing.

Daly, K. (2000) 'Revisiting the Relationship Between Retributive and Restorative Justice', in H. Strang and J. Braithwaite (eds), *Restorative Justice: Philosophy to Practice*, Burlington, VA: Ashgate Publishing.

Daly, K. (2002) 'Restorative Justice: The Real Story', *Punishment & Society*, 4(1): 55–79.

Daly, K. (2003) 'Making Variation a Virtue: Evaluating the Potential and Limits of Restorative Justice', in E.G.M. Weitekamp and H.-J. Kerner (eds), *Restorative Justice in Context*, Cullompton: Willan Publishing.

Daly, K. (2006) 'Restorative Justice and Sexual Assault: An Archival Study of Court and Conference Cases', *British Journal of Criminology*, 46(2): 334–356.

Daly, K. and Immarigeon, R. (1998) 'The Past, Present, and Future of Restorative Justice: Some Critical Reflections', *Contemporary Justice Review*, 1(1): 21–45.

Denscombe, M. (2010) *Good Research Guide: For Small-Scale Social Research Projects*, 4th edn, Maidenhead: Open University Press.

Dhami, M.K., Mantle, G. and Fox, D. (2009) 'Restorative Justice in Prisons', *Contemporary Justice Review*, 12(4): 433–448.

Dignan, J. (2005) *Understanding Victims and Restorative Justice*, Maidenhead: Open University Press.

Dzur, A.W. and Olson, S.M. (2004) 'The Value of Community Participation in Restorative Justice', *Journal of Social Philosophy*, 35(1): 91–107.

Dzur, A.W. and Wertheimer, A. (2002) 'Forgiveness and Public Deliberation', *Criminal Justice Ethics*, 21(1): 3–20.

Fattah, E. (1997) 'From Crime Policy to Victim Policy – The Need for a Fundamental Policy Change', in M. McShane and F. Williams III (eds), *Victims of Crime and the Victimization Process*, New York: Garland Publishing.

Fattah, E. (1998a), 'Restorative and Retributive Justice Models: A Comparison', in E. Fattah and T. Peters (eds), *Support for Crime Victims in a Comparative Perspective*, Leuven: Leuven University Press.

Fattah, E. (1998b), 'Some Reflections on the Paradigm of Restorative Justice and its Viability for Juvenile Justice', in L. Walgrave (ed.), *Restorative Justice for Juveniles: Potentialities, Risks and Problems*, Leuven: Leuven University Press.

Fattah, E. (2012) 'The Dawning of a New Era in Social Reaction to Crime: Promise, Potential and Limitations of Restorative Justice', *7th International Conference of the European Forum for Restorative Justice*, Helsinki, Finland.

Feest, J. and Paul, B. (2007) 'Abolitionismus. Einige Antworten auf oft gestellte Fragen', *Kriminologisches Journal*, 40(1): 6–20.

Fox, K.J. (2012) 'Redeeming Communities: Restorative Offender Reentry in a Risk-Centric Society', *Victims & Offenders*, 7(1): 97–120.

Garland, D. (2001) *The Culture of Control: Crime and Social Order in Contemporary Society*, Oxford: Oxford University Press.

Gavrielides, T. (2007) *Restorative Justice Theory and Practice: Addressing the Discrepancy*, Helsinki: European Institute for Crime Prevention and Control.

Gavrielides, T. (2011) *Restorative Justice and the Secure Estate: Alternatives for Young People in Custody*, London: Independent Academic Research Studies.

Green, S., Johnstone, G. and Lambert, C. (2013) 'What Harm, Whose Justice? Excavating the Restorative Movement', *Contemporary Justice Review*, 16(4): 445–460.

Greene, D. (2013) 'Repeat Performance: Is Restorative Justice Another Good Reform Gone Bad?', *Contemporary Justice Review*, 16(3): 359–390.

Griffin, D. (2007) 'Restorative Justice, Diversion and Social Control: Potential Problems', in K. Lalor, F. Ryan, M. Swymour and C. Hamilton (eds), *Young People and Crime: Research, Policy and Practice*, Dublin: Centre for Social and Educational Research.

Groenhuijsen, M. (2004) 'Victims' Rights and Restorative Justice: Piecemeal Reform of the Criminal Justice System or a Change of Paradigm?', in H. Kaptein and M. Malsch (eds), *Crime, Victims, and Justice: Essays on Principles and Practice*, Aldershot: Ashgate Publishing.

Hagemann, O. (2003) 'Restorative Justice in Prison?', in L. Walgrave (ed.), *Repositioning Restorative Justice*, Cullompton: Willan Publishing.

Hayes, H. and Daly, K. (2004) 'Conferencing and Re-offending in Queensland', *Australian and New Zealand Journal of Criminology*, 37(2): 167–191.

Hopkins, B. (2004) *Just Schools: A Whole School Approach to Restorative Justice*, London: Jessica Kingsley Publishing.

Hopkins, B. and Wright, M. (2009) 'Restorative Practices: Should the European Forum Take a Broad or Narrow View?', *European Forum for Restorative Justice*, 10 (1): 3.

Hoyle, C. (2002) 'Securing Justice for the "Non-Participating" Victim', in C. Hoyle and R. Young (eds), *New Visions of Crime Victims*, Oxford: Hart Publishing.

Hoyle, C. (2012) 'Victims, the Criminal Process, and Restorative Justice', in M. Maguire, R. Morgan and R. Reiner (eds), *The Oxford Handbook of Criminology*, Oxford: Oxford University Press.

Hudson, B. (1998) 'Restorative Justice: The Challenge of Sexual and Racial Violence', *Journal of Law and Society*, 25(2): 237–256.

Hudson, B. (2002) 'Restorative Justice and Gendered Violence: Diversion or Effective Justice?', *British Journal of Criminology*, 42(3): 616–634.

Hudson, B. (2003) 'Victims and Offenders', in A.V. Hirsch, J.V. Roberts, A.E. Bottoms, K. Roach and M. Schiff (eds), *Restorative Justice & Criminal Justice: Competing or Reconcilable Paradigms?*, Oxford: Hart Publishing.

Hudson, B. (2005) 'The Culture of Control: Choosing the Future', in M. Matravers (ed.), *Managing Modernity: Politics and the Culture of Control*, London: Routledge.

Johnstone, G. (ed.) (2003) *A Restorative Justice Reader: Texts, Sources, Context*, Cullompton: Willan Publishing.

Johnstone, G. (2007) 'Restorative Justice and the Practice of Imprisonment', *Prison Service Journal*, 174: 15–20.

Johnstone, G. (2011) *Restorative Justice: Ideas, Values, Debates*, 2nd edn, London: Routledge.

Johnstone, G. and Van Ness, D. (2007) 'The Meaning of Restorative Justice', in G. Johnstone and D. Van Ness (eds), *Handbook of Restorative Justice*, Cullompton: Willan Publishing.

Latimer, J., Dowden, C. and Muise, D. (2005) 'The Effectiveness of Restorative Justice Practices: A Meta-Analysis', *The Prison Journal*, 85(2): 127–144.

Levrant, S., Cullen, F.T., Fulton, B. and Wozniak, J.F. (1999) 'Reconsidering Restorative Justice: The Corruption of Benevolence Revisited?', *Crime & Delinquency*, 45(1): 3–27.

Liebmann, M. (2007) *Restorative Justice: How it Works*, London: Jessica Kingsley Publishers.

Llewellyn, J.J. (2006) 'Restorative Justice in Transitions and Beyond: The Justice Potential of Truth-Telling Mechanisms for Post-Peace Accord Societies', in A.T. Borer (ed.), *Telling the Truths: Truth Telling and Peace Building in Post-Conflict Societies*, Notre Dame, IN: University of Notre Dame Press.

Marshall, T. (1996) 'The Evolution of Restorative Justice in Britain', *European Journal of Criminal Policy and Research*, 4(4): 21–43.

Maxwell, G. (2013) 'Justice, Power, and Restorative Solutions', *Restorative Justice: An International Journal*, 1(1): 52–54.

McCold, P. (1998) 'Restorative Justice: Variations on a Theme', in L. Walgrave (ed.), *Restorative Justice for Juveniles: Potentialities, Risks and Problems*, Leuven: Leuven University Press.

McCold, P. (2000) 'Toward a Holistic Vision of Restorative Juvenile Justice: A Reply to the Maximalist Model', *Contemporary Justice Review*, 3(4): 357–414.

McCold, P. (2001) 'Primary Restorative Justice Practices', in A. Morris and G. Maxwell (eds), *Restorative Justice for Juveniles: Conferencing, Mediation and Circles*, Oxford: Hart Publishing.

Mesmaecker, V.D. (2013) 'Victim-offender Mediation Participants' Opinions on the Restorative Justice Values of Confidentiality, Impartiality and Voluntariness', *Restorative Justice: An International Journal*, 1(3): 334–361.

Miers, D. (2004) 'Situating and Researching Restorative Justice in Great Britain', *Punishment and Society*, 6(1): 23–46.

Miller, S.L. (2011) *After the Crime: The Power of Restorative Justice Dialogues between Victims and Violent Offenders*, New York: New York University.

Ministry of Justice (New Zealand) (2014) *Reoffending Analysis for Restorative Justice Cases 2008–2011*, Wellington: Ministry of Justice.

Mirsky, L. (2009) *Hull, UK: Toward a Restorative City*, www.iirp.edu/pdf/Hull.pdf.

Moore, D., Forsythe, L. and O'Connell, T. (1995) *A New Approach to Juvenile Justice: An Evaluation of Family Group Conferencing in Wagga Wagga*, Wagga Wagga: Criminology Research Council (Australia).

Morris, A. (2002) 'Critiquing the Critics: A Brief Response to Critics of Restorative Justice', *British Journal of Criminology*, 42(3): 596–615.

Morris, A. and Maxwell, G. (2000) 'The Practice of Family Group Conferences in New Zealand: Assessing the Place, Potential and Pitfalls of Restorative Justice', in A. Crawford and J. Goodey (eds), *Integrating a Victim Perspective within Criminal Justice: International Debates*, Aldershot: Ashgate Publishing.
Morris, A. and Maxwell, G. (2001) 'Restorative Conferencing', in G. Bazemore and M. Schiff (eds), *Restorative Community Justice: Repairing Harm and Transforming Communities*, Cincinnati, OH: Anderson.
Morris, A. and Young, W. (2000) 'Reforming Criminal Justice: The Potential of Restorative Justice', in H. Strang and J. Braithwaite (eds), *Restorative Justice: Philosophy to Practice*, Aldershot: Ashgate.
Nussbaum, M.C. (2004) *Hiding from Humanity: Disgust, Shame, and the Law*, Princeton, NJ: Princeton University Press.
Pali, B. and Pelikan, C. (2014) 'Con-texting Restorative Justice and Abolitionism: Exploring the Potential and Limits of Restorative Justice as an Alternative Discourse to Criminal Justice', *Restorative Justice: An International Journal*, 2(2): 142.
Pavlich, G. (2005) *Governing Paradoxes of Restorative Justice*, London: Glass House Press.
Pelikan, C. (2010) 'On the Efficacy of Victim-Offender Mediation in Cases of Partnership Violence; or, Men Don't Get Better, but Women Get Stronger: Is it Still True? Outcomes of an Empirical Study', *European Journal on Crime Policy and Research*, 16(1): 49–67.
Peters, T. and Aertsen, I. (2000) 'Towards Restorative Justice: Victimisation, Victim Support and Trends in Criminal Justice', in C.O. Europe (ed.), *Crime and Criminal Justice in Europe*, Baden-Baden: Koelblin.
Polk, K. (1994) 'Family Conferencing: Theoretical and Evaluative Questions', in C. Alder and J. Wundersitz (eds), *Family Conferencing and Juvenile Justice*, Canberra: Australian Institute of Criminology.
Pollard, C. (2001) 'If Your Only Tool is a Hammer, All Your Problems Will Look Like Nails', in H. Strang and J. Braithwaite (eds), *Restorative Justice and Civil Society*, Cambridge: Cambridge University Press.
Pranis, K. (2001) 'Restorative Justice, Social Justice and the Empowerment of Marginalized Populations', in G. Bazemore and M. Schiff (eds), *Restorative Community Justice: Repairing Harm and Transforming Communities*, Cincinnati, OH: Anderson Publishing.
Raye, B.E. and Roberts, A.W. (2007) 'Restorative Processes', in G. Johnstone and D. Van Ness (eds), *Handbook of Restorative Justice*, Cullompton: Willan Publishing.
Robert, L. and Peters, T. (2003) 'How Restorative Justice is Able to Transcend the Prison Walls: A Discussion of the "Restorative Detention" Project', in E.G.M. Weitekamp and H.-J. Kerner (eds), *Restorative Justice in Context: International Practice and Directions*, Cullompton: Willan Publishing.
Roberts, J.V. and Roach, K. (2003) 'Restorative Justice in Canada: From Sentencing Circles to Sentencing Principles', in A.V. Hirsch, J. Roberts, A.E. Bottoms, K. Roach and M. Schiff (eds), *Restorative Justice and Criminal Justice: Competing or Reconcilable Paradigms?* Oxford: Hart Publishing.
Roberts, P. (2003) 'Restoration and Retribution in International Criminal Justice', in A.V. Hirsch, J. Roberts, A.E. Bottoms, K. Roach and M. Schiff (eds), *Restorative Justice & Criminal Justice: Competing or Reconcilable Paradigms*, Oxford: Hart Publishing.

Roche, D. (2006) 'Dimensions of Restorative Justice', *Journal of Social Issues*, 62(2): 217–238.

Shapland, J. (2012) 'Comparing Conferencing and Mediation: Some Evaluation Results Internationally', in E. Zinsstag and I. Vanfraechem (eds), *Conferencing and Restorative Justice: International Practices and Perspectives*, Oxford: Oxford University Press.

Shapland, J., Atkinson, A., Atkinson, H., Colledge, E., Dignan, J., Howes, M., Johnstone, J., Robinson, G. and Sorsby, A. (2006) 'Situating Restorative Justice within Criminal Justice', *Theoretical Criminology*, 10(4): 505–532.

Shapland, J., Robinson, G. and Sorsby, A. (2011) *Restorative Justice in Practice: Evaluating what Works for Victims and Offenders*, New York: Routledge.

Sherman, L., Strang, H., Barnes, G., Braithwaite, J., Inkpen, N. and Teh, M. (1998) *Experiments in Restorative Policing: A Progress Report on the Canberra Reintegrative Shaming Experiments*, Canberra: Australian National University.

Sherman, L., Strang, H. and Woods, D. (2000) *Reoffending Patterns in the Canberra Reintegrative Shaming Experiments (RISE)*, Canberra: Australian National University.

Strang, H. (2002) *Repair or Revenge: Victims and Restorative Justice*, Oxford: Oxford University Press.

Strang, H., Barnes, G., Braithwaite, J. and Sherman, L. (1999) *Experiments in Restorative Policing: A Progress Report on the Canberra Reintegrative Shaming Experiments (RISE)*, Canberra: Australian National University.

Strang, H. and Sherman, L.W. (2003) 'Repairing the Harm: Victims and Restorative Justice', *Utah Law Review*, 15(1): 15–42.

Strang, H., Sherman, L.W., Mayo-Wilson, E., Woods, D. and Ariel, B. (2013) 'Restorative Justice Conferencing (RJC) Using Face-to-Face Meetings of Offenders and Victims: Effects on Offender Recidivism and Victim Satisfaction. A Systematic Review', *Campbell Systematic Reviews*, 9(12): 1–59.

Stubbs, J. (2007) 'Beyond Apology? Domestic Violence and Critical Questions for Restorative Justice', *Criminology and Criminal Justice*, 7(2): 169–187.

Sullivan, D. and Tifft, L. (2004) 'What are the Implications of Restorative Justice for Society and Our Lives', in H. Zehr and B. Toews (eds), *Critical Issues in Restorative Justice*, Cullompton: Willan Publishing.

Sullivan, D. and Tifft, L. (2006) 'Gross Human Rights Violations and Transitional Justice', in D. Sullivan and L. Tifft (eds), *Handbook of Restorative Justice: A Global Perspective*, New York: Routledge.

Tomporowski, B. (2014) 'Restorative Justice and Community Justice in Canada', *Restorative Justice: An International Journal*, 2(2): 218–224.

Tyler, T. (1990) *Why People Obey the Law*, New Haven, CT: Yale University Press.

Umbreit, M. (1999) 'Avoiding the Marginalization and "McDonaldization" of Victim-Offender Mediation: A Case Study in Moving Towards the Mainstream', in G. Bazemore and L. Walgrave (eds), *Restorative Juvenile Justice: Repairing the Harm of Youth Crime*, Monsey, NY: Criminal Justice Press.

Umbreit, M.S. and Armour, M.P. (2011) *Restorative Justice Dialogue: An Essential Guide for Research and Practice*, New York: Springer.

Umbreit, M.S. and Stacey, S.L. (1996) 'Family Group Conferencing Comes to the U.S.: A Comparison with Victim Offender Mediation', *Juvenile and Family Court Journal*, 47(2): 29–39.

Umbreit, M.S., Vos, B., Coates, R.B. and Brown, K.A. (2003) *Facing Violence: The Path of Restorative Justice and Dialogue*, Monsey, NY: Criminal Justice Press.

Van Camp, T. and Wemmers, J. (2013) 'Victim Satisfaction with Restorative Justice: More than Simply Procedural Justice', *International Review of Victimology*, 19(2): 117–143.

Van Ness, D. (2002) 'Creating Restorative Systems', in L. Walgrave (ed.), *Restorative Justice and the Law*, Cullompton: Willan Publishing.

Van Ness, D. (2005) 'An Overview of Restorative Justice around the World', *Eleventh United Nations Congress on Crime Prevention and Criminal Justice*, Bangkok, Thailand.

Van Ness, D. and Strong, K.H. (2010) *Restoring Justice: An Introduction to Restorative Justice*, 4th edn, Cincinnati, OH: Anderson.

Vanfraechem, I. (2007) 'Community, Society and State in Restorative Justice: Some Reflections', in R. Mackay, M. Bosjnak, J. Deklerck, C. Pelikan, B.V. Stokkom and M. Wright (eds), *Images of Restorative Justice Theory*, Frankfurt am Main: Verlag fur Polizei und Wissenschaft.

Vanfraechem, I., Aertsen, I. and Willemsens, J. (eds) (2010) *Restorative Justice Realities: Empirical Research in a European Context*, The Hague: Eleven International Publishing.

Vanfraechem, I. and Walgrave, L. (2009) 'Restorative Practices: Should the European Forum Take a Broad or Narrow View?', *European Forum for Restorative Justice*, 10 (1): 1–2.

Varona, G. (2014) 'ETA Terrorism Victims' Experience with Restorative Encounters in Spain', in I. Vanfraechem, A. Pemberton and F.M. Hdahinda (eds), *Justice for Victims: Perspectives on Rights, Transition and Reconciliation*, Abingdon: Routledge.

Wachtel, T. (2013) *Dreaming of a New Reality: How Restorative Practices Reduce Crime and Violence, Improve Relationships and Strengthen Civil Society*, Pipersville, PA: The Piper's Press.

Wachtel, T. and Mirsky, L. (eds) (2008) *Safer Saner Schools: Restorative Practices in Education*, Bethlehem, PA: International Institute for Restorative Practices.

Wachtel, T., O'Connell, T. and Wachtel, B. (2010) *Restorative Justice Conferencing: Real Justice and the Conferencing Handbook*, Pipersville, PA: The Piper's Press.

Walgrave, L. (1995) 'Restorative Justice for Juveniles: Just a Technique or a Fully Fledged Alternative?', *Howard Journal*, 34(3): 228–249.

Walgrave, L. (1998) 'What is at Stake in Restorative Justice for Juveniles?', in L. Walgrave (ed.), *Restorative Justice for Juveniles: Potentialities, Risks, and Problems for Research*, Leuven: Leuven University Press.

Walgrave, L. (1999) 'Community Service as a Cornerstone of a Systematic Restorative Response to Juvenile Justice', in G. Bazemore and L. Walgrave (eds), *Restorative Juvenile Justice: Repairing the Harm of Youth Crime*, Monsey, NY: Criminal Justice Press.

Walgrave, L. (2000) 'How Pure Can a Maximalist Approach to Restorative Justice Remain?', *Contemporary Justice Review*, 3(4): 415–432.

Walgrave, L. (2006) 'Integrating Criminal Justice and Restorative Justice', in G. Johnstone and D. Van Ness (eds), *Handbook of Restorative Justice*, Cullompton: Willan Publishing.

Walgrave, L. (2008) *Restorative Justice, Self-Interest and Responsible Citizenship*, Cullompton: Willan Publishing.

Walgrave, L. (2012) 'The Need for Clarity about Restorative Justice Conferences', in E. Zinsstag and I. Vanfraechem (eds), *Conferencing and Restorative Justice: International Practices and Perspectives*, Oxford: Oxford University Press.

Walgrave, L. (2013a), 'From Civilising Punishment to Civilising Criminal Justice: From Punishment to Restoration', in D.J. Cornwell, J. Blad and M. Wright (eds), *Civilising Criminal Justice: An International Restorative Agenda for Penal Reform*, Winchester: Waterside Press.

Walgrave, L. (2013b), 'Words on "Words on Words"', *Restorative Justice: An International Journal*, 1(1): 77–85.

Walgrave, L., Aertsen, I., Parmentier, S., Vanfraechem, I. and Zinsstag, E. (2013) 'Why Restorative Justice Matters for Criminology?', *Restorative Justice: An International Journal*, 1(2): 159–167.

Walters, M.A. and Hoyle, C. (2012) 'Exploring the Everday World of Hate Victimization through Community Mediation', *International Review of Victimology*, 18(1): 7–24.

Weitekamp, E.G.M. (1992) 'Can Restitution Serve as a Reasonable Alternative to Imprisonment?', in H. Messmer and H.U. Otto (eds), *Restorative Justice on Trial: Pitfalls and Potentials of Victim-Offender Mediation*, Dordrecht and Boston, MA: Kluwer Academic.

Weitekamp, E.G.M. (2002) 'Restorative Justice: Present Prospects and Future Directions', in E.G.M. Weitekamp and H.-J. Kerner (eds), *Restorative Justice: Theoretical Foundations*, Cullompton: Willan Publishing.

Weitekamp, E.G.M., Parmentier, S., Vanspauwen, K., Valiñas, M. and Gerits, R. (2006) 'How to Deal with Mass Victimization and Gross Human Rights Violations: A Restorative Justice Approach', in U. Ewald and K. Turkovic (eds), *Large-Scale Victimisation as a Potential Source of Terrorist Activities: Importance of Regaining Security in Post-Conflict Societies*, Amsterdam: IOS Press.

Wheeldon, J. (2009) 'Finding Common Ground: Restorative Justice and its Theoretical Construction(s)', *Contemporary Justice Review*, 12(1): 91–100.

Woolford, A. (2009) *The Politics of Restorative Justice: A Critical Introduction*, Halifax: Fernwood.

Wright, M. (1996a), 'Can Mediation be an Alternative to Criminal Justice?', in B. Galaway and J. Hudson (eds), *Restorative Justice: International Perspectives*, Monsey, NY: Criminal Justice Press.

Wright, M. (1996b), *Justice for Victims and Offenders: A Restorative Response to Crime*, 2nd edn, Winchester: Waterside Press.

Wright, M. (2010) *Towards a Restorative Society: A Problem-Solving Response to Harm*, www.makejusticework.org.uk/wp-content/uploads/Martin-Wright-Towards-a-Restorative-Society.pdf.

Wright, M. (2013a), 'Could a Restorative System of Justice be more Civilised than a Punitive One?', in D.J. Cornwell, J. Blad and M. Wright (eds), *Civilising Criminal Justice: An International Restorative Agenda for Penal Reform*, Winchester: Waterside Press.

Wright, M. (2013b), 'Restorative Justice: The Search for the mot juste', *Restorative Justice: An International Journal*, 1(1): 85–90.

Young, R. (2001) 'Just Cops Doing "Shameful" Business? Police-Led Restorative Justice and the Lessons of Research', in A. Morris and G. Maxwell (eds), *Restoring Justice for Juveniles: Conferences, Mediation and Circles*, Oxford: Hart Publishing.

Zehr, H. (1990) *Changing Lenses: A New Focus for Crime and Justice*, Scottdale, PA: Herald Press.

Zehr, H. (2002) *The Little Book of Restorative Justice*, Intercourse, PA: Good Books.

Zehr, H. and Mika, H. (1998) 'Fundamental Concepts of Restorative Justice', *Contemporary Justice Review*, 1(1): 47–55.

Zinsstag, E. (2012) 'Conferencing: A Developing Practice of Restorative Justice', in E. Zinsstag and I. Vanfraechem (eds), *Conferencing and Restorative Justice: International Practices and Perspectives*, Oxford: Oxford University Press.

2 Restorative justice's problematic appeals to community

As the previous chapter demonstrates, attempts to explain the principles and goals of restorative justice necessarily include several references to the term 'community'. In fact, since its inception, advocates have presented the community as an essential pillar of restorative justice theory and practice (see Zehr 1990). No wonder, then, the frequent use of the word 'community' within discourses of restorative justice, the prominence of 'community service' amidst currently known and accepted forms of reparation, and the overall emphasis placed by restorativists on 'community involvement' in restorative justice practices. However, whilst there has been considerable academic focus on other themes – such as the potential of restorative justice to satisfy victims – the role of community in restorative justice remains an under-researched topic, both theoretically and empirically.

In fact, although restorative justice theory has yet to be fully realised, and further theoretical work is required, appeals to community are particularly imprecise. Within the morass of restorative justice's appeals, the rationale for *why* and *how* community is essential to restorative justice remains under-developed and largely unchallenged. With this in mind, the aim of this chapter is threefold. First, I draw on the restorative justice literature to identify and explore restorative justice's appeals to community: *why do restorativists promote (and, indeed, fiercely defend) the involvement of the community in restorative practices?* Second, I show how the notion of community involvement has been conceived and operationalised throughout time and across different contexts of restorative justice: *how has the community typically been involved in restorative justice programmes?* Third, I revisit and problematise restorative justice's appeals to community: *what remains unclear about the role of community in restorative justice?* In other words, I shall attempt to identify the theoretical 'justifications' for restorativists' promotion of the community in restorative justice processes, and provide an overview of the means by which they have sought to realise community involvement. In so doing, I shall be able to identify some of the unanswered questions centring on the role of community in restorative justice, and it is against this theoretical background that I shall proceed to analyse my empirical findings.[1]

2.1 'Why' should the community be involved?

As has been argued in the previous chapter, from a restorative justice perspective, crime affects a tripartite relationship between the offender, the victim and the community (Gormally 2002). Ideally, therefore, restorative justice processes should bring all three parties into communication to collectively define the harm and develop a plan to repair it (McCold 2000). One of restorative justice's premises, then, is that the community should be involved in the process of restorative justice. But why, precisely, should the community be involved?

Because conflicts also belong to the community

Most of the theoretical justifications for community involvement in restorative justice processes start from the premise that 'stolen' conflicts should be returned to their owners (Christie 1977). Restorativists have enthusiastically taken up the argument that because offending has conventionally been conceived of as a violation against the state, decisions on how crime should be dealt with have traditionally been reached through detached and impersonal justice processes led and dominated by professionals who represent the state and who marginalise those affected by crime (Morris 2002; Morris and Young 2000). Restorative justice, by contrast, aims to change the traditional way of doing justice by placing the decision of how to deal with a particular offence in the hands of those most (directly) affected by it. This means returning decision making to the community as well as the offender and victim, since crime also causes harm to what Walgrave (2002) has referred to as the 'living' community. Restorative justice then focuses on putting right the wrongs caused by criminal offences, and again, that means (insofar as possible) repairing the harms done to victims *and* the victimised community.

This is not to suggest that the spillover effects of crime on the community were not acknowledged before the rise of restorative justice, but rather to make the point that conventionally, for advocates of restorative justice, 'the idea that the community has a stake in an offense – that apart from direct victims, a larger social network might also be a harmed party – is incorporated into mainstream criminal justice practice only in abstract, highly formalized ways' (Dzur and Olson 2004: 93).[2] Restorative justice proponents argue that 'apart from participation as silent jurors and, upon request, as witnesses, community members do not, themselves, speak out in criminal justice proceedings'; instead, prosecutors and judges proclaim to provide a voice for whoever (or whatever) might have been victimised, from the direct (individual or corporate) victim to society at large (Dzur and Olson 2004: 93; see also Vanfraechem 2007).

By involving community representatives in restorative justice processes, scholars and practitioners (explicitly or implicitly) claim to be involving a party ('the community') that is more directly victimised by the occurrence of an offence than the remote and detached figures of state and society (typically represented by professionals) (Walgrave 2002). That is, through the discourse that 'stolen' conflicts should be returned to their owners, restorative justice theorists hope to bring about changes in the way criminal justice systems handle the community harm generated by crime as they suggest that restorative justice programmes are capable of establishing more concrete ways of involving the (victimised) community in mainstream criminal justice practice (Dzur and Olson 2004).

Because community should find the ability to solve its own conflicts

Linked to the discourse of giving conflict back to the community is the idea that the community should be able to shoulder its own conflicts. By involving members of the community in restorative justice processes, it is hoped that the community will emerge stronger, more capable of resolving its own conflicts, and thus more capable of controlling crime (Bazemore 1998; Christie 1977). For restorative justice advocates, '[t]he more the public participates, the more it takes back the authority for social control ceded to the state' (Dzur 2008: 184). As Dzur and Olson (2004: 96) explain:

> When the public is more involved in the criminal justice system, people meet one another, neighbors are no longer strangers, and informal social control is increased. [...] Participation ideally strengthens the social ties that empower community members to deter crime and shame and reintegrate offenders.

So, restorative justice is aimed at not just returning conflicts to the community but empowering the community to take control over the resolution of its own conflicts. As such, it is often described as a 'community-based movement', which rejects 'notions of experts and the consolidation of professional power', and ventures 'to explore – or revive – a more communitarian and assessable means for community members to take back power that institutions stole from their lives' (Erbe 2004: 289). The idea is that the community should have ownership over the restorative justice process, and the authorities should not be the arbiters of justice. In fact, it is argued, whenever decisions are made by the authorities, or whenever authorities interfere with the workings of restorative encounters, the process should be referred to as 'authoritarian restorative justice', if it is recognised as restorative justice at all (Wright 2000).

Along these lines, restorative justice is also very much about changing government/community relations, or more precisely, the relationships between communities and their criminal justice systems (Dzur and Olson 2004; Erbe 2004). Indeed, beyond increasing community access to criminal justice, restorative justice aims at changing 'the essential role of the citizen from service recipient to decision maker with a stake in what services are provided and how they are delivered' (Bazemore 1998: 334). Within a restorative justice framework, then, the state's role in the crime control system, or indeed the role of its representatives, is limited mainly to that of an enabler or resource provider, just as Christie (1977: 12) had suggested:

> And [...] if we find [professionals] unavoidable in certain cases or at certain stages, [l]et us try to get them to perceive themselves as resource-persons, answering when asked, but not domineering, not in the centre. They might help to stage conflicts, not take them over.

In this vein, restorative justice is as much about involving the community as it is about *how* community involvement should occur. Or, as argued by Erbe (2004: 294):

> The movement is not about the community participating in the sanctioning of the offender, or the system allowing for community involvement. Rather, it is about the community taking ownership of its problems and being equal partners with mainstream, criminal justice institutions.

This brings us to two other theoretical justifications for community participation in restorative justice practices: the benefits of lay participation, and the power of the so-called 'community of care'.

Because laypeople are better than criminal justice professionals at certain tasks

In many restorative justice programmes across the globe, the notion of community involvement has been developed to mean, more specifically, the involvement of *laypeople* in the processes of restorative justice. These members of the public are not invited as 'behaviour experts' (Christie 1977) or as lawyers; in fact, they are not involved in the process due to their professional expertise at all, but due to their attachment to the community that has been affected by a particular crime or series of crimes. They are involved in the process of conflict resolution because they 'own' the conflict, and because, it is argued, we should dispel the idea that professionals are better able to decide how those directly involved in the conflict should be helped or responded to. Here Christie's ideas of conflicts as property once again come to the fore, particularly where he calls for 'an extreme degree of lay-orientation' in the handling of crime (Christie 1977).

Over time, the rereading and repackaging of Christie's ideas, oftentimes influenced by different theoretical foundations or movements (particularly by communitarian theories and informal justice ideals), has led restorative justice advocates to aggregate some very ambitious assumptions around the benefits of laypeople controlling or directing mainstream criminal justice practice. Some advocates go as far as to suggest that 'laypeople are better able than criminal justice professionals at certain key tasks, such as reprobation and reintegration of offenders and communicating sympathy for victims' (Dzur and Olson 2004: 94). Arguments of that kind are normally rooted in assumptions about the benefits of informal over formal social control. Indeed, according to Clear and Karp (1999: 18), community members are a 'more powerful agent of social control, if for no other reason than the fact that parents, teachers, or neighbors provide a level of surveillance that can never be matched by the police in a free, democratic society'.

The line of reasoning leading to the assumption that laypeople are better able than professionals to carry out certain criminal justice tasks, as presented by Dzur and Olson (2004: 95), could be summarised as follows: members of the community 'have a better sense of who is doing what, when, and where in their neighborhoods', plus they 'can be more intrusive into their own lives than can state officials'. Therefore, 'the informal monitoring of criminal activity has deterrence effects unmatched by the formal efforts of the police'. When crime occurs, again we should turn to lay members of the community in the process of conflict resolution, because, it is said, non-professionals '"speak the same language" as the offender and are therefore thought to communicate disapproval better than criminal justice professionals, who might be seen as "part of the system"' (Dzur and Olson 2004: 95). In fact, restorativists often contend that lay members of the community are better than criminal justice professionals at 'connecting' with the conflicting parties (Olson and Dzur 2003), or, indeed, that lay members of the community should be involved in restorative justice processes because 'offenders are more likely to care about their opinion than that of justice professionals, and thus community members are more able to achieve rehabilitative and reintegrative effects' (Olson and Dzur 2003: 63; see also Braithwaite 2002). The overall idea is to try to control crime by involving community representatives in crime prevention and penal decision making (Green 2014).

Such high expectations around the benefits of lay participation have been caused by, and in turn have caused, an ever-growing scepticism around the role of professionals in restorative justice. In fact, restorative justice theorists often present a dichotomous picture of lay members of the community and criminal justice professionals, with the latter appearing as a threat to genuine restorative justice endeavours. One restorative justice enthusiast has gone as far as to alert us to the dangers of 'academic superstars' whom he thinks may be dismissing community members in the development of practice and discourse regarding restorative justice (Erbe 2004). So, while some restorative justice writers choose to focus more on the potential benefits of lay involvement, others focus on the potential threats posed by professionals. However, despite subtle differences, all recognise that if conflicts are to be returned to their owners – and not appropriated by the state and its representatives – professionals should be kept as far away as possible from (or as inactive as possible in) the process of restorative justice.

Because the offender's 'community of care' is better able than criminal justice professionals to persuade the offender to take responsibility

Above, I have drawn attention to the fact that in many restorative justice programmes, the increasing involvement of community members has come to mean the involvement of *laypeople* not necessarily known to the offender or to the victim, such as residents of a local area where a particular offence has been committed. It is important to say, however, that another quite different rationale for community participation in restorative practices has developed in parallel to (and perhaps ahead of) the assumptions laid out above regarding lay participation. It has to do with the idea that certain people known to the offender may be more capable of influencing the offender's attitudes within processes of restorative justice.

Indeed, the involvement of the 'community' in restorative processes has also come to mean the involvement of the so-called 'community of care' of both offenders and victims. That is, besides involving members of the (affected but rather detached) community who may not be acquainted with the victim or with the offender, restorative justice programmes have also sought to include the family groups, peers, friends, colleagues, and so forth, of victims and offenders (Morris and Maxwell 2000). The rationales underpinning the involvement of the victim's community of care come down to the idea of providing victims with a meaningful net of support during restorative justice encounters, given that, while aspiring to be rewarding, they can be painful experiences. However, it is important to note the less obvious – but rather influential – reasons why it is considered helpful to involve the offender's community of care in restorative practices.

Drawing explicitly or implicitly on Braithwaite's notions of reintegrative shaming (Braithwaite 1989), restorative justice advocates have argued that the involvement of the community in restorative justice processes is also important for bringing together people who are more likely to persuade the offender to take responsibility for his or her behaviour. Again, this is more evident in practices such as restorative conferences and circles, whereby offenders are confronted with the victims' suffering but also with the suffering of their own loved ones (e.g. their mother, their father, their best friends, etc.). This 'suffering of their own loved ones', it is argued, can be much more powerful in leading the offender to take full responsibility for the offence than the moralising speech of a judge in a court session, for example, or even than the victims' story of suffering (Harris *et al.* 2004). In turn, within the 'emotional dynamics' of a restorative encounter, where it is expected that offenders will feel shame 'especially because their wrongfulness is exposed in the eyes of those who care for them and for whom they care', offenders are better persuaded to repair the harm they have caused and ultimately to refrain from further offending behaviour (Harris *et al.* 2004; Johnstone 2011; Walgrave 2008). Finally, the offender's community of care, it is said, can provide the kind of support that offenders need in their efforts to keep out of trouble (Johnstone 2011).

Hopefully, it should have become clear by now that although I have attempted to explain them separately, the theoretical justifications for community participation in restorative justice are all very much interrelated and should not be seen in isolation. Buried in all the reasons for involving the community in restorative justice practice is the idea that conflicts should be returned to their owners, and the belief that the community is one of the owners of all conflicts generated by the occurrence of a crime. In fact, it is apparent that there is a clear tendency among restorative justice theorists to dichotomise state and community. Accordingly, all reasons for community involvement highlight the many possible benefits of having the community, as opposed to the state using professionals, in charge of the process of reparation and conflict resolution. All in all, Fitzpatrick's (1992: 200) description of the 'Community Boards Program in San Francisco' is equally relevant here, as restorative justice practices should also:

> [...] stand opposed to the alienating professionalism of the state, to its formality and its 'record-keeping apparatus', to its insensitivity in the face of the real needs of individuals and communities, and to its illimitable arrogation of conflicts and other matters that can only be dealt with adequately by individuals and neighbourhoods.

2.2 'How' should the community be involved?

Possibly more problematic than the question of *why* is the question of *how* the community should be involved in restorative justice programmes. Whilst restorative justice aims to establish more concrete and meaningful ways of involving the community in mainstream criminal justice practice, the truth is that 'different views of community have led to conflicting goals and divergent practices' (McCold 2004: 157). As a matter of fact, in practice, choices about how to involve the community entail establishing how many and which people should be involved in the restorative justice process as 'community representatives' (or on behalf of the community), and also what tasks they should (and should not) perform. Over time, different restorative justice programmes have made different choices.

That said, although it is quite difficult to generalise, the restorative justice literature seems to identify four more obvious ways of involving members of the community in restorative processes: through lay (but trained) volunteers serving as mediators; through the networks of both victim and offender helping to shape (and monitor) restoration plans; through local residents helping to shape (and monitor) restoration plans; and through lay (but trained) volunteers helping to shape (and monitor) restoration plans. Although these by no means exhaust the range of alternatives of community involvement, they are sufficiently distinct to illustrate the different perceptions of community within current restorative justice rhetoric and practice.

Through lay (but trained) volunteers serving as mediators

In the first modern expressions of restorative justice, in the late 1970s, community participation was generally limited to the involvement of lay volunteers serving as mediators (McCold 2004). That was and still is the case with most victim–offender mediation programmes, which involve direct or indirect dialogue between the victim and offender in the presence of a lay facilitator or with a lay facilitator acting as a go-between (Johnstone 2011; Wright 1998). In such programmes, the task of the lay facilitator (or mediator) is not to propose or impose a decision on the parties, but to act as an intermediary or as a channel of communication between victim and offender (Dignan 2005). Another important mandate that may be assigned to (or assumed by) mediators is the responsibility for preparing the parties, which involves contacting them separately before mediation sessions take place to explain the process and assess their readiness to participate (Aertsen *et al.* 2004). Finally, victim–offender mediation services (and, thus, mediators on their behalf) may also assume the responsibility for post-session monitoring, enforcement and follow-up, although that may be done by, or under the close guidance of, criminal justice agencies (and, thus, professionals) (Aertsen *et al.* 2004).

So, in short, mediators are involved in victim–offender mediation programmes primarily to enable and facilitate a dialogical process between the victim and the offender, although some authors suggest that they are also there to represent symbolically 'the macro-community' or 'the interests of society in general' (McCold 2004: 155). Be that as it may, the truth is that they do not tend to provide a voice for secondary victims, nor are they there as part of a community of care for the victim or the offender; they normally act as a neutral party in a process that is very much focused on the ideal of reconciliation between the victim and the offender.

Advocates of victim-offender mediation programmes have traditionally argued that the involvement of a larger number and a wider range of community members would be undesirable and unnecessary. For many, 'the advantages in allowing only victim, offender, and mediator to participate, are that more time is allowed for victim input and that victims who might feel intimidated in a larger group may feel empowered to speak' (Bazemore 1998: 342–343). Some also argue that the presence of too many people (or of too many adults, in the particular case of young offenders) may be so intimidating to offenders that they may not feel sufficiently safe or comfortable to take responsibility fully for their criminal behaviour and provide an honest account of their actions (Haines 1997; Umbreit and Stacey 1996). Ultimately, it has been argued that 'the bottom-line objectives of involving the victim, gaining reparation, and holding the offender accountable for his or her crime do not necessarily require the larger community' (Bazemore 1998: 342–343).

Through the networks of victims and offenders helping to shape (and monitor) restoration plans

As has been suggested above, the involvement of the community in restorative justice processes has also come to mean the involvement of the so-called 'community of care' of both offenders and victims. Indeed, particularly from the 1990s, there has been something of a departure from the highly abstract notion of having the 'wider society' represented in the justice process; restorative justice programmes reworked the notion of community involvement and tied it to the inclusion of those who, in addition to the victim and the offender, are most directly affected by (or emotionally connected to) a particular offence (Bolivar 2012; McCold 2004; Morris and Maxwell 2000). On the one hand, the notion of community participation is broadened in that a group of people, instead of just one mediator, is involved in the process. On the other hand, the perception of community is narrowed to those family members, friends and others with whom the offender and the victim have meaningful personal relationships, whilst practices become more concerned with harms caused to these specific individuals rather than with 'the cumulative effect of crime on neighborhoods or society, and the resulting loss of sense of public safety' (McCold 2004: 157). To use McCold's (2004) terms, instead of involving random local citizen volunteers to represent symbolically the 'macro-community', some restorative practices have preferred to include the victim's and offender's 'micro-community'.

Family group conferences are probably the best examples of this. In contrast to victim–offender mediation programmes, the involvement of this community of intimates (particularly the offender's family) is viewed as essential to, and an integral part of family group conferences (Bazemore 1998; Morris and Maxwell 2000; Umbreit and Stacey 1996). Accordingly, those people who are part of a community of care for the victim or for the offender have an active role in helping to resolve the offence. In fact, 'they can offer reactions to the crime, restitution ideas, and opportunities for implementation', and what is more, 'they also frequently stay involved with the victim and/or offender afterwards, contributing support and monitoring of the restitution agreement' (Umbreit and Stacey 1996: 33). In other words, unlike mediators, members of the victim's and of the offender's community of care do actually take part in the decision-making process. That said, as with victim–offender mediation schemes, family group conferences also employ a facilitator to enable communication between the parties, although in family group conferences the role of the facilitator as a community representative is less obvious or obfuscated by the role of community played by the parties' acquaintances or significant others (Morris and Maxwell 2000).

It should be stressed that in victim–offender mediation programmes the parties are sometimes (and ever more often) allowed to bring family members or other supporters to a meeting. This is particularly the case in mediation schemes involving young offenders, when the parents are usually present

(McCold 2001). In such cases, victim–offender mediation programmes are rather similar to family group conferences in that they also involve the parties' 'community of care'. Nevertheless, an important distinction remains: victim–offender mediation programmes remain personally focused on the dialogue between the victim and the offender, with the result that often only expressions of feelings by the victim and the offender are encouraged whilst any support people present may even be asked not to speak at all until the end of the meeting (Shapland 2012; Umbreit and Stacey 1996). In contrast to that, in family group conferences, the young person and her community of care work out a plan proposal together, which is then discussed by everyone in the meeting (Morris and Maxwell 2000; Smull *et al.* 2012).

Through local residents helping to shape (and monitor) restoration plans

Experiments with restorative justice may also involve an even larger number and wider range of community members, who are recruited from the local community where crime has occurred, but who are not necessarily acquainted with the victim and the offender (unlike in family group conferences), and yet are expected to take part actively in shaping and monitoring restoration plans (unlike in victim–offender mediation programmes) (Johnstone 2011).

A good example would be restorative circles (e.g. sentencing circles), where local residents are invited to come along, take a seat (in a circle), and 'speak from their heart' about their concerns for victims, offenders and their families; about the situations in the community that enabled the offence to happen and the obligations that the community might have towards the parties and/or towards other residents; about their hope that the circle will find a way of healing all affected parties and preventing future occurrences; and so on (McCold 2001). Here, 'the effort to blur the distinction between crime and more general problems in social relationships, social justice, and spirituality provides a philosophical justification for this openness to citizen participation' (Bazemore 1998: 350; see also Pranis 2003).

In this context, there is not really a limit on the number of attendees: 'the number of participants in circle sentencing is apparently limited only by the size of the facility available (and to those citizens who do not present a disruptive influence by drinking or drug use)' (Bazemore 1998: 343). Besides victims, offenders and their respective communities of care, virtually any other members of the local community are welcome to come along. More importantly, as a 'talking piece' is passed from person to person around the circle, opportunity is given to each and every participant to express their views and opinions in a controlled and therefore safe environment (Raye and Roberts 2007). Further, each person's interests and concerns are integrated into the decision-making process (Umbreit and Armour 2011). The idea is to encourage extensive, real and not just token, community participation. In this, circles broaden the notion of community participation in restorative justice processes to its full extent:

> These peace forums are at the expansive end of the continuum of stakeholder participation, moving from the 'community of care' of much restorative justice writing to a 'community of life'. They seek to govern the future rather than simply restore a balance that has been upset in the past.
>
> (Braithwaite and Strang 2001: 3)

Indeed, 'the principal intent of circles, regardless of their overt goals, is to develop or strengthen the community' (Umbreit and Armour 2011: 183). That means that the whole process revolves equally around every member of the circle, as victims, offenders, communities of care and other local residents are all equally regarded as members of the victimised community.

Having said that, it should be noted that restorative circles often involve criminal justice professionals (e.g. judges, prosecutors, court officials, police officers). Nevertheless, instead of taking the role of primary decision makers, these professionals will normally share with lay members of the community the responsibilities of selecting, sanctioning and following up the cases. In fact, in circle processes, lay members of the community may play crucial roles at virtually all stages of the 'criminal' (actually, 'restorative') process as they may be involved in deciding whether to accept an applicant for a sentencing circle, in planning and preparing the circle process, in deciding the sentence to be served by the offender, and also in the later stages of monitoring, enforcing and following up the decisions reached by the circle (Bazemore 1998; Umbreit and Armour 2011). As such, it is said, circles are perhaps the practical expressions of restorative justice that come the closest to realising the restorative ideal of retaining control of community issues within the community (Erbe 2004; Raye and Roberts 2007).

Through lay (but trained) volunteers helping to shape (and monitor) restoration plans

Some restorative programmes have also sought to increase community participation through the involvement of local citizens in the process, but when compared to circles, they do so in more formal, less spontaneous and less inclusive ways. They involve the community in a more systematically institutionalised fashion, as the court orders a small number of *lay (but trained) volunteers* to meet with the offender (and possibly with the victim and their communities of care) to help shape (and monitor) restoration plans. Clear examples here would be local citizens reparative boards in the USA (see Bazemore 1998; Karp and Drakulich 2004; Lockhart 2002).

In the Vermont model (see Boyes-Watson 2004; Karp 2001; Olson and Dzur 2003), for example, judges sentence non-violent offenders to probation with the proviso that they must appear before a local reparative board. The board – which is typically composed of five or six citizen volunteers, and assisted by a member of staff – meets with the offender for the first time to negotiate a reparative agreement. This reparative agreement includes a set of tasks that are assigned to the offender to be completed during his/her probationary period. Victims and other affected parties, such as parents of young offenders, are invited to attend this meeting, although victim attendance rates have been reported to be very low (Karp 2001; Karp and Drakulich 2004). Typically, offenders return to the board for a review meeting halfway through their probationary period, and then again for a closure meeting before discharge. Finally, the board members have the authority to return offenders to court for resentencing if they refuse to sign the agreement or if they fail to comply with the requirements of the reparation agreement.

As far as community involvement is concerned, such practices are hybrid in that they resemble features of the other models described above. So, for example, like facilitators in victim-offender mediation programmes, community members in reparative boards are chosen from a pool of volunteers who are trained to perform that role. Nevertheless, as in circles, they are not there as a neutral third party acting to facilitate the communication between victim and offender; they are themselves parties acting on behalf of the community and, as such, are actively involved (or even take the lead) in the decision-making process. Furthermore, as in family group conferences, the community of care is normally present and may help to shape the restoration plan by bringing their own ideas on how the offender could make good the harms done.

In later chapters (particularly in Chapter 6), when analysing the context within which the community is involved in referral orders and youth offender panels in England and Wales, I will return to these different 'models' of community involvement. For the time being, this overview suffices to provide a theoretical backdrop for the following discussion over what remains unclear about the role of community in restorative justice.

2.3 What remains unclear about the role of community in restorative justice?

It is important to note that restorative justice's appeals to community sit within a wider 'late modern' criminal justice landscape where the limitations of the state's capacity to control crime are increasingly apparent, and where professional specialism in the handling of crime is viewed with increasing scepticism (Garland 2001). According to Bartkowiak and Jaccoud (2008: 209), communities' prerogatives and identities became more prominent 'when the state (at least in Western countries) decided to withdraw to some extent from its role as a service provider and first port of call for citizens'. Neoliberal ideologies, decentralisation movements and the crises linked with state agencies' loss of legitimacy, they argue, have all 'contributed to an increase in the potency of the idea of community in several domains' (Bartkowiak and Jaccoud 2008: 209). Similarly, in his explanation of the process by which appeals to community have been assimilated into contemporary criminal justice policies, Green (2014: 52) writes:

> If policies cannot affect the rate of crime, the task becomes one of political management [...] The government has to be seen to be strong on law and order whilst simultaneously extricating itself from blame in regard to rising crime. The only pragmatic solution to this conundrum was to shift the responsibility for crime onto social structures such as the family and the community.

So, actually, the idea of 'community involvement' is common to other 'non-restorative justice' movements or initiatives, which influence and may be influenced by restorative justice. For example, in searching for reasons why the community has been involved with other criminal justice initiatives, ranging from Neighbourhood Watch to volunteer involvement in community service orders, Lacey and Zedner (1995: 302) found two decades ago that:

> [...] institutional initiatives have sought to incorporate the community in combating crime, in order to encourage self-help and active co-operation or even partnership with the formal agencies of crime control. In so doing, they also seek to dispel the idea that crime is the problem of government, to be dealt with away from the community's gaze.

Garland (1996: 452) characterises this mode of governing as 'responsibilisation strategy', and according to him:

> This involves the central government seeking to act upon crime not in a direct fashion through state agencies (police, courts, prisons, social work, etc.) but instead by acting indirectly, seeking to activate action on the part of non-state agencies and organizations.

In such a climate it is not surprising that restorative justice has gathered momentum. However, if discourses of community participation in criminal justice practice have become increasingly common, what then remains unique about restorativists' appeals to community? Perhaps the promise that restorative justice programmes provide a better framework for community participation than other current criminal justice initiatives. But do they?

Although the restorative justice literature has been quite convincing in its arguments that we need to find more meaningful ways of involving the community in criminal justice practice, I would argue that it has not yet provided a coherent framework for operationalising community involvement in restorative justice programmes. All the theoretical justifications for community involvement, as laid out above, are intuitively appealing – and the means by which restorative justice programmes have sought to realise community involvement are indeed interesting. Nevertheless, thorough reviews of the restorative justice literature leave a distinct impression that there has been too little effort at drawing a clearer line between the empirical authenticity of community (what community can actually do) and its normative appeals (what community is expected to do) (Crawford 2000). Instead, the restorative justice literature has perpetuated some old myths around the benefits of community involvement in criminal justice, added some new 'restorative myths', and largely overlooked the limitations upon realising community involvement on the ground. All in all, some very important questions around the role of community in restorative justice have been left without satisfactory answers, and I would like to bring some of these to the fore.

How more concrete can community involvement get?

As mentioned above, a common criticism among restorativists is that the notion of community harm generated by crime has conventionally been incorporated into mainstream criminal justice practice in only very abstract ways – for example, through the participation of community members as silent jurors or as witnesses on request (Dzur 2008). In response to that, 'restorative justice proponents call for more public participation in the criminal justice process so that the harm to community is more clearly brought to the attention of the offender' (Dzur and Olson 2004: 93). There are at least two underlying assumptions here: first, that the notion of community harm can be incorporated into criminal justice practice in more concrete ways, and second, that the way to do this is by increasing the involvement of community members in criminal/restorative justice processes.

The problem is that harm to community remains a notoriously abstract idea: 'almost any communal interest can be said to be set back by a criminal act' (Von Hirsch 1998: 675). Increased insecurity, fear of crime, weakened social ties, decline in trust, etc., are the sorts of collective harms that could be brought to the attention of the offender. So what are we actually expecting from community members once they get involved in restorative justice processes? Are we expecting them to communicate such harms more persuasively than has been done before? Are we expecting them to bring to the fore creative ideas on how these sorts of harms could be repaired by the offender? Are we expecting them to help offenders realise the goals of the damaged community? In which case, are justice agencies prepared to take creative ideas on board, given their typically risk-averse (or health and safety-focused) professional culture (Crawford and Newburn 2003)? Ultimately, how can the greater involvement of community members – for example, the changing role from mere witness to facilitator – help to fully incorporate community harm into criminal justice in day-to-day practice, rather than in the rarefied world of restorative justice academics? While we have a considerable amount of empirical data on the experiences of victims and offenders in restorative processes, it is clear that more research is needed to explore how, and to what effect, 'community representatives' have been communicating the harms done to the community, particularly to offenders.

What is so good about lay involvement?

The widespread idea that lay members of the community can be more effective in the process of reparation and conflict resolution than professionals is rooted in a series of assumptions. To start with, it is argued that lay members of the community know who is doing what and when in their neighbourhoods, and can be more intrusive in their neighbours' lives. In turn, it is thought, they are better than professionals at the task of deterring their neighbours from committing crimes; and then when crime occurs, of reintegrating the offender back into the community. In other words, besides the apparent assumptions about the benefits of informal over formal social control, it is also assumed that lay members of the community have better 'local intelligence' or 'personal knowledge' than professionals do (Shapland 2008).

However, as Hudson (1998: 251) reminds us, 'most of us now inhabit not "communities", but shifting, temporary alliances which come together on the basis of private prudentialism'. Hence, the truth is that in contemporary, urban contexts, people may know very little about the locality in which they live and about their 'neighbours'. In fact, because of their jobs, professionals may well have better local knowledge than lay members of the community. What is more, it is not clear '[...] why people who are trained and are paid for their work cannot be at the same time committed members of their community' (Walgrave 2012: 38).

The idea that lay members of the community have better 'local knowledge' than professionals also entails the assumption that restorative justice programmes will always be able to recruit a pool of lay volunteers that properly represents the community in which the crime has occurred – although, in reality, the recruited community members may represent a very limited section of the population living in that community. Indeed, 'there is no guarantee that unpaid people being motivated and able to facilitate conferences do really represent the community in which the offence has occurred' (Walgrave 2012: 38).

Furthermore, as Walgrave (2012: 38) notes, 'facilitating a conference must be done with all the methodical skills that are indispensable to do this'; it is not like organising a party with neighbours, he reminds us. Indeed, the myth 'that a stranger with minimal training can, in the course of an hour's meeting, resolve deep-rooted, long-standing conflicts between intimates' should not be propagated (Abel 1982: 304). The irony, though, is that '[t]he more volunteers are trained in methods and the more they gradually build experience, the less they remain real volunteers and risk turning into unpaid professionals' (Walgrave 2012: 38). In fact, continuing training and years of practice may enhance the quality of mediation and other 'restorative justice services', but on the flip side, volunteers may well 'begin to look and behave more like "quasi-professionals" than ordinary lay people' (Crawford 2000: 214).

What is more, as Abel (1982: 303) anticipated decades ago, '[m]ediators, like all other categories of service providers, will seek to professionalize, i.e., to control entry into the occupation and to enhance its status and perquisites'. That is, the pressure towards professionalisation may well come from the lay volunteers themselves. Although at the time Abel was analysing the contradictions of 'informal justice' – not 'restorative justice', a term little known in the early 1980s – his observations are applicable today and resonate beyond the experiences of early victim–offender mediation experiments.

Indeed, in 2011, the Restorative Justice Council (RJC) – an independent third sector membership body for the field of restorative practices in the UK – launched a national register of 'restorative practitioners'. Today, perhaps confirming Abel's projection, those who have 'at least one year's experience of delivering restorative processes' in the UK can be awarded an 'accredited practitioner status' by the RJC, with the proviso that they abide to certain codes of practice, and with the benefit of being able to use the so-called 'RJC Practitioner Quality Mark'. Lizzie Nelson, the former director of the RJC, explained the rationale underpinning the national register: 'The practitioners doing this skillful and effective work deserve *professional* recognition; and the public deserves transparent assurance that they are being offered a safe and effective process' (emphasis added).[3] The Ministry of Justice has been supportive of the RJC's registration/accreditation initiatives, and it is likely that in the not so distant future only accredited practitioners will be able to act as mediators, facilitators or community panel members in (at least the official or statutory) restorative justice schemes in the UK.[4] In fact, the Ministry of Justice recently tasked the RJC with delivering a clear set of standards and a quality mark for services that meet these standards. The resulting 'Restorative Service Quality Mark' (RSQM) has been developed and, as part of their general election pre-manifesto, the Liberal Democrat Party pledged to make the RSQM 'a mandatory pre-requisite for commissioning restorative justice services'.[5] Similar developments can be seen in other jurisdictions. For example, in 2012, the Canadian Restorative Justice Consortium was established 'to promote restorative justice at the national level and support practitioners, programmes, agencies and networks/associations' (Tomporowski 2014: 221). It will not be long before they too begin to deliver quality marks to further professionalise restorative justice services.

What is so problematic about the professionalisation of lay members of the community? Well, at the least, the professionalisation of lay members of the community goes against the deprofessionalising goals of restorative justice. Ultimately, further research needs to be conducted into the expectations around the involvement of lay members of the community in restorative justice programmes, and into how participants (including the lay volunteers themselves) understand the involvement of laypeople in restorative justice processes.

What does the community get through its involvement in restorative justice practices?

As Bolivar (2012: 18) argues, '[w]hereas there is an important amount of literature assessing the impact of RJ [restorative justice] on victims and offenders, there are few studies evaluating its effects upon communities'. Indeed, it is not clear what, effectively, the community gets through its involvement in restorative justice practices.

Advocates of restorative justice often argue that community participation in criminal justice practices *strengthens the social ties* that empower the community to actually handle its own conflicts. Nevertheless, it remains unclear how restorative justice 'events' may further strengthen social ties. Opportunities could be created for neighbours to meet each other, and even bond, after participating in a series of healing or peace-making circles, but restorative justice processes often include a one-off 'restorative encounter' between small numbers of people who do not know each other, and who will not want to 'keep in touch'. Before propagating the idea that restorative justice processes 'strengthen social ties', we need to reflect upon questions such as: in practice, how often is it the case that community members are already acquainted with victims and offenders before the restorative processes take place? That is, how often are there 'social ties' to strengthen? Also, how often do community members feel comfortable facilitating a meeting involving victims and/or offenders whom they already know? How many of them think it is appropriate to stay in touch with the offender after the process has finished? Finally, do fellow community volunteers tend to become friends, or do they tend to build a 'quasi-work' relationship with their 'quasi-colleagues'?

The assumption that community participation increases community skills in problem solving and conflict resolution is also unproved. Indeed, it is assumed that processes of restorative justice will generally allow for the creation of informal support systems or safety nets for victims and offenders, when, on the ground, limited community resources may hinder any conceivable substantive changes in the structure of communities. For example, is it realistic to expect that community members participating in restorative justice encounters will offer education and/or employment opportunities to youth at risk of becoming involved in further offending behaviour? It is clear that further research needs to explore the benefits to community of its involvement in restorative justice practices.

What are the dangers of community involvement?

While there is a widespread and compelling enthusiasm around the potential benefits of community involvement in restorative justice practices, some scholars have warned of the dangers that such an involvement may pose (Pavlich 2004; Weisberg 2003). According to them, instead of moving rapidly towards greater community participation, restorative justice programmes need to learn from past mistakes. For example, Weisberg (2003: 363) draws on the 'sad history' of deinstitutionalisation that happened to American state mental hospitals in the 1970s to illustrate 'the dangers of assuming that there is some independent social phenomenon called the community'. According to him, '[i]t is now an axiom that deinstitutionalization caused the contemporary epidemic of homelessness for the mentally ill' (Weisberg 2003: 364), and

> [...] this public disaster was the entrancement of people out in society generally, mental health professionals, and some politicians, with the notion that there was something out there called the community to which drugged and incarcerated mental patients could return, and where they would be respected, if not cured, and thrive far better.
>
> (Weisberg 2003: 363)

As Sullivan and Tifft (2001: 81) remind us, 'it is easy to suggest that reintegration is best achieved in places where a strong sense of community exists, where relationships based in mutual aid thrive', but 'what possibility is there for social reintegration to occur in a community or family when no prior integration exists?' According to them, restorative justice advocates should be asking, 'reintegration into what?' (Sullivan and Tifft 2001). This speaks to questions of community capacity. As Crawford and Clear (2003: 221) argue, 'not all communities share the same access to resources, nor can they feasibly restore victims or reintegrate offenders in the same way or to the same extent'. In this context, restorative justice's 'deprofessionalising' impetus must be tempered by concerns for the varying levels of community capacity – indeed, some communities may well need more state (or professional) intervention (or support) than others. Perhaps more precisely, one danger of transferring 'power' to the community is that some communities may do better than others – with more affluent communities probably featuring among those that would do better.

Along these lines, there are many potential risks involved in putting discretionary power in the hands of the community – and concerns about the reproduction of power imbalances are amongst the most worrying of them (Pavlich 2004, 2005). Indeed, among the risks of involving the community in mainstream restorative/criminal justice practice is the imposition of white, middle-class, ethnocentric biases. In this respect, some lessons can be drawn from the criticisms that came to dominate the informal justice literature in the 1980s:

> Community production of services, whether these involve justice, legality, social control, or regulation, is a nonautonomous mode of production. At most it has a merely negative autonomy – the freedom not to depend on the state for the performance of certain services. There is no positive autonomy – the capacity to struggle for measures and services that,

> though structurally possible, are functionally incompatible with the corporate interests of the dominant class.
>
> (Santos 1982: 261)

In fact, the 'romanticization of community' (McEvoy and Mika 2002) is dangerous. It is dangerous to assume that there is something good out there called 'community', which is homogeneous and comprises relations of equality, where people are all friendly and understanding, and into which the victim and the offender can be effortlessly reintegrated (Bauman 2001). The danger is 'an assumption buried in the celebration of community that the status quo is fair' (Weisberg 2003: 370), when, on the ground, by aiming at the restoration of the status quo, restorative justice interventions may be apt to compound pre-existing power and status differentials in the community (Delgado 2000).

What is more, whilst restorative justice's theoretical appeals to community are strongly motivated by the restorative value of inclusiveness (discussed in Chapter 1), the involvement of the community in restorative justice programmes may well produce the unwanted effects of exclusion. Strategies need to be put in place to prevent the involvement of certain community representatives in ways that may marginalise other (less privileged or more vulnerable) members of the community. This is particularly relevant in the context of youth justice, where young offenders are typically in more vulnerable positions than their adult counterparts.

Finally, instead of assuming that greater community involvement necessarily leads to less formal, less professionalised and less managerial justice processes, restorative justice advocates should be wary of the danger of simply replicating a formal justice system within communities (Bartkowiak and Jaccoud 2008). Indeed, community involvement in restorative justice processes may well turn out to be 'an illusion in order to allow more social control and a way for government institutions to regain lost legitimacy and justification' (Bartkowiak and Jaccoud 2008: 229).

All in all, more research is needed to explore the potential dangers of community involvement in restorative justice programmes, both to test empirically if those dangers already articulated by some theorists are real, and to reveal other, as yet unforeseen, dangers.

2.4 Concluding comments

Since the 1970s, as Bartkowiak and Jaccoud (2008: 209) remind us, 'the concept of "community" has become a much discussed topic which researchers in criminal justice and socio-legal studies have been trying to define'. As Crawford (2000: 210) notes, '[i]t has become an academic *cliché* [...] to protest that there are few concepts in social science as nebulous as "community"'. I agree, and do not intend to join the protest. Like Walgrave (2002), I believe that the notion of community *cannot* be defined, and more importantly, I do not think it needs to be. I am persuaded that a coherent theory of restorative justice can be developed without a concrete and precise definition of community. However, I depart paths from Walgrave (2002) in wishing to hold on to the term 'community'. As Weisberg (2003: 374) notes, '[t]o say it is a confused set of concepts and performative tropes is not to suggest the feasibility or even desirability of eradicating the vocabulary of "community" from our discourse'. Instead of getting rid of the term, I think, we should be asking the right questions.

In this vein, as Medawar (1967) suggests, science is the 'art of the soluble', meaning that 'there is no point in asking questions which by their nature are not capable of being answered through scientific instruments at our disposal' (King and Wincup 2008: 21). '*What is community?*', then, is the wrong question. Indeed, nearly five decades ago, Hillery (1955) identified 94 different definitions of community, with one commonality between them: all of them deal with people. Another researcher, after summarising much of the available literature on community, concludes: 'In other words, the nature and extent of one's community is largely a matter of individual definition' (Anderson 1960: 27). In a similar vein, Alper and Nichols (1981: 3) argue that it is 'impossible to find two people who interpret or define it [community] alike'. Clearly, there is no one definition of community.

The truth is that restorativists' attempts to define community have not translated into a more coherent framework for community involvement in restorative justice programmes. For example, according to McCold and Wachtel (2003: 294), '[c]ommunity is a feeling, a perception of connectedness – personal connectedness both to other individual human beings and to a group'. However elegant, this definition does not help to operationalise community involvement in restorative justice programmes. Likewise, restorativists' clichéd mention of Ferdinand Tönnies's (see Harris 2001) distinction between *Gemeinschaft* ('community') and *Gesellschaft* ('society') – and their contention that 'community in restorative justice is more akin to the concept of *Gemeinschaft* than *Gesellschaft*' (Hoyle, in Cunneen and Hoyle 2010: 19) – has not been helpful in clearing up the ambiguities surrounding the role of community in restorative justice programmes.[6]

It is what restorativists expect from 'community involvement' that needs to be more clearly defined. There may be (very) good reasons to involve lay members of the community in restorative justice programmes, but we need further clarification on what, precisely, the community can actually bring to processes of restoration and conflict resolution. We also need to explore further what the community can take back from its involvement in such processes. Moreover, the possible 'dangers' of community involvement in restorative justice need to be taken more seriously. We need to assess whether our hopes on community involvement are not too high, not as a means of discouraging it, but rather as a means of avoiding expectations that are impossible to meet. By keeping (high) expectations under control, we shall hopefully avoid falling into an unrewarding 'mood of impossibilism' (Daly 2003) around restorative justice's appeals.

All things considered, I would like to argue that we should be further reflecting on the questions of *why* (that is, *for what purposes*) and *how* (that is, *within what limits and under which conditions*) the community should be involved in restorative justice practices. Indeed, taking as a truth that community and restorative justice form an inseparable couple (Pranis and Bazemore 2000), we need to sort out the precise terms of this relationship. The questions of *why* and *how* the community should be involved in restorative justice practices, I would argue, summarise all the other more specific questions that I have raised throughout this chapter. The aim of the following chapters is not to provide an empirical evaluation of whether restorative justice *works* or, more precisely, if community involvement *works*. Rather, the primary aim of this study, as introduced at the beginning of this book, is to advance our empirical and theoretical understanding of what 'community involvement' means and what work it does in restorative justice.

Notes

1 A shorter version of this discussion was originally published as part of Rosenblatt, F.F. (2014), 'Community Involvement in Restorative Justice: Lessons from an English and Welsh Case Study on Youth Offender Panels', *Restorative Justice: An International Journal*, 2(3): 280–301 (Hart Publishing, used by permission of Bloomsbury Publishing Plc).

2 Dzur and Olson (2004) quotes have been reproduced with kind permission from John Wiley and Sons.

3 Her quote and further details about who can become an accredited practitioner and the benefits linked to the accredited practitioner status can be found on the RJC website: www.restorativejustice.org.uk.

4 About the Ministry of Justice's support for the initiatives of the RJC, see: www.restorativejustice.org.uk/news/new_national_rjc_restorative_practitioner_register_launched_with_justice_minister_crispin_blunt/#.UKux-qXxa0t.

5 RJC members e-bulletin, 17 September 2014. For more information about the RSQM, see: www.rsqm.org.uk/find_out_more/governance/.

6 If anything, restorative justice commentators tend to hold onto Tönnies's characterisation of community to make their romantic appeal to an inaccurate recollection of the past (and the need to restore it), almost always ignoring that Tönnies himself 'was anxious to insist that attributes of both "Gemeinschaft" and "Gesellschaft" were latent and co-existent within all political and legal orders at all periods in history' (Harris 2001: xviii).

References

Abel, R.L. (ed.) (1982) *The Politics of Informal Justice*, New York: Academic Press.

Aertsen, I., Mackay, R., Pelikan, C., Wright, M. and Willemsens, J. (2004) *Rebuilding Community Connections: Mediation and Restorative Justice*, Strasbourg: Council of Europe.

Alper, B.S. and Nichols, L.T. (1981) *Beyond the Courtroom: Programs in Community Justice and Conflict Resolution*, Lexington, KY: Lexington Books.

Anderson, N. (1960) *The Urban Community: A World Perspective*, New York: Henry Holt.

Bartkowiak, I. and Jaccoud, M. (2008) 'New Directions in Canadian Justice: From State Workers to Community "Representatives"', in J. Shapland (ed.), *Justice, Community and Civil Society: A Contested Terrain*, Cullompton: Willan Publishing.

Bauman, Z. (2001) *Community: Seeking Safety in an Insecure World*, Cambridge: Polity.

Bazemore, G. (1998) 'The "Community" in Community Justice: Issues, Themes, and Questions for the New Neighbourhood Sanctioning Models', in D. Karp (ed.), *Community Justice: An Emerging Field*, Lanham, MD: Rowman & Littlefield.

Bolivar, D. (2012) 'Community of Care from a Victim Perspective: A Qualitative Study', *Contemporary Justice Review*, 15(1): 17–37.

Boyes-Watson, C. (2004) 'The Value of Citizen Participation in Restorative/Community Justice: Lessons from Vermont', *Criminology & Public Policy*, 3(4): 687–692.

Braithwaite, J. (1989) *Crime, Shame, and Reintegration*, Cambridge: Cambridge University Press.

Braithwaite, J. (2002) *Restorative Justice and Response Regulation*, Oxford: Oxford University Press.

Braithwaite, J. and Strang, H. (2001) 'Introduction: Restorative Justice and Civil Society', in H. Strang and J. Braithwaite (eds), *Restorative Justice and Civil Society*, Cambridge: Cambridge University Press.

Christie, N. (1977) 'Conflicts as Property', *British Journal of Criminology*, 17(1): 1–15.

Clear, T.R. and Karp, D.R. (1999) *The Community Justice Ideal: Preventing Crime and Achieving Justice*, Boulder, CO: Westview Press.

Crawford, A. (2000) 'Contrasts in Victim-Offender Mediation and Appeals to Community in France and England', in D. Nelken (ed.), *Contrasting Criminal Justice*, Aldershot: Ashgate.

Crawford, A. and Clear, T. (2003) 'Community Justice: Transforming Communities through Restorative Justice', in E. McLaughlin, R. Fergusson, G. Hughes and L. Westmarland (eds), *Restorative Justice: Critical Issues*, London: SAGE Publications.

Crawford, A. and Newburn, T. (2003) *Youth Offending and Restorative Justice: Implementing Reform in Youth Justice*, Cullompton: Willan Publishing.

Cunneen, C. and Hoyle, C. (2010) *Debating Restorative Justice*, Oxford: Hart Publishing.

Daly, K. (2003) 'Making Variation a Virtue: Evaluating the Potential and Limits of Restorative Justice', in E.G.M. Weitekamp and H.-J. Kerner (eds), *Restorative Justice in Context*, Cullompton: Willan Publishing.

Delgado, R. (2000) 'Goodbye to Hammurabi: Analyzing the Atavistic Appeal of Restorative Justice', *Stanford Law Review*, 52(4): 751–776.

Dignan, J. (2005) *Understanding Victims and Restorative Justice*, Maidenhead: Open University Press.

Dzur, A.W. (2008) *Democratic Professionalism: Citizen Participation and the Reconstruction of Professional Ethics, Identity, and Practice*, University Park: Pennsylvania State University Press.

Dzur, A.W. and Olson, S.M. (2004) 'The Value of Community Participation in Restorative Justice', *Journal of Social Philosophy*, 35(1): 91–107.

Erbe, C. (2004) 'What is the Role of Professionals in Restorative Justice?', in H. Zehr and B. Toews (eds), *Critical Issues in Restorative Justice*, Monsey, NY: Criminal Justice Press.

Fitzpatrick, P. (1992) 'The Impossibility of Popular Justice', *Social & Legal Studies*, 1 (2): 199–215.

Garland, D. (1996) 'The Limits of the Sovereign State: Strategies of Crime Control in Contemporary Society', *British Journal of Criminology*, 36(4): 445–471.

Garland, D. (2001) *The Culture of Control: Crime and Social Order in Contemporary Society*, Oxford: Oxford University Press.

Gormally, B. (2002) 'The Third Corner and the Second Pillar: The Community and Restorative Justice in Northern Ireland', *ERA Forum*, 3(1): 14–18.

Green, S. (2014) *Crime, Community and Morality*, Abingdon: Routledge.

Haines, K. (1997) 'Some Principled Objections to a Restorative Justice Approach to Working with Juvenile Offenders', in L. Walgrave (ed.), *Restorative Justice for Juveniles: Potentialities, Risks and Problems for Research*, Leuven: Leuven University Press.

Harris, J. (ed.) (2001) *Tönnies: Community and Society*, Cambridge: Cambridge University Press.

Harris, N., Walgrave, L. and Braithwaite, J. (2004) 'Emotional Dynamics in Restorative Conferences', *Theoretical Criminology*, 8(2): 191–210.

Hillery, G.A. (1955) 'Definitions of Community: Areas of Agreement', *Rural Sociology*, 20(1): 779–791.

Hudson, B. (1998) 'Restorative Justice: The Challenge of Sexual and Racial Violence', *Journal of Law and Society*, 25(2): 237–256.

Johnstone, G. (2011) *Restorative Justice: Ideas, Values, Debates*, 2nd edn, London: Routledge.

Karp, D.R. (2001) 'Harm and Repair: Observing Restorative Justice in Vermont', *Justice Quarterly*, 18(4): 727–758.

Karp, D.R. and Drakulich, K. (2004) 'Minor Crime in a Quaint Setting: Practices, Outcomes, and Limits of Vermont Reparative Probation Boards', *Criminology & Public Policy*, 3(4): 655–686.

King, R. and Wincup, E. (2008) 'The Process of Criminological Research', in R. King and E. Wincup (eds), *Doing Research on Crime and Justice*, Oxford: Oxford University Press.

Lacey, N. and Zedner, L. (1995) 'Discourses of Community in Criminal Justice', *Journal of Law and Society*, 22(3): 301–325.

Lockhart, B. (2002) 'Restorative Justice: State-led or Community-led', *ERA Forum*, 3 (1): 18–22.

McCold, P. (2000) 'Toward a Holistic Vision of Restorative Juvenile Justice: A Reply to the Maximalist Model', *Contemporary Justice Review*, 3(4): 357–414.

McCold, P. (2001) 'Primary Restorative Justice Practices', in A. Morris and G. Maxwell (eds), *Restorative Justice for Juveniles: Conferencing, Mediation and Circles*, Oxford: Hart Publishing.

McCold, P. (2004) 'What is the Role of Community in Restorative Justice Theory and Practice?', in H. Zehr and B. Toews (eds), *Critical Issues in Restorative Justice*, Monsey, NY: Criminal Justice Press.

McCold, P. and Wachtel, B. (2003) 'Community is Not a Place: A New Look at Community Justice', in G. Johnstone (ed.), *A Restorative Justice Reader*, Cullompton: Willan Publishing.

McEvoy, K. and Mika, H. (2002) 'Restorative Justice and the Critique of Informalism in Northern Ireland', *British Journal of Criminology*, 42(3): 534–562.

Medawar, P.B. (1967) *The Art of the Soluble: Creativity and Originality in Science*, London: Methuen.

Morris, A. (2002) 'Critiquing the Critics: A Brief Response to Critics of Restorative Justice', *British Journal of Criminology*, 42(3): 596–615.

Morris, A. and Maxwell, G. (2000) 'The Practice of Family Group Conferences in New Zealand: Assessing the Place, Potential and Pitfalls of Restorative Justice', in A. Crawford and J. Goodey (eds), *Integrating a Victim Perspective within Criminal Justice: International Debates*, Aldershot: Ashgate Publishing.

Morris, A. and Young, W. (2000) 'Reforming Criminal Justice: The Potential of Restorative Justice', in H. Strang and J. Braithwaite (eds), *Restorative Justice: Philosophy to Practice*, Aldershot: Ashgate.

Olson, S.M. and Dzur, A.W. (2003) 'Reconstructing Professional Roles in Restorative Justice Programs', *Utah Law Review*, 57(1): 57–89.

Pavlich, G. (2004) 'What are the Dangers as Well as the Promise of Community Involvement?', in H. Zehr and B. Toews (eds), *Critical Issues in Restorative Justice*, Monsey, NY: Criminal Justice Press.

Pavlich, G. (2005) *Governing Paradoxes of Restorative Justice*, London: Glass House Press.

Pranis, K. (2003) *Peacemaking Circles: From Crime to Community*, St Paul, MN: Living Justice Press.

Pranis, K. and Bazemore, G. (2000) *Engaging the Community in the Response to Youth Crime: A Restorative Justice Approach*, Washington, DC: Department of Justice OJDP.

Raye, B.E. and Roberts, A.W. (2007) 'Restorative Processes', in G. Johnstone and D. Van Ness (eds), *Handbook of Restorative Justice*, Cullompton: Willan Publishing.

Santos, B.d.S. (1982) 'Law and Community: The Changing Nature of State Power in Later Capitalism', in R. Abel (ed.), *The Politics of Informal Justice*, New York: Academic Press.

Shapland, J. (2008) *Justice, Community and Civil Society: A Contested Terrain*, Cullompton: Willan Publishing.

Shapland, J. (2012) 'Comparing Conferencing and Mediation: Some Evaluation Results Internationally', in E. Zinsstag and I. Vanfraechem (eds), *Conferencing and Restorative Justice: International Practices and Perspectives*, Oxford: Oxford University Press.

Smull, E., Wachtel, J. and Wachtel, T. (2012) *Family Power: Engaging and Collaborating with Families*, Bethlehem, PA: International Institute for Restorative Practices.

Sullivan, D. and Tifft, L. (2001) *Restorative Justice: Healing the Foundations of Our Everyday Lives*, Monsey, NY: Willow Tree Press.

Tomporowski, B. (2014) 'Restorative Justice and Community Justice in Canada', *Restorative Justice: An International Journal*, 2(2): 218–224.

Umbreit, M.S. and Armour, M.P. (2011) *Restorative Justice Dialogue: An Essential Guide for Research and Practice*, New York: Springer.

Umbreit, M.S. and Stacey, S.L. (1996) 'Family Group Conferencing Comes to the U.S.: A Comparison with Victim Offender Mediation', *Juvenile and Family Court Journal*, 47(2): 29–39.

Vanfraechem, I. (2007) 'Community, Society and State in Restorative Justice: Some Reflections', in R. Mackay, M. Bosjnak, J. Deklerck, C. Pelikan, B.V. Stokkom and

M. Wright (eds), *Images of Restorative Justice Theory*, Frankfurt am Main: Verlag fur Polizei und Wissenschaft.

Von Hirsch, A. (1998) 'Penal Theories', in M. Tonry (ed.), *The Handbook of Crime & Punishment*, New York: Oxford University Press.

Walgrave, L. (2002) 'From Community to Dominion: In Search of Social Values for Restorative Justice', in E.G.M. Weitekamp and H.-J. Kerner (eds), *Restorative Justice: Theoretical Foundations*, Cullompton: Willan Publishing.

Walgrave, L. (2008) *Restorative Justice, Self-Interest and Responsible Citizenship*, Cullompton: Willan Publishing.

Walgrave, L. (2012) 'The Need for Clarity about Restorative Justice Conferences', in E. Zinsstag and I. Vanfraechem (eds), *Conferencing and Restorative Justice: International Practices and Perspectives*, Oxford: Oxford University Press.

Weisberg, R. (2003) 'Restorative Justice and the Danger of "Community"', *Utah Law Review*: 343–374.

Wright, M. (1998) 'Victim/Offender Conferencing: The Need for Safeguards', in L. Walgrave (ed.), *Restorative Justice for Juveniles: Potentialities, Risks and Problems*, Leuven: Leuven University Press.

Wright, M. (2000) 'Restorative Justice: For Whose Benefit?', in European Forum for Victim-Offender Mediation and Restorative Justice (ed.), *Victim-Offender Mediation in Europe: Making Restorative Justice Work*, Leuven: Leuven University Press.

Zehr, H. (1990) *Changing Lenses: A New Focus for Crime and Justice*, Scottdale, PA: Herald Press.

3 Selecting a case study of community involvement in restorative justice

As mentioned in the previous chapter, the primary aim of this study is to reach a better empirical and theoretical understanding of what 'community involvement' means and what work it does in restorative justice. In this vein, I have adopted a case study approach in the research design, to examine the involvement of the community in one selected practice of restorative justice, namely youth offender panels in England and Wales. The decision to adopt a case study approach, along with the motives for selecting youth offender panels as a case study, is explained in this chapter. In this way, while exploring the history and operation of referral orders, the first part of the chapter sets out the legal and theoretical framework underpinning youth offender panels. Then, drawing on the notions of restorative justice introduced in Chapter 1, it is argued that youth offender panels were designed to operate on restorative justice principles – and, thus, that they constitute a 'typical case' (Denscombe 2010) of community involvement in restorative justice practices. The fact that they are explicitly aimed at involving the community – in a way that other restorative justice programmes (e.g. victim–offender mediation) never have – is also noted. Attention is drawn to the fact that there is no up-to-date study on the conduct of referral orders and youth offender panels, further indicating the relevance and timeliness of this (empirical) study. Finally, the empirical aims of the study are set out.

3.1 The introduction of restorative justice into the youth justice system of England and Wales

The enthusiasm for restorative justice as an alternative way of dealing with crime, especially prominent in the youth offending arena, has led many youth justice systems across the world to seek transformation by adopting and developing restorative justice principles (O'Mahony and Doak 2009). This has been the case in England and Wales, particularly after the introduction of referral orders by the Youth Justice and Criminal Evidence Act 1999 (Earle and Newburn 2001). Before discussing this act, however, and in order to better understand the theoretical contours of youth offender panels, I will sketch the legal (and political) landscape that was in place in the UK prior to the introduction of referral orders.

A brief (and modern) history of youth justice in England and Wales

The history of youth justice in England and Wales – which, as in other countries, is pitted with 'conflict, contradictions, ambiguity and compromise' (Muncie and Hughes 2002: 1) – is a difficult one to tell. Commitments to 'evidence-based policy' have been contradicted by the launch of electorally popular punitive programmes; centralised managerial control has challenged expressed preferences for 'governing at a distance'; inclusionary and participatory aspirations have been eclipsed by exclusionary and net-widening actions, to name but a few contending themes (Crawford and Newburn 2003; Goldson 2010; Muncie 2001). All in all, we are in the territory of 'a rather complex and messy' history (Earle and Newburn 2001: 11) and any attempt to summarise its course is likely to be open to the charge of trivialisation. That said, whilst a detailed examination of the history of Anglo-Welsh youth justice is beyond the scope of this study, it is important to revisit some of the main aspects of this trajectory so as to give an idea of the political forces that were at play in the emergence of restorative justice practices with young offenders in England and Wales.

For much of the twentieth century, the youth justice system in England and Wales operated under the competing discourses of 'punishment' and 'welfare' – that is, under the rival slogans of the 'justice' and the 'welfare' models (Burnett and Appleton 2004; Crawford and Newburn 2003; Pitts 2005; Pratt 1989). This entails an ideological indecision between formal and informal court proceedings, determinate and indeterminate sentencing, providing treatment or sanctioning behaviour, responding to individual needs or respecting individual rights, emphasising the role of child care experts or that of lawyers, among many other dichotomies (Pratt 1989). In the latter part of the century, the unresolved tensions between the aims of retribution and the ambitions of treatment-type interventions culminated in the decline of the 'rehabilitative ideal' (Earle and Newburn 2001) and, thereafter, according to Pratt (1989), a third model of youth justice called 'corporatism' emerged.

This is not to say that the tensions were over, or that a fully fledged model arose. Quite the reverse: traces of the welfare and the justice models can still be found today, and new tensions have been added to the 'old' ones (Tomlinson 2005). In fact, what happened in the late 1980s was that the debate about justice and welfare became something of a 'sideshow' while 'efficient and effective "management" of the offending population came to the fore, underpinned by the rediscovery that "something works"' (Earle and Newburn 2001: 3). Indeed, the corporatist model of youth justice 'presaged the slightly later emergence of what Feeley and Simon (1994) have termed the "new penology" in which actuarial techniques of risk assessment and classification come to dominate much penal decision-making and administration' (Crawford and Newburn 2003: 10).

In the early 1990s, the managerialist and actuarialist discourses of the previous decade were fuelled by the embrace of 'populist punitiveness' by politicians of all hues (Crawford and Newburn 2003: 10; see also Garland 2001) – and the scenario for the coming elections was then set:

> Rising levels of juvenile crime, a [sic] increasing popular and political belief that the youth justice system was ineffective, and widespread concern about the moral health of contemporary youth inspired by a number of high-profile cases involving young offenders [...] provided the backdrop against which New Labour sought to redefine itself in the law and order landscape.
>
> (Crawford and Newburn 2003: 10)

The question of how to respond to youth crime and antisocial behaviour became 'the major focus of New Labour's criminal justice concerns in the run up to the 1997 General Election' (Earle and Newburn 2001: 4). Since then (up to 2010), 'three successive New Labour administrations have subjected the English youth justice system to a seemingly endless sequence of reforms' (Goldson 2010: 155). Whilst trying to unravel the complexities of youth justice policy within this jurisdiction, several commentators have observed an overall emphasis on 'tough on crime' discourses (Burnett and Appleton 2004; Goldson 2010; Muncie 2001). Indeed, youth justice in England and Wales has typically witnessed the implementation of a wide range of American-inspired policies that are 'obsessed with not being seen to be soft on crime' (Muncie 2001: 29), such as boot camps, curfews, electronic monitoring, 'three strikes and you're out' rules, antisocial behaviour legislation, to name but a few. Yet, despite the 'political imperative to appear tough' (Goldson 2010: 171), one cannot overlook the fact that some space has been made for more progressive practices to emerge, such as multi-agency working and diversionary responses to youth crime. Indeed, 'much of the governmental "style" has been to "talk tough" whilst behind the scenes enabling sometimes more enlightened practices to be developed and promulgated' (Crawford and Newburn 2003: 11). It was within this more progressive context that restorative justice-inspired practices have emerged and been introduced into the youth justice system of England and Wales.

The Crime and Disorder Act 1998

In early 1997, a series of consultative documents setting out New Labour's plans for 'a major reform of youth justice' were published (Home Office 1997a, 1997b, 1997c, 1997d, 1997e, 1997f). The result was the introduction of the Crime and Disorder Act 1998 (hereafter, the 1998 Act), 'an ambitious and wide-ranging programme of legislative and organizational change' (Souhami

2007: 11). In the White Paper *No More Excuses* (Home Office 1997d: 7), which preceded the 1998 Act, the government said that there was 'confusion about the purpose of the youth justice system', and that 'concerns about the welfare of young people have too often been seen as in conflict with the aims of protecting the public, punishing offences and preventing offending'. It accepted that 'children need protection from the full rigour of criminal law', but argued that there is no conflict 'between protecting the welfare of a young offender and preventing that individual from offending again' (Home Office 1997d: 7). In this vein, the 1998 Act established 'preventing offending by children and young persons' (in section 37) as the principal aim of the youth justice system.

The 1998 Act also introduced the key elements of Labour's 'new youth justice' (Goldson 2010): the establishment of inter-agency Youth Offending Teams (YOTs); the creation of a new non-departmental public body, called the Youth Justice Board for England and Wales (YJB); and the restructuring of the non-custodial orders available to the Youth Court. Since then, YOTs have become responsible for the delivery of 'the bulk of youth justice services' (Souhami 2007: 19), and are still in operation in every local authority area in England and Wales (National Audit Office 2010).[1] They replaced the 'youth justice teams', which mainly comprised social workers, and brought together the various agencies that had been involved with young offenders (Burnett 2005). Indeed:

> Stimulated by a concern with efficiency and consistency on the one hand, and by a pragmatic belief in multi-agency working on the other, the New Labour's new model YOTs had to include a probation officer, a local authority social worker, a police officer, a representative of the local health authority, and someone nominated by the chief education officer.
>
> (Crawford and Newburn 2003: 12)

On the national level, the YJB was established 'to monitor the operation of the youth justice system and the provision of youth justice services' (section 41). That is, the YJB's role 'is one of supervision and guidance rather than direct management', as it 'monitors the performance of YOTs against targets and standards, identifies and promotes "effective practice", issuing guidance for practitioners accordingly' (Souhami 2007: 20). Following the 2010 General Election, the Conservative–Liberal Democrat coalition government announced a plan to cut public spending through the abolition of a large number of non-departmental public bodies or quasi-autonomous non-governmental organisations ('quangos') (Cabinet Office 2011), and among the list of those to be abolished was the YJB. There was strong opposition to this move, however, and the government finally reached the decision to grant a temporary reprieve – although, as with other 'quangos', the YJB has been subjected to triennial reviews in which it needed to justify its continuing existence (see Puffet 2013). According to Goldson (2010: 156), taken together, the YJB and the YOTs have 'transformed the architecture of the youth justice apparatus; radically reconfigured lines of power, management and responsibility; and facilitated substantial system growth'.

The detail that is most relevant to my story, though, is that restorative justice measures featured quite prominently throughout the 1998 Act. For example, a new power was introduced (in section 67), enabling courts to impose 'Reparation Orders', where young offenders are required to make reparation either directly to the victim (provided they are agreeable) or to 'the community at large'. Reparation orders are still available to the Youth Court today, and in the White Paper *No More Excuses* (Home Office 1997d: 14) they were explained in the following terms:

> The Crime and Disorder Bill will provide a new penalty – the reparation order – which courts will have to consider imposing on young offenders in all cases where they do not impose a compensation order. The order will require reparation to be made in kind, up to a maximum of 24 hours' work within a period of three months. The reparation might involve writing a letter of apology, apologising to the victim in person, cleaning graffiti or repairing criminal damage. Of course, not all victims want reparation. The Government's proposals ensure that the victim's views will be sought before an order is made. Where a victim does not want direct reparation, the reparation may be made to the community at large.

Another order introduced by the 1998 Act, which also had 'a strong restorative justice component to it' (Dignan 1999), was the Action Plan Order – 'a short, intensive programme of community intervention combining punishment, rehabilitation and reparation to change offending behaviour and prevent further crime' (Home Office 1997d: 18).[2] According to Green (2014), the 1998 Act borrows much from a report by the National Association for the Care and Resettlement of Offenders (NACRO), entitled *A New Three Rs for Young Offenders: Towards a New Strategy for Children who Offend* (NACRO 1997), which 'delved into the possible advantages of using a restorative model of justice for young offenders and was largely based upon the success of family group conferencing in New Zealand and Australia' (Green 2014: 60). This helps to explain why restorative justice measures are scattered throughout the 1998 Act.

Although these reforms hardly amount to a 'restorative justice revolution' or to a 'paradigm shift' (Dignan 1999: 58; see also Morris and Gelsthorpe 2000), '[t]here can be little doubt that there was a concerted effort by New Labour to make both victims' views and reparation more central aspects of youth justice than previously had been the case' (Crawford and Newburn 2003: 18).[3] In this context, particularly because of the prominence it affords to 'reparation', the 1998 Act is often referred to as the first enabling legislation for the use of restorative justice with young offenders in England and Wales (Dignan 1999; Earle and Newburn 2001). However, the 'most significant expression of restorative justice principles in the youth justice arena' (Earle and Newburn 2001: 4) arrived with the creation of the Referral Order as part of the Youth Justice and Criminal Evidence Act 1999 (hereafter, the 1999 Act).

3.2 The 1999 Act, referral orders and youth offender panels[4]

The 1999 Act – which was later consolidated in the Powers of Criminal Courts (Sentencing) Act 2000 (hereafter, the Sentencing Act) – introduced referral orders as a primary sentencing disposal for 10–17-year-olds pleading guilty and convicted for the first time. Referral orders were introduced as a *compulsory* sentence – that is, courts were *required* to make a referral order on *all* young offenders aged 10 to 17 years, provided that they had *no previous convictions* and *pleaded guilty*, and unless the offence was one for which the sentence was fixed by law, or the court considered it appropriate to give a custodial sentence, an absolute discharge or make a hospital order (see section 16 of the Sentencing Act).

Some years later, the Criminal Justice and Immigration Act 2008 amended the Sentencing Act, extending the circumstances in which young people may receive a referral order. Since then, besides the compulsory referral order conditions – where courts are required to make a referral order, but only if the young offender has not previously been convicted and pleads guilty – there are circumstances in which a *discretionary* referral order can be made. For example, the court *may* make a referral order if the offender has one previous conviction but is pleading guilty to the present offence and has *not* previously had a referral order; if the offender has previously had a referral order, but an appropriate officer (e.g. a YOT member) recommends to the court as suitable for the offender a *second* referral order; or if the court considers that there are exceptional circumstances that justify the making of a referral order (see section 17 of the Sentencing Act).[5] These legislative changes came into force on 27 April 2009, and this was the legislation in force when the vast majority of my field research was conducted. Towards the end of my study, however, the Sentencing Act was again amended, this time by the Legal Aid, Sentencing and Punishment of Offenders Act 2012, which allows for the repeated use of referral orders. That is, since 3 December 2012, when these more recent legislative changes came into effect, a young offender may receive not (only) a second, but multiple referral orders.

What is a referral order?

When making a referral order, the court specifies the YOT responsible for implementing the order, and how long the order will last – which must not be less than three nor more than 12 months, depending on the seriousness of the offence (see section 18 of the Sentencing Act). It is important to highlight that the court shall not decide upon the *content* of the order, but only upon its appropriate *length*. Indeed, a referral order involves *referring* the young offender to a 'youth offender panel', *and it is the panel that decides the content of the order*. Also, where a referral order has been made, it is the duty of the YOT (as specified by court) to establish a youth offender panel for the offender, to arrange for the first meeting of the panel to be held, and subsequently to arrange for the holding of any further meetings of the panel.

The initial panel meeting should be held within 20 working days of a referral order being made in court, and must be attended by the young person and, when the young offender is under 16, by her 'appropriate person' (i.e. a parent, a guardian, or a representative of the local authority if the young person is looked after by a local authority) (section 22 of the Sentencing Act; see also Ministry of Justice 2009). The panel may also allow other people to attend panel meetings, but they are 'voluntary attendees': any person who appears to the panel to be a victim of, or otherwise affected by the offence in respect of which the offender was referred to the panel; a supporter of the victim (chosen by the victim and with the agreement of the panel); a supporter of the young person (e.g. a parent, even when the young person is not under 16); and any person who appears to the panel to be someone capable of having a good influence on the offender. According to Crawford and Newburn (2003: 61), it is 'to encourage the restorative nature of the process' that a variety of other people may be invited to attend given panel meetings.

In this initial meeting the panel will agree a 'youth offender contract' with the young offender, her family and, where present, the victim (Home Office 2002; Ministry of Justice 2009). This contract stands for the *content* of the order, and it lasts for the duration of the referral order.

What is a youth offender panel?

The youth offender panel is a panel comprising at least two members of the community and one YOT member. It is the duty of the YOT specified in the order to recruit and train these 'community panel members', and the Home Office (together with the YJB) has frequently published *Guidance* on how YOTs should do this. The work of youth offender panels is governed by 'the restorative justice principles of responsibility, reparation and reintegration' (Ministry of Justice 2009: 9). As such, in the meeting with the young offender, her family and (if possible) the victim, the panel reviews the offence and its consequences, and then agrees the aforementioned contract. In turn, the contract should always include an element of reparation to the victim or to the wider community, as well as a programme of activities aimed at preventing reoffending. The referral order does not begin until this contract has been signed at the initial panel meeting.

Thereafter, the panel oversees the contract by way of reviews (or 'progress meetings', as they are termed in the Sentencing Act), which need to be conducted at least every three months. Lastly, towards the end of the order, a final meeting is held to decide whether the offender's compliance with the terms of the contract has been such as to justify the discharge of the referral order. This all means that if a young person is given a six-month referral order, for example, she will probably meet the panel three times: at the initial panel meeting, to agree the contract; at the review panel meeting, to discuss her progress or any breach of the contract; and at the final meeting, to review her overall compliance with the contract.

If the young person does not comply with the contract, the youth offender panel may return her to court to be resentenced for the original offence, in which case the court will be able to impose any sentence that it could have imposed when the young person first appeared before it (including *another* referral order), but in so doing it will have to take into account the extent to which the young person complied with the contract. Further details about the overall referral order process will be provided in Chapter 5, when I shall contrast the theory and practice of youth offender panels.

The pilots and the national rollout of referral orders

Following the 1999 Act, and before the national rollout, referral orders were piloted in 11 areas: Blackburn with Darwen, Cardiff, Nottingham, Nottinghamshire, Oxfordshire, Swindon, Suffolk, Wiltshire, and three London boroughs (Hammersmith and Fulham, Kensington and Chelsea, and Westminster). According to Crawford and Newburn (2003: 63), '[t]he introduction of the first referral order pilots was slightly staggered across the pilot areas over the summer 2000', with the first referral orders being made in the week beginning 3 July, and the first panels meeting on 24 July 2000. The national rollout of referral orders only began on 1 April 2002, so when the empirical component of the present study was conducted, the YOTs I visited had been operating referral orders for at least 10 years.

The **Guidance**

Since the introduction of referral orders, various sets of guidance on the conduct of referral orders and youth offender panels have been published, all of which supplement the statutory provisions. Although new *Guidance* was published in December 2012, most of my data analysis was done against the backdrop of the 2002 *Guidance* (which was the first guidance provided to YOTs after the national rollout of referral orders) and the 2009 *Guidance* (which replaced the 2002 *Guidance*, and was therefore the one in force when the vast majority of my field research was conducted). This will become clear in later chapters, particularly in Chapter 5. Although I conducted a few observations and interviews in 2013, the panel members had not yet been retrained in line with the new *Guidance*. In fact, some were not even aware that new *Guidance* had been published. On the other hand, I still refer to the 2002 *Guidance*, not only because it remained unaltered in varied aspects, but also because many of the interviewed and observed community panel members, who have been doing panels for over three years, still appear to operate under, or to be influenced by, its text.

Having said that, it is important to note that the 2012 *Guidance* does not bring any substantial change with regards to the functioning of panel meetings. In fact, although in the introduction it is stated that this guidance 'also updates and improves the *Guidance* in the light of experience of the practical application of referral orders since their introduction nationally in 2002' (Ministry of Justice 2012: 7), the 'new' *Guidance* is practically identical to the previous one. If anything, it only amends the circumstances in which a court must or may make a referral order – that is, it takes into account the recent legislative change that allows for the repeated use of referral orders. It should be stressed that my criticism of referral orders (introduced particularly in Chapters 6 and 7) have not been addressed in any way by the 2012 *Guidance*, and thus remain current concerns.

3.3 Youth offender panels as a case study

The key characteristic of the case study approach is its focus on just one or a few instances of the 'phenomenon' being researched, 'with a view to providing an in-depth account of events, relationships, experiences or processes occurring in that particular instance' (Denscombe 2010: 52). With case studies, '[t]he aim is to illuminate the general by looking at the particular' (Denscombe 2010: 53). In this vein, instead of examining the involvement of the community in various restorative justice programmes – for example, youth offender panels *and* victim–offender mediation *and* family group conferencing *and* sentencing circles, etc. – I have selected just one of these programmes so as to allow for an in-depth study of this particular practice. The aim, ultimately, is to illuminate more *general* discussions about the role of community in restorative justice by looking at the *particular* English and Welsh experience of youth offender panels.

A frequent criticism of the case study approach is that concerning '*the credibility of generalizations* made from its findings' (Denscombe 2010: 62, emphasis in the original). In particular, critics are sceptical of the value of single-case studies or, indeed, of the ability of extrapolating conclusions to a broader phenomenon by studying a single case (George and Bennett 2005). These concerns, however, are not exclusive to case study research – for example, a common criticism of qualitative studies is that they may not be generalisable (Silverman 2013). In fact, although they can take either a qualitative or quantitative approach, case studies are typically viewed as relying on qualitative data and interpretive methods rather than quantitative data and statistical procedures. In our 'bigger is better culture' (George and Bennett 2005: 17), the statistical methods (with their large numbers of 'cases') are often deemed more reliable than the case study method (with its 'suspicious' single-case approach).

In order to address the abovementioned issues and concerns, case study researchers need 'to be particularly careful to allay suspicions and to demonstrate the extent to which the case study is similar to, or contrasts with, others of its type' (Denscombe 2010: 62). That is, case study researchers should include 'sufficient details about how the case was selected' and 'how it compares with others in the class', 'so that the reader can make an informed judgement about how far the findings have relevance to the class as a whole and how far they are limited to just the case study example' (Jones 2010: 4). Whilst the motives for selecting youth offender panels will be dealt with below, in later chapters (particularly Chapters 6 and 7) I shall be careful to contrast my empirical data with previous findings of community involvement in other restorative justice initiatives.

Of course, there is no ideal method, each having limitations and 'particular advantages in answering certain kinds of questions' (George and Bennett 2005: 17). It should be noted that '[c]ase studies are generally strong precisely where statistical methods and formal models are weak' (George and Bennett 2005: 19). As Denscombe argues:

> The main benefit of using a case study approach is that the focus on one or a few instances allows the researcher to *deal with the subtleties and intricacies* of complex social situations. In particular, it enables the researcher to grapple with relationships and social processes in a way that is denied to the survey approach. The analysis is holistic rather than based on isolated factors.
>
> (Denscombe 2010: 62, original emphasis)

Other perceived advantages are that the case study approach allows for (or, indeed, encourages) the use of multiple methods ('in order to capture the complex reality under scrutiny'); fosters the use of multiple sources of data (which, as will be further explored in Chapter 4, 'facilitates the validation of data through triangulation'); and possesses an enhanced capacity for theory building and theory testing (Denscombe 2010: 62). These advantages were all important reasons in my decision to use a case study approach.

The restorative justice 'spirit' of youth offender panels

Despite some criticism concerning the restorative justice nature of youth offender panels (e.g. Walgrave 2008), if one takes a closer look at the guidelines, legislation, and the policy documents leading up to the introduction of referral orders (and those in force today), it becomes clear that panels were (and continue to be) *intended* as a restorative justice practice. In fact, as mentioned above, youth offender panels have the *stated* purpose to 'operate on the *restorative principles* of responsibility, reparation and reintegration' (Home Office 2002: 5, emphasis added). Moreover, the consultation documents leading to the 1998 Act and the 1999 Act, the legislation itself and the related *Guidance* documents that have been published since the introduction of referral orders all explicitly mention, in one way or another, 'the Government's strategy to prevent offending by young people, providing for *a restorative justice approach within a community context*' (Home Office 2002: 5, emphasis added).

Unsurprisingly, within the restorative justice literature, referral orders and youth offender panels are often referred to as 'the most significant attempt by the British government to integrate restorative justice into the heart of the youth justice system' (Crawford 2002: 116; see also Crawford and Newburn 2002, 2003; Earle and Newburn 2001). In addition, edited books in the field of restorative justice often include a chapter on the experiences of youth offender panels (e.g. Johnstone 2003; Spuy *et al.* 2007; Walgrave 2002), and in the United Nations *Handbook on Restorative Justice Programmes*,[6] youth offender panels are mentioned among the 'examples of restorative programmes for youth' (UNODC 2006: 27). Indeed, referral orders are widely recognised as a significant milestone in the history of restorative justice in the UK. For example, Lizzie Nelson, the former director of the RJC, described recent legislation introducing restorative justice for victims of adult offenders in England and Wales (the Crime and Courts Act 2013) as 'the biggest development for restorative justice in England and Wales *since legislation introduced referral order panels to the youth justice system in 1999*' (emphasis added).[7]

As Crawford (2007: 3) reminds us, youth offender panels embody the following factors with regard to their place in restorative justice: they draw on the experiences of family group conferencing; they involve lay members of the community in facilitating proceedings; they seek to involve victims in a dialogue about the offence and the response to it; and they seek to involve family members or other members of the young person's (and the victim's) community of care, who might have a beneficial impact upon deliberations. Although we might want to discuss their 'restorativeness' on the ground – which I shall do in Chapter 7, based on the empirical component of this study – youth offender panels do have that restorative justice 'spirit' described in Chapter 1. Moreover, while one of the main criticisms of youth offender panels is the low level of victim involvement (Newburn *et al.* 2002; Newbury 2011), it should be noted that this is also a main concern in other restorative justice initiatives (see Dignan 2005). In fact, as will become apparent from discussions in later chapters, youth offender panels have much in common with other initiatives across the world: they are very similar, for example, to the reparative boards in Vermont (see Boyes-Watson 2004). Thus, as Crawford writes:

> I believe that *an analysis of youth offender panels is of interest to international debates about restorative justice*, less because they constitute a principled institutionalisation of restorative ideals (which they do not), and more because they are hybrid cross-fertilisation (and compromise) of diverse ideas, values and interests. Their hybridity reflects the kind of

> ambiguous compromise that is evident in much criminal justice policy. This is especially apparent with regard to youth justice where, a 'general trend from welfare to justice to restoration and responsibility' has culminated in 'a particularly complex agglomeration of competing and contradictory policies'.
>
> (Crawford 2007: 3, emphasis added)

On the whole, youth offender panels constitute a 'typical' instance of restorative justice practice in line with the use of the term 'typical' by Denscombe (2010: 57):

> The most common justification to be offered for the selection of a particular case is that it is typical. The logic being invoked here is that the particular case is similar in crucial respects with the others that might have been chosen, and that the findings from the case study are therefore likely to apply elsewhere.

The focus on community involvement

It was not the government's original intention to involve lay members of the community in the youth offender panel process; for example, there is no reference to this in the *No More Excuses* White Paper (Crawford and Newburn 2003). Having said that, some commentators have argued that 'both the Crime and Disorder Act and the Labour administration have been heavily influenced by the communitarian movement' (Green 2014: 59), and particularly by a communitarian ideology developed in the USA by Amitai Etzioni (1995, 1996).[8] This perhaps helps to explain why the legislation and all the *Guidance* documents following the introduction of referral orders are explicit in their focus on community involvement. Indeed, according to the 2002, 2009 and 2012 *Guidance*, the primary aim of referral orders is 'to prevent young people offending and provide a restorative justice approach *within a community* context' (Home Office 2002: 5; Ministry of Justice 2009: 7; Ministry of Justice 2012: 8; emphasis added). And 'one of the stated purposes of having (at least) two lay members of the community as part of the panel is *to engage local communities in dealing with young offenders*' (Crawford and Burden 2005: 6, emphasis added). All together, youth offender panels are explicitly aimed at involving the community, and in a way that other restorative justice programmes, such as victim–offender mediation, never have. This focus on community involvement in the heart of youth justice, I would argue, makes youth offender panels an 'intrinsically interesting' case. According to Denscombe (2010: 59):

> If a case is intrinsically interesting then it can prove an attractive proposition. The findings are likely to reach a wider audience and the research itself is likely to be a more exciting experience. There are even some

experts in the field who would go as far as to argue that selection on the basis of being intrinsically interesting is a sufficient justification in its own right.

Another gap in the literature

A Home Office evaluation of the pilot areas (Newburn *et al.* 2002) was conducted prior to the national rollout. This was based on an in-depth 18-month study undertaken by a consortium from Goldsmiths College (University of London) and the Universities of Leeds and Kent, and is still the most comprehensive study on referral orders and youth offender panels. In fact, most of the book chapters I mention above are based on the findings of this national study which was conducted over 10 years ago. Apart from this milestone, there have been a couple of other smaller studies of youth offender panels. In 2005 Crawford and Burden (2005) evaluated the work of the Restorative Justice Team within the Leeds Youth Offending Service, but this was a study concerning victim involvement and input into referral orders and youth offender panels. In 2003, Gray and colleagues (2003) carried out a study to evaluate the effectiveness of one particular restorative justice programme, developed by Plymouth YOT. Others have studied YOTs with a particular focus on their multi-agency approach (see, for example, Burnett and Appleton 2004; and Souhami 2007). However, there has been no up-to-date study of the restorative component of referral orders, and certainly not on the role of community in youth offender panels. This further indicates the relevance and timeliness of this (empirical) study.

My empirical aims

In all, my *empirical* aims are as follows: 1 to explore *why* (that is, *for what purposes*) the community is involved in the youth offender panel process; 2 to examine *how* (that is, *within what limits* and *under which conditions*) the community is involved in the youth offender panel process; and 3 to investigate the overall role of community in the referral order process. The next chapter details the methods of data collection and analysis employed – that is, it sets out a clear plan for achieving the aforementioned empirical aims.

Notes

1 Many YOTs across England and Wales have chosen to rebadge themselves as a 'Youth Offending Service' (instead of 'Youth Offending Team'). In fact, most YOTs I visited called themselves a service, only because they had grown into a 'team' of various 'sub-teams'. However, to be concise, and in order to avoid confusion of terms, this book will use the term 'YOT'.

2 The Action Plan Order, along with other community sentences (e.g. Curfew Order, Supervision Order, etc.), was later replaced by the Youth Rehabilitation Order (YRO), which came into effect on 30 November 2009, as part of the Criminal Justice and

Immigration Act 2008. The YRO 'is a generic community sentence for children and young people who offend and combines a number of existing sentences into one generic sentence'. As such, it is 'the standard community sentence used for the majority of children and young people who offend'. More information about YROs can be found on the Ministry of Justice website, at www.justice.gov.uk.

3 In fact, apart from the 1998 Act, the home secretary at the time, Jack Straw, spoke out publicly in support of restorative justice, and strongly endorsed the restorative cautioning scheme in the Thames Valley Police area (Hoyle *et al.* 2002; Young and Hoyle 2003). Also Tony Blair, the prime minister at the time, often expressed an interest in the philosophy of communitarianism. Altogether, although New Labour's policy messages were somewhat mixed (for example, not only the communitarian philosophy, but populism characterised Blair's approach to law and order), many of them were 'ostensibly much more favourable towards the future prospects for restorative justice' than previously had been the case (Dignan 2005: 50; see also Earle and Newburn 2001).

4 A part of this section was first published in Rosenblatt, F.F. (2014), 'Community Involvement in Restorative Justice: Lessons from an English and Welsh Case Study on Youth Offender Panels', *Restorative Justice: An International Journal*, 2(3): 280–301 (Hart Publishing, used by permission of Bloomsbury Publishing Plc).

5 In any case, it remains that a referral order shall *not* be made where the court considers appropriate a custodial sentence, an absolute discharge or a hospital order, or where the offence is one for which the sentence is fixed by law.

6 This handbook was prepared for the United Nations Office on Drugs and Crime (UNODC) by Yvon Dandurand and Curt T. Griffiths, and reviewed by many other leading experts in the field of restorative justice, such as Ivo Aertsen, Paul McCold, Daniel Van Ness and Martin Wright.

7 RJC quarterly newsletters (26 April 2013). This quotation from the former director of the RJC, Lizzie Nelson, is repeated (though unattributed) on the RJC website at: www.restorativejustice.org.uk/news/rjlaw/#.Ujm8ZRZ9nww.

8 This theme (Etzioni's communitarianism) is returned to in more detail in Chapter 7.

References

Boyes-Watson, C. (2004) 'The Value of Citizen Participation in Restorative/Community Justice: Lessons from Vermont', *Criminology & Public Policy*, 3(4): 687–692.

Burnett, R. (2005) 'Youth Offending Teams', in T. Bateman and J. Pitts (eds), *The RHP Companion to Youth Justice*, Dorset: Russell House.

Burnett, R. and Appleton, C. (2004) 'Joined-up Services to Tackle Youth Crime', *British Journal of Criminology*, 44(1): 34–54.

Cabinet Office (2011) *Public Bodies Reform: Proposals for Change*, London: Cabinet Office.

Crawford, A. (2002) 'The State, Community and Restorative Justice: Heresy, Nostalgia and Butterfly Collecting', in L. Walgrave (ed.), *Restorative Justice and the Law*, Cullompton: Willan Publishing.

Crawford, A. (2007) 'Situating Restorative Youth Justice in Crime Control and Prevention', in E. van der Spuy, S. Parmentier and A. Dissel (eds), *Restorative Justice: Politics, Policies and Prospects*, Cape Town: Juta.

Crawford, A. and Burden, T. (2005) *Integrating Victims in Restorative Youth Justice*, Bristol: The Policy Press.

Crawford, A. and Newburn, T. (2002) 'Recent Developments in Restorative Justice for Young People in England and Wales: Community Participation and Representation', *British Journal of Criminology*, 42(3): 476–495.

Crawford, A. and Newburn, T. (2003) *Youth Offending and Restorative Justice: Implementing Reform in Youth Justice*, Cullompton: Willan Publishing.

Denscombe, M. (2010) *Good Research Guide: For Small-scale Social Research Projects*, 4th edn, Maidenhead: Open University Press.

Dignan, J. (1999) 'The Crime and Disorder Act and the Prospects for Restorative Justice', *Criminal Law Review*: 48–60.

Dignan, J. (2005) *Understanding Victims and Restorative Justice*, Maidenhead: Open University Press.

Earle, R. and Newburn, T. (2001) 'Creative Tensions? Young Offenders, Restorative Justice and the Introduction of Referral Orders', *Youth Justice*, 1(3): 3–13.

Etzioni, A. (1995) *The Spirit of Community: Rights, Responsibilities and the Communitarian Agenda*, London: Fontana.

Etzioni, A. (1996) *The New Golden Rule: Community and Morality in a Democratic Society*, New York: Basic Books.

Feeley, M. and Simon, J. (1994) 'Actuarial Justice: The Emerging New Criminal Law', in D. Nelken (ed.), *The Futures of Criminology*, London: SAGE Publications.

Garland, D. (2001) *The Culture of Control: Crime and Social Order in Contemporary Society*, Oxford: Oxford University Press.

George, A.L. and Bennett, A. (2005) *Case Studies and Theory Development in the Social Sciences*, Cambridge, MA: MIT Press.

Goldson, B. (2010) 'The Sleep of (Criminological) Reason: Knowledge-Policy Rupture and New Labour's Youth Justice Legacy', *Criminology and Criminal Justice*, 10(2): 155–178.

Gray, P., Moseley, J. and Browning, R. (2003) *An Evaluation of the Plymouth Restorative Justice Programme*, Plymouth: University of Plymouth.

Green, S. (2014) *Crime, Community and Morality*, Abingdon: Routledge.

Home Office (1997a), *Community Safety Order: A Consultation Document*, London: Home Office.

Home Office (1997b), *Getting to Grips with Crime*, London: Home Office.

Home Office (1997c), *New National and Local Focus on Youth Crime: A Consultation Paper*, London: HMSO.

Home Office (1997d), *No More Excuses: A New Approach to Tackling Youth Crime in England and Wales*, London: Home Office.

Home Office (1997e), *Tackling Delays in the Youth Justice System: A Consultation Paper*, London: HMSO.

Home Office (1997f), *Tackling Youth Crime: A Consultation Paper*, London: Home Office.

Home Office (2002) *Referral Orders and Youth Offender Panels: Guidance for Courts, Youth Offending Teams and Youth Offender Panels*, London: Home Office/Lord Chancellor's Department/Youth Justice Board.

Hoyle, C., Young, R. and Hill, R. (2002) *Proceed with Caution: An Evaluation of the Thames Valley Police Initiative in Restorative Cautioning*, York: Joseph Rowntree Foundation.

Johnstone, G. (ed.) (2003) *A Restorative Justice Reader: Texts, Sources, Context*, Cullompton: Willan Publishing.

Jones, G. (2010) 'A Case Study Approach to Social Research', in M. Walter (ed.), *Social Research Methods*, 2nd edn, Oxford: Oxford University Press.

Ministry of Justice (2009) *Referral Order Guidance*, London: Ministry of Justice/Department for Children, Schools and Families/Youth Justice Board.

Ministry of Justice (2012) *Referral Order Guidance*, London: Ministry of Justice/Youth Justice Board.

Morris, A. and Gelsthorpe, L. (2000) 'Something Old, Something Borrowed, Something Blue, but Something New? A Comment on the Prospects for Restorative Justice under the Crime and Disorder Act 1998', *Criminal Law Review* (January): 18–30.

Muncie, J. (2001) 'A Deal for Youth? Early Intervention and Correctionalism', in J. Muncie and E. McLaughlin (eds), *Crime Prevention and Community Safety*, London: SAGE Publications.

Muncie, J. and Hughes, G. (2002) 'Modes of Youth Governance: Political Rationalities, Criminalization and Resistance', in J. Muncie, G. Hughes and E. McLaughlin (eds), *Youth Justice: Critical Readings*, London: SAGE Publications.

NACRO (1997) *A New Three Rs for Young Offenders: Towards a New Strategy for Children who Offend*, London: National Association for the Care and Resettlement of Offenders.

National Audit Office (2010) *The Youth Justice System in England and Wales: Reducing Offending by Young People*, London: NAO.

Newburn, T., Crawford, A., Earle, R., Goldie, S., Hale, C., Hallam, A., Masters, G., Netten, A., Saunders, R., Sharpe, K. and Uglow, S. (2002) *The Introduction of Referral Orders into the Youth Justice System: Final Report*, Home Office Research Study 242, London: Home Office.

Newbury, A. (2011) '"I Would Have Been Able to Hear What They Think": Tensions in Achieving Restorative Outcomes in the English Youth Justice System', *Youth Justice*, 11(3): 250–265.

O'Mahony, D. and Doak, J. (2009) 'Restorative Justice and Youth Justice: Bringing Theory and Practice Closer Together in Europe', in J. Junger-Tas and F. Dünkel (eds), *Reforming Juvenile Justice*, Dordrecht: Springer.

Pitts, J. (2005) 'The Recent History of Youth Justice in England and Wales', in T. Bateman and J. Pitts (eds), *The RHP Companion to Youth Justice*, Dorset: Russell House Publishing.

Pratt, J. (1989) 'Corporatism: The Third Model of Juvenile Justice', *British Journal of Criminology*, 29(3): 236–254.

Puffet, N. (2013) 'Fresh Review of YJB Announced', *Children and Young People Now*.

Silverman, D. (2013) *Doing Qualitative Research*, 4th edn, London: SAGE Publications.

Souhami, A. (2007) *Transforming Youth Justice: Occupational Identity and Cultural Change*, Abingdon: Routledge.

Spuy, E. van der, Parmentier, S. and Dissel, A. (eds) (2007) *Restorative Justice: Politics, Policies and Prospects*, Cape Town: Juta.

Tomlinson, R. (2005) 'Youth Justice at the Local Level', in T. Bateman and J. Pitts (eds), *The RHP Companion to Youth Justice*, Dorset: Russell House Publishing.

UNODC (2006) *Handbook on Restorative Justice Programmes*, New York: United Nations.

Walgrave, L. (2002) 'From Community to Dominion: In Search of Social Values for Restorative Justice', in E.G.M. Weitekamp and H.-J. Kerner (eds), *Restorative Justice: Theoretical Foundations*, Cullompton: Willan Publishing.

Walgrave, L. (2008) *Restorative Justice, Self-Interest and Responsible Citizenship*, Cullompton: Willan Publishing.

Young, R. and Hoyle, C. (2003) 'New Improved Restorative Justice?: Action-Research and the Thames Valley Initiative in Restorative Cautioning', in A. Von Hirsch, J. Roberts, A.E. Bottoms, K. Roach and M. Schiff (eds), *Restorative Justice and Criminal Justice: Competing or Reconcilable Paradigms?* Oxford: Hart Publishing.

4 Notes on an empirical study

As discussed in more detail in Chapter 3, for the empirical component of this research, an exploratory case study approach was used to examine the involvement of the community in one selected practice of restorative justice, namely youth offender panels in England and Wales. Closely aligned with the qualitative objective of understanding a phenomenon through the perspectives of those who actually experience it and make sense of it (Bachman and Schutt 2011; Rubin and Rubin 2012), data collection was through interviews with the key stakeholders involved in the process of referral orders, as well as through observation of panel meetings, and the analysis of various related documents. The reasons why a case study design was chosen, along with the motives for selecting youth offender panels as a case study, were detailed in the previous chapter. This chapter briefs the methods of data collection and analysis employed.

4.1 The research sites

As King and Wincup (2008: 27) observe, '[r]esearch designs vary in the extent to which they prioritize breadth over depth and *vice versa*'. When looking at it this way, the case study design clearly emphasises depth over breadth of understanding as it typically entails 'the detailed and intensive analysis of a single case' (Bryman 2012: 66; see also Denscombe 2010) – in the present study, a detailed and intensive analysis of youth offender panels (and the involvement of the community therein). Having said that, instead of concentrating efforts on one single research site, I have attempted to broaden the focus of this study by studying more than one setting, which, according to Bachman and Schutt (2011: 265), 'almost always [...] makes the findings more generalizable'.

Over a 16-month period beginning in February 2012, data were gathered in 12 areas in England and Wales (three of them in Wales and the others in England, including three London boroughs). These areas are not claimed to be representative of all YOTs in England and Wales,[1] but were selected to incorporate a broad cross-section in terms of size, geographic distribution and character of the area. There are YOTs covering very urban to largely rural areas. There are YOTs covering areas with both high and low proportions of minority ethnic groups. Some YOTs are relatively large and particularly busy, whereas others comprise smaller teams. There are YOTs covering some of the most deprived areas in England and Wales, as well as some of the wealthiest. All in all, the selected YOTs represent a wide geographical spread, cover regions in both England and Wales, and are as varied in number and scope as they were in previous research on referral orders and youth offender panels (see Crawford and Newburn 2003).

It is important to note, however, that assurances of confidentiality made to these YOTs and to all research participants mean that data are not attributed to specific YOTs, and that therefore comparison between them is precluded. While comparison would be informative, the amount of data collected is not substantial enough to permit inferences to be drawn on the extent to which geographical area (or characteristics of that area) influence the involvement of the community in youth offender panels. That said, at the least, the variety of research sites means that the results of this study do not reflect a particular geographical area (or characteristics of that area).

4.2 The process of data collection

In order to achieve 'triangulation', and therefore enhance the quality and reliability of this study, multiple sources of data and a variety of collection strategies were used (Arksey and Knight 1999; Bachman and Schutt 2011; Denzin 1970; Hagan 2007). The three methods of data collection employed were semi-structured interviews, non-participant observations and documentary analysis. While the three methods are discussed separately below, in the processes of data collection and analysis they were often mutually dependent. For example, the opportunity to find out about (and obtain) certain documents (e.g. YOT reports) typically came from interviewing a YOT worker, a community panel member, or observing a panel meeting. Also, in the process of data analysis, interview transcriptions were often analysed along with observational field notes and documents, so as to allow for the cross-checking of information and interpretations.

Semi-structured interviews

A total of 127 semi-structured interviews were conducted with three sets of stakeholders involved in the process of referral orders: 52 YOT workers, 50 community panel members and 25 young offenders. The size of the sample was determined by the principle of saturation, described by Bachman and Schutt (2011: 275) as 'the point when new interviews seem to yield little additional information'. In this study, saturation was reached when no new information emerged from the interviews carried out with each type of respondent. It should be noted, however, that in order to achieve a more balanced number of participants from each research site, some interviews with

YOT workers and community panel members were conducted even after I felt that the saturation point was reached.

Interviews with all research participants were undertaken on a face-to-face basis, and nearly all of them on a one-to-one basis. Among the exceptions to the one-to-one approach were eight interviews where the young offender's parent or carer was also present (although in every case, silent). Another exception was a case where a referral order coordinator ignored my request to interview panel members separately, and booked them all in at the same time. When this YOT worker entered the room followed by four panel members, I realised that I had been unwittingly 'thrown' into a focus group situation. As the panel members had given up their time to be there, I felt I could not ask three of them to come back sometime later. To my surprise, the experience of conducting a group interview with four panel members proved interesting. Besides, this irregular interview served the purpose of what Denzin (1970: 301) calls 'within-method' triangulation insofar as, although unwittingly, I have applied two different techniques within the same method (single and group interviews). Of course, 'triangulation is not just about using as many different methods or sources of data collection as possible' (Arksey and Knight 1999: 21), but this one-off group interview provided another insight on how panel members make sense of their role in the process of referral orders. I return to this case in Chapter 6.

The semi-structured approach was achieved by devising interview schedules tailored to each type of participant – namely, YOT workers, panel members and young people. Each of the three interview schedules consisted of a series of standard (but open-ended) questions, as well as a few prompt questions to encourage the interviewees to elaborate on their answers (Denscombe 2010). Some of the items were adapted from previous studies on referral orders and youth offender panels (Crawford and Burden 2005; Crawford and Newburn 2003), while others were new. As the period of fieldwork progressed, I made minor changes to each of these schedules as a means of focusing attention on my research questions, opening up research themes, or rephrasing certain questions for clarity.

Young people were interviewed in relation to their experiences of referral orders and panel meetings, with no questions being asked in relation to the offence or their personal life circumstances (although in all cases I knew which offence had been committed as I had observed their panel meeting and/or read their report). With respect to panel members, interviews mainly covered their views and experiences of sitting on panels, as well as their reasons for becoming a panel member. Finally, YOT workers were interviewed in relation to their general views about the referral order process (vis-à-vis other orders available in the youth court), and their more specific views on the role of panel members within that process.

All but one interview was carried out in a room set aside for the purpose, either at the YOT or at a community venue where some panel meetings took place. The exception was an interview undertaken in a panel member's own home, as she felt that this would be more convenient for her. Interviews with all YOT workers and panel members were digitally recorded and fully transcribed for analysis (I hired a native speaker to transcribe all the interviews). With respect to young offenders, I only made use of a digital recorder on two occasions; I found that the digital recorder made them less at ease. Besides, young offenders' responses were short enough to take notes during the interview, and on very rare occasions where a more elaborate response was given, I would take note of key elements during the interview and write a full account immediately after (Noaks and Wincup 2004).

Confidentiality and anonymity can be difficult to achieve in case studies given that with one single case (or with a small number of cases) it is easier to identify who said what (Denscombe 2010). I therefore deployed a few strategies to outweigh the risk of unintentionally revealing the respondent's identity. For example, I avoided mention of the respondent's gender, unless this was of particular relevance – hence the use of 'she' and 'her' as indeterminate pronouns. Also, quotations from respondents are referenced only by respondent type, such as: 'one of the *YOT workers* stated that ...', 'as argued by a *panel member* ...', 'according to a *young offender* ...', and so on. Moreover, I have excluded any descriptive references that could identify the respondent. All in all, I am persuaded that anonymity has been achieved and that promises of confidentiality have been respected.

Non-participant observations

Throughout the period of 16 months (February 2012–June 2013) I attended a total of 59 panel meetings for observation purposes, but in 18 cases the young person failed to attend, and in two further cases the mother or the young person asked for me to leave the room. This meant that I have actually observed a total of 39 panel meetings, comprising 18 initial, nine review, two breach, one extension and nine final panel meetings. As well as all the possible types of meetings, my observations covered a wide range of referral offences, as well as all the possible lengths of a referral order (i.e. the full range of 3–12 months). Unlike most other observation studies of restorative practices, my particular focus was on the voices of panel members (the 'community representatives'): what they said, how they intervened, what verbal and body language they used, and their attitudes towards the young person.

I deemed it inappropriate to digitally record panel meetings. After observing the first meeting, I realised that much of the discussion was centred on matters that were too personal to the young offender and her parents and irrelevant to my research. And much of what needed to be recorded, the digital recorder could not capture: people's demeanours. Whilst I will discuss this in more detail in later chapters, for the time being it is enough to say that I felt ethically bound not to use my digital recorder at panel meetings. Hence, I have relied on the more traditional method of note taking (Bachman and

Schutt 2011), which I did during the meeting (in most cases), or immediately after it (in a couple of cases, where I felt that my taking notes during the meeting was distracting the young people or their parents).

Documentary analysis

In addition to interviews and observational data, I have also used documentary evidence as an adjunct source of information, as well as to confirm interviewee accounts and identify inconsistencies.[2] This meant a piecing together, and a critical analysis, of statutory instruments (e.g. the 1999 Act); statutory guidance (e.g. Ministry of Justice/YJB referral order guidance); YOT reports produced for panel members; referral order contracts; training packages for volunteers (e.g. the YJB's 'Panel Matters' programme); reports provided by inspection bodies (e.g. on the use of restorative justice provided by the Criminal Justice Joint Inspectorates); and various information leaflets (e.g. NACRO pamphlet on spent conviction). I also asked each YOT to provide me with a table showing the socio-demographic profile (age, gender and ethnicity) of their panel members.

4.3 The process of data analysis

In some respects, I began analysing my data early in the data collection process by writing reflective notes, which I refer to as my 'research diaries'. My early attention to analysis meant that I could refine my interview schedules early in the data collection process, adding different questions that could open up potential research themes (e.g. the young offenders' views on the *voluntary* role of panel members), or shelving irrelevant queries (e.g. about the young person's current occupation). Also because data collection and analysis occurred, to a certain extent, simultaneously, I was able to 'test' some of my ideas and themes with participants, and improve the way I was conducting observations.[3]

Having said that, I did most of my data analysis once I had my final set of data – that is, after the interviews had been transcribed. Indeed, since I acquired professional support to transcribe all recorded interviews, I could only fully familiarise myself with the data once the transcriptions were done and I had proofread them. That was when I started to review my data as a whole, and to organise all my field notes and interview materials into emerging themes and subthemes. At this point, I made the decision *not* to use analytic software packages such as NVivo. Like Wincup (1997, as cited by Noaks and Wincup 2004: 125), I felt that too much time would be spent sorting and retrieving data at the expense of interpreting and writing. Hence, instead of NVivo, I have used Microsoft Word headings, along with its copy and paste facility, to sort out the themes and generally help to organise the data.

The data were analysed using a grounded theory approach; that is, instead of testing a hypothesis, my attempt was to discover hypotheses implicit in the data (Glaser and Strauss 1967). This is not to say that I have gone into the field with no preconceived ideas about potential research themes (not least because I conducted a review of the literature before entering the field), but rather that my analysis has allowed for additional research themes to emerge from the fieldwork (Mruck and Mey 2007; Noaks and Wincup 2004). After I gathered and made preliminary interpretations of my data, I looked for more literature (particularly on 'community') so as to enrich my understanding of my own data. In this context, a continuous process of moving back and forth from a new review of the literature to the interpretation of the analysed data played a central role: I often 're-entered' the data and wrestled with it to locate supporting or refuting evidence for the themes that were emerging or that have emerged in previous studies (Mruck and Mey 2007).

It is fair to say that the process of data analysis ended when the last full stop was keyed, and this book was finished. Indeed, for me, just as suggested by Coffey and Atkinson (1996: 109), the writing stage represented the culmination of the analysis process:

> Writing makes us think about data in new and different ways. Thinking about how to represent our data forces us to think about the meanings and understandings, voices and experiences present in the data. As such, writing actually deepens our level of analytic endeavour. Analytical ideas are developed and tried out in the process of writing and representing.

Having outlined the research process, the findings and analysis of this empirical study form the bulk of the next three chapters.

Notes

1 There are 158 YOTs in England and Wales (National Audit Office 2010).
2 See Hudson (2011) on treating documentary materials as empirical research.
3 On the benefits of simultaneous data collection and analysis, see King and Wincup 2008: 36.

References

Arksey, H. and Knight, P.T. (1999) *Interviewing for Social Scientists: An Introductory Resource with Examples*, London: SAGE Publications.

Bachman, R. and Schutt, R. (2011) *The Practice of Research in Criminology and Criminal Justice*, 4th edn, London: SAGE Publications.

Bryman, A. (2012) *Social Research Methods*, 4th edn, Oxford: Oxford University Press.

Coffey, A. and Atkinson, P. (1996) *Making Sense of Qualitative Data*, London: SAGE Publications.

Crawford, A. and Burden, T. (2005) *Integrating Victims in Restorative Youth Justice*, Bristol: The Policy Press.

Crawford, A. and Newburn, T. (2003) *Youth Offending and Restorative Justice: Implementing Reform in Youth Justice*, Cullompton: Willan Publishing.

Denscombe, M. (2010) *Good Research Guide: For Small-scale Social Research Projects*, 4th edn, Maidenhead: Open University Press.

Denzin, N.K. (1970) *The Research Act in Sociology*, Chicago, IL: Aldine.

Glaser, B.G. and Strauss, A.L. (1967) *The Discovery of Grounded Theory: Strategies for Qualitative Research*, Chicago, IL: Aldine Publishing Company.

Hagan, F.E. (2007) *Essentials of Research Methods in Criminal Justice and Criminology*, 2nd edn, Boston, MA: Pearson.

Hudson, B. (2011) 'Critical Reflections as Research Methodology', in P. Davies, P. Francis and V. Jupp (eds), *Doing Criminological Research*, 2nd edn, London: SAGE Publications.

King, R. and Wincup, E. (2008) 'The Process of Criminological Research', in R. King and E. Wincup (eds), *Doing Research on Crime and Justice*, Oxford: Oxford University Press.

Mruck, K. and Mey, G. (2007) 'Grounded Theory and Reflexivity', in A. Bryant and K. Charmaz (eds), *The SAGE Handbook of Grounded Theory*, London: SAGE Publications.

National Audit Office (2010) *The Youth Justice System in England and Wales: Reducing Offending by Young People*, London: NAO.

Noaks, L. and Wincup, E. (2004) *Criminological Research: Understanding Qualitative Methods*, London: SAGE Publications.

Rubin, H.J. and Rubin, I. (2012) *Qualitative Interviewing: The Art of Hearing Data*, Thousand Oaks: SAGE Publications.

Wincup, E. (1997) 'Waiting for Trial: Living and Working in a Bail Hostel', unpublished PhD thesis, Cardiff University.

5 Youth offender panels

A play in three acts

As explained in Chapter 3, while the court sets the length of the referral order (3–12 months, depending on the seriousness of the offence), its content should be agreed by a panel comprising at least two members of the community and one YOT member: the 'youth offender panel'. Drawing mainly on the experiences of the family group conferencing model in New Zealand (Morris and Maxwell 2000) and the Scottish Children's Hearings system (Hallett *et al.* 1998), the intention is for panels to 'provide a forum away from the formality of the court where the young offender, his or her family and, where appropriate, the victim can consider the circumstances surrounding the offence(s) and the effect on the victim' (Crawford and Burden 2005: 5). In this spirit, within 20 working days of a referral order being made in court, an initial panel meeting needs to be held to devise a 'youth offender contract' (Youth Justice Board 2009). The contract should always include an element of reparation to the victim or to the community, as well as a programme of interventions aimed at preventing reoffending; the length of the referral order only starts from the time the contract is signed.

It is worth reiterating here that 'one of the stated purposes of having (at least) two community members as part of the panel is to engage local communities in dealing with young offenders' (Crawford and Burden 2005: 6). In fact, a core rationale for referral orders is the intention to broaden lay community involvement in the youth justice system. Accordingly, at panel meetings, 'the discussion with the offender, victims and family members and the drawing up of the contract should be led by the community panel members', while YOT workers sitting on panels have a merely advisory role (Ministry of Justice 2009: 11). In the same vein, the *Guidance* recommends that community panel members should be encouraged to suggest activities for inclusion in contracts 'that draw on community rather than just youth offending team resources' (Home Office 2002: 7; Ministry of Justice 2009: 11). Altogether, the stated role of the community panel members in the referral order process is seen as one of great significance: it is their responsibility to lead all panel meetings; the decision on returning young offenders back to court (for a breach) lies in their hands; they have the 'power' to 'sign off' the young offender once the referral order has been successfully completed; and so forth.

In theory, thus, the community panel members are heavily involved in the operation of referral orders, not least because *they determine the directions and outcomes of panel meetings.*

In practice, however, there is little evidence of this occurring. Indeed, as will be argued below, the panel meetings that I have observed look more like theatre productions: the producers (YOT workers) write the script (the initial or progress report) and closely monitor its execution (as they sit on the panel); the actors (community panel members) read the script and rehearse for the performance (at a pre-panel meeting); the spectators (the young person and her parent) arrive at the theatre (YOT premises) and take a seat; finally the play begins, and it lasts for three acts (the initial meeting, the review meeting(s) and the final meeting). The interaction with the audience, which is afforded by the script, may happen to a greater or lesser extent depending on everyone's communication skills and the spectators' willingness to step on stage. Interestingly, though, the spectators have also read the script beforehand and they know how the play is expected to end, meaning that even the most engaged audiences do not actually help in the creation of an original performance – they also, to a certain extent, 'follow the script', with few opportunities genuinely to 'ad-lib'. Directors generally tolerate some improvisation, but not all actors have improvisational skills. Besides, more often than not, like in plays that have been running for many years, the more creative improvisation tends to be integrated into the script, regardless of who is sitting in the audience that particular evening.

This chapter provides a detailed narrative description of this 'play', but one that also goes behind the scenes to provide a bigger picture of how youth offender panels operate on the ground. In fact, it aims to weave the story of how the referral order process works, and is therefore of a more descriptive or narrative nature. Nonetheless, in 'telling the story', it inevitably starts to raise some important issues around the artificiality of the role of community in youth offender panels which the subsequent chapters will explore further. The following account is based largely on observation data gathered during the research fieldwork – more precisely, on the observation of 39 panel meetings (including initials, reviews and finals). It also draws on nearly 130 interviews with YOT workers, community panel members and young offenders, although in this chapter I use interview data mainly as a means of cross-checking the reliability of my observations (a more detailed analysis of the interviews will be provided in the next chapter). Finally, this chapter also draws on documentary evidence, or more precisely, on the nearly 40 panel reports and 20 youth offender contracts collected at my research sites.

5.1 A 'behind the scenes' look at youth offender panels

If one takes the example of a six-month referral order, during which time there will probably be three panel meetings, it is not hard to work out that most of the referral order process runs offstage – that is, outside the planned panel meetings – and, therefore, under the auspices of YOT workers rather than community panel members. Indeed, the local YOT is responsible for recruiting and training the community panel members, establishing a youth offender panel for each offender, assessing offenders prior to initial panel meetings, engaging with victims and convening all panel meetings (Ministry of Justice 2009; see also the legislation discussed in Chapter 3). During panel meetings, YOT members provide information and advice on services, the legal framework, proportionality and, at the end of the day, it is their duty to ensure that the contract is 'effective and fair', and that it 'includes appropriate reparation and activities to reduce reoffending risk' (Ministry of Justice 2009: 22). Once it is agreed and signed, the local YOT must ensure that all parts of the contract are delivered within the period of the order, that any reparation undertaken by the young person is risk assessed, and that all appropriate health and safety provisions are in place (Ministry of Justice 2009). All in all, as will be discussed in detail below, behind the scenes, YOT workers are responsible for a considerable amount of work in the operation of referral orders and youth offender panels – and in such context, exercise great control over the whole process.

The recruitment and training of community panel members

The *Guidance* has always made clear (Home Office 2002; Ministry of Justice 2009) that there should be no unnecessary restrictions on recruitment; the aim, ultimately, is to have a diverse group of panel members that is properly representative of the local community. To this end, the strategy should be to recruit people from a broad age range (over 18) and from a wide experiential background. In fact, the opportunity for participation in youth offender panels should be open to all, 'regardless of age, ethnic or racial origin, gender, sexual orientation, social background, religion, disability or any other irrelevant factor' (Ministry of Justice 2009: 25). Furthermore, the *Guidance* calls for the selection criteria to be based on personal qualities rather than professional qualifications, such as 'communication skills', 'sound temperament', and 'commitment and reliability' (Ministry of Justice 2009: 23). This all seems to be respected on the ground. Indeed, in terms of recruitment, the following comments from YOT workers were typical:

> It's an open door. I am not interested in GCSE [General Certificate of Secondary Education] or degree; I don't care. I am interested in how they engage with people in general. […] They can have strong views but I don't want them dictating or being judgemental. I like people who communicate, who don't judge. We have had sex offenders before the panel, and I want people who can sit there and be shocked but still treat them with respect.
>
> (YOT11, WORKER1)

> I want a mix of community; so to say I want a particular type of person would rob that diversity. I could look for people with particular skillsets, but I want that breadth of community. When a young person sits before the panel I want someone to be horrified at what they've done, and someone who thinks it's not that serious, because that's what communities are like. [...] I think one of the problems that young people have in court is there's no relationship with the court because they're not like the defendant. And I want the young person to come into a panel and see that there's someone who is like them. [...] If they see community as being just one type of person, and they're not that kind of person, they're instantly excluded. They need to see that community is broad and diverse, and full of mad people and cross people and friendly people, because the better they understand that, the better they can fit in.
>
> (YOT2, WORKER1)

Other YOT workers commented on the recruitment of volunteers who are ex-offenders:

> We don't necessarily turn people away who had offences in the past, but it would depend on what these offences were, how long ago they were, and the circumstances of the situation.
>
> (YOT1, WORKER1)

> We had an excellent panel member who was an ex-drug user, who had been to custody a lot when he was young, got his life back on track, got a young family, [was] working locally.
>
> (YOT2, WORKER2)

> We have a couple of people on the panel who have been there themselves. We've got a couple of people who are ex-offenders, so they'll have the view, they'll have the experience they can use. Or we've got a couple of parents of youngsters who have been in trouble.
>
> (YOT1, WORKER2)

Generally speaking, YOTs still use the same advertising methods that were recommended back in the 2002 *Guidance*, with advertising in local media (newspaper or magazine) and word of mouth being by far the most frequently used methods. Having said that, some YOTs have turned to other, more creative advertising methods – for example, having the young people deliver leaflets, as part of their reparation, informing that the YOT is recruiting for volunteers. A couple of YOTs included in this study have also visited universities in order to get younger people on board. In one area, for example, a YOT worker had given a talk at the local university to the criminology, psychology and youth studies students, providing information about the process and on how students could get involved. It is noteworthy, however, that many

YOT workers see the recruitment of students as controversial. They argue that students are less reliable for they often become panel members 'to get a tick on their CV [curriculum vitae]' – and then 'they're off'. In this vein, the following comments were typical:

> People become panel members for a variety of motives: because they want to be magistrates and can't, because they want to work with young people, […] because they want to get a job in the YOT – and, again, they don't come to represent the community, but to get a tick on their CV.
>
> (YOT4, WORKER1)

> Previously I'd say it was wanting to give something back, being productive or being useful. More recently, it's about … people see it as a step on getting employment. That actually they can put on a CV that they've done voluntary work.
>
> (YOT1, WORKER1)

> Some of them are students, some of them work full time. The ones that tend to work are more reliable than the students.
>
> (YOT10, WORKER1)

The student panel members I interviewed generally admitted that they were interested in becoming a panel member for 'CV purposes'. The following comment from one of them was typical of others: 'Because of, like, the lack of jobs going on … I was struggling, you know, with the "you've got the qualification but you've not got the experience"? So I just literally tapped in "voluntary work" on Google' (YOT1, CPM1). It should be noted, however, that 'gaining work experience' was a common theme for many non-student panel members as well. One community member, for example, said: 'I am volunteering in a number of different places because for 11 years I was a corporate solicitor […] and last year I decided to resign and do a different career' (YOT12, CPM1). Another community member wanted to become a magistrate:

> I was turned down to be a magistrate, and the reason when I asked was that they said I didn't have enough experience of youth crime in the area that I live in. I live in quite a safe area, there isn't a great deal of crime, so it wasn't something I was going to learn just living there. So I started checking websites and there's a very good website called doit.org, and I put in youth offending, and up it came with 'have you considered volunteering as a panel member?' […]
>
> (YOT7, CPM1)

I would therefore argue that if YOTs need to get younger panel members on board, targeting students is a way forward. Indeed, the interview data show that by avoiding the students, YOTs do not avoid attracting volunteers who become involved in youth offender panels 'to get a tick on their CV'.

Whereas during the pilot period, 'attracting, recruiting and retaining a sufficient number of community panel members' was seen as a 'major issue' (Crawford and Newburn 2003: 72), YOTs nowadays often have a waiting list of people who would like to become a panel member. One YOT worker noted: 'What we found after two runs of adverts is that word of mouth is sufficient, so now we don't need to advertise and I always have a waiting list of around 20–30 people waiting to join the panel' (YOT2, WORKER1). Nonetheless, and despite the open recruitment strategies, YOTs still struggle to recruit community panel members who are male, younger and/or from minority ethnic groups – as they did during the pilot period (see Crawford and Newburn 2003; Newburn *et al.* 2002). Altogether, YOTs generally reported having 'enough' community panel members, but were concerned that these were not properly representative of the local community.[1]

With regards to training, the YJB has created two programmes, the 'Foundation Programme' and the 'Panel Matters Programme', which YOTs use to train their community panel members.[2] The first programme provides core learning for all those who are interested in volunteering in the youth justice system (as panel members, appropriate adults, reparation supervisors and so on). Panel members then need to take part in an additional training specifically tailored for them – the 'Panel Matters Programme' (hereafter, *Panel Matters*).[3] Finally, before serving as panel members, they attend a few panel meetings for observation purposes. Thereafter, 'community panel members should receive at least one day of further training per year' (Ministry of Justice 2009: 21). In interviews, nearly all panel members expressed satisfaction with the range and quality of initial and continuing training courses.

The young person's first meeting

After the making of the referral order, and while still in court, a YOT officer explains the process to the young people and their parent(s) and sets a date for them to come to the YOT office and meet with an allocated worker. The purpose of this first meeting, which some YOT workers refer to as the 'referral order interview', is mainly to carry out the ASSET assessment of the young offender. The ASSET – or Young Offender Assessment Profile – is a structured assessment tool (or, in simplistic terms, a comprehensive questionnaire) that asks questions about the young person's offence(s), and identifies a multitude of factors or circumstances (from lack of educational attainment to mental health problems) that may have contributed to the offending behaviour and may put them at risk of further offending.[4] YOT workers are expected to complete the ASSET 'to ensure they have a good understanding of the risks and needs of the young person', and if applicable, 'the risk of serious harm to others' (Youth Justice Board 2010a: 11).

Also at the referral order interview, the YOT worker should explain to the young person the referral order and panel procedures. Given this pre-panel preparation, it is perhaps not surprising that young offenders, in interviews with me, often reported that they already knew from 'their' YOT worker what sort of things would be included in the contract. One young offender, when asked 'Did someone give you information about referral orders and youth offender panels in preparation for the initial panel meeting?', responded: 'Yeah. I knew everything that was gonna happen' (YOT4, YP1). Similarly, when asked if she thought the actual panel meeting was an important part of the referral order process, one YOT worker responded: 'No. The contract is largely decided as you do the report, and you agree things then. The structure is agreed at the assessment. You meet them [the young people] once or twice before the panel, and their parents. So they know what's coming at the panel' (YOT4, WORKER2). On top of that, one YOT worker said she revises the report with the young people minutes before their initial meeting, so as to make sure they know exactly what to expect:

> [...] before the young person comes in we'd have a brief discussion to see if they've got any questions or issues with the report, any issues with the recommendations, we'd discuss that, so we'd know exactly what's going to happen in the meeting. Just a 10-minute discussion.
>
> (YOT7, WORKER1)

Therefore, although the referral order does not formally begin until the contract has been signed at the initial *panel* meeting, from a young offender point of view, the first meeting actually happens between them and the YOT worker writing the report. In fact, by the time the young offender sits on her first panel meeting, she may already have heard three explanations of the referral order process and its possible outcomes (or, indeed, likely terms of the contract): from the magistrates making the order, from the YOT officer at court, and from the YOT worker who carries out the ASSET. What is more, before entering the initial panel meeting, the young person (and whoever is accompanying) gets the chance to read the report, so they also read the report's recommendations which, as will be explained below, often become the very terms of the contract. In this context, some young offenders do not understand the relevance of, or reason for, the initial panel meeting. One young offender, when asked what she thought the purpose of the panel meeting was, responded: 'To be honest, I don't have a clue. I feel I just came here to read my report and sign some papers' (YOT7, YP3). Yet this is the first opportunity for them to meet the panel members, those from their 'community'.

It is worth emphasising that the referral order interview is a one-on-one meeting between the young person and the allocated YOT worker – or when young offenders are accompanied, a meeting between them, their 'appropriate person' and the allocated YOT worker. That is, community panel members are not involved at this stage of the process, although it is at this stage that the discussions around the terms of the contract actually begin.

The panel report

On the basis of the ASSET and any information available from the police or the Crown Prosecution Service (or any other agencies), the YOT worker will produce a report for the youth offender panel. According to the *Guidance*, the panel report should include an outline of the offence and its consequences (including the victim perspective, when possible), and the key positive and risk factors identified in the ASSET. Also based on the ASSET, and using a tiered approach to interventions named the 'Scaled Approach', the YOT worker should recommend the most suitable level of intervention for managing the young person: standard, enhanced or intensive (Youth Justice Board 2010a, 2010b). The intervention level determines the minimum number of contacts the young offender should have with the YOT – that is, it suggests how frequently, during the referral order period, the young person should meet with her caseworker (or other assigned professionals, such as a nurse, substance misuse worker, etc.). Table 5.1 summarises the Scaled Approach framework.

In the analysed reports, YOT workers typically highlighted the recommended level of intervention as follows:

Table 5.1 The Scaled Approach and supervision levels

Young person profile	*Intervention level*	*Minimum number of contacts per month for first three months of order*	*Minimum number of contacts per month for remainder of order*
Low likelihood of reoffending and low risk of serious harm to the public	Standard	2	1
Medium likelihood of reoffending and medium risk of serious harm	Enhanced	4	2
High likelihood of reoffending and high (or very high) risk of serious harm	Intensive	12	4

Source: Adapted from Youth Justice Board 2010a, 2010b.

> The likelihood of [YP][5] re-offending and causing serious harm to others is assessed as low. His risk of self-harm is also assessed as low. [YP] is assessed as requiring a 'standard' level of supervision under the 'scaled approach', which will require his attendance at fortnightly sessions, for the length of the Order.
>
> (Report 1)

> [YP's] reporting frequency will be weekly for the first three months, in accordance with the Enhanced Level under [the] Scaled Approach.
>
> (Report 2)

The report should be 'balanced, impartial, focused and analytical, free from discriminatory language or stereotypes, verified and factually accurate and understandable to the young person and their parent/carer' (Ministry of Justice 2009: 33). Also, 'panel members should have updated information on the range of reparation and intervention opportunities which are currently available and can be included in the contract for any particular case' (Ministry of Justice 2009: 33). Finally, the most difficult advice to follow: the report 'should not make specific recommendations regarding the content of the contract' (Ministry of Justice 2009: 33). We should remember that when following all the guidelines, the YOT worker writing the report has to suggest the level of intervention (e.g. 'attendance at fortnightly sessions'), highlight the risk factors identified in the ASSET (e.g. 'during the assessment, [YP] appeared to justify and minimise his actions by saying that he "forgot" he had the lock knife in his pocket'), provide information about the range of reparation and intervention opportunities that are currently available (e.g. 'knife crime programme'), to name but a few responsibilities. Unsurprisingly, even if it is not the YOT worker's intention to make specific recommendations, by following all the guidelines, the recommended interventions become self-evident.

Indeed, it comes as no surprise that nearly all of the reports that were analysed included recommendations, although these would usually be found under a different heading such as 'YOS Member Statement', 'Areas of Need', and 'Range of Interventions Available'. In some YOTs, though, the report openly makes recommendations under sections entitled 'Suggested Interventions', 'Conclusion and Recommendations', or 'Recommendations for Contract'. In any case, regardless of the heading, the following phrasings were commonplace:

> The Panel may feel it appropriate to include the following suggestions in [YP's] contract: [...]
>
> (Report 3)

> I would suggest that the Panel consider the following interventions for [YP's] contract on his Referral Order: [...]
>
> (Report 4)

> Based on the information contained in this report, it is my assessment that [YP] would benefit from work focused on the following areas: [...]
>
> (Report 5)

> The Panel may also consider that [YP] visit the Headway Project[6] which would give him an insight into the affects on victims affected by head injuries.
>
> (Report 6)

> The panel may also consider imposing as part of [YP's] contract for him to undertake the Knife Story Programme during supervision. This will be to address the seriousness of knife crime and the potential consequences associated with knife crime offending.
>
> (Report 7)

According to the *Guidance*, the report should be made available to community members a minimum of two working days before the panel meeting (Ministry of Justice 2009). In practice, however, half of the YOTs I visited only made the report available on the day of – and often, half an hour before – the meeting. The main justification given by YOT workers for not sending reports out in advance was data protection. A few others, however, provided a more principled reason:

> We don't send out reports before, and we don't give too much time before, because a lot of it is about listening to what comes out in the meeting and deciding what's appropriate – rather than going with a pre-judged idea of 'they need X, Y and Z'.
>
> (YOT2, WORKER2)

> I'm thinking of the recent case we discussed yesterday with six young people. Because that was robbery or conspiracy to rob, it'd been reported in the local paper. You've got that element of risk of if you're getting [the report] two days early, you could look up all sorts of things and be all 'ooh, you awful young people, look at what you've done!'
>
> (YOT5, WORKER1)

What is interesting to mention is that where the routine practice was to have the report sent out in advance, community panel members tended to complain that they were not given enough time – they would usually get the report one or two days before the meeting, when they would rather have received it a week in advance. However, where they had been trained to think that having the report in advance would lead to unwelcome pre-judgement, community panel members were generally happy to read the report minutes before the meeting:

> I would be worried about prejudging ahead. Thirty minutes is enough, and you can discuss it as a panel. To sit at home and read it on your own may give you a closed mind – you are not a court.
>
> (YOT6, CPM1)

The rehearsal

Panel members normally hold 'pre-panel meetings'. This is when community and YOT members come together as a panel for the first time to discuss the most varied issues: who is attending (e.g. 'mum is coming'); any issues related to them (e.g. 'mum and dad are getting divorced'); any questions about the report (e.g. 'is the young person currently in education?'); where people will sit; and so forth (see *Panel Matters*). Part of the pre-panel meeting is also to decide who will chair the meeting, and who will lead on which part of the discussions (for example, panel members who are ex-teachers tend to lead discussions about school/education). Although these organisational issues account for most of the pre-meeting discussions, as a rule, it was also during pre-panel meetings that panel members agreed on the extent of reparation to be imposed.

On one occasion I was too late to observe the pre-panel meeting, so I had to stay outside the room, where the young offender was also waiting. From the improvised waiting room, both of us could hear nearly everything that was being discussed in the pre-panel meeting. When the YOT panel member came out and asked the young person if there was anything in the report that she was not happy with, the reply was that the caseworker had probably got her wrong when stating that she thought she could reoffend if she was bored. Coincidently (or not), that was precisely what the panel members were discussing during the pre-panel meeting. YOTs need to take the necessary precautions to prevent this from happening. The possibility of young people 'paying lip service', as a community panel member once put it, may be increased if they can hear what is being discussed at pre-panel meetings.

5.2 Act one: the initial panel meeting

In line with the goal that referral orders 'provide a restorative justice approach *within a community context*', the guidance has always been that panel meetings should be held in community venues (Ministry of Justice 2009: 7, emphasis added). Generally speaking, 'venues should be community-based, informal and non-institutional', so, for example, meetings should occur in 'community sports and leisure centres, adult education centres, family centres, youth clubs and schools, rather than youth offending team premises or police stations' (Home Office 2002: 30; Ministry of Justice 2009: 37). In practice, however, nearly all panel meetings observed in this study occurred in YOT premises. In fact, only four of the 12 YOTs I visited reported holding panel meetings in community venues such as libraries, civic centres, adult learning centres and town halls.

What is noteworthy is that my observation data show no noticeable differences in the functioning of panel meetings held in community venues compared with those held in YOT premises. In fact, it was in a public library (and therefore, in a community venue) that I witnessed probably the most unhelpful (or indeed, non-restorative) of all initial panels observed. It was a very emotional meeting, where the young person had cried, and where the mother asked for me and another observer[7] to leave the room. We were waiting in the room next door, when a member of the library staff walked into the panel meeting, asking everyone to leave the building because it was closing. The YOT panel member asked if she could wait until that meeting was finished, but the library staff member abruptly declared that she had been waiting for too long already. Everyone had to leave the library immediately; there was no time left to discuss the contract and, what is worse, the young offender and her mother had to leave while in an intensely emotional state. All in all, if the meeting that day had occurred at the YOT office, it probably would have been better.

Although I do accept the rhetorical importance of having panel meetings 'in the community', I would argue that there is no added benefit in using public libraries, adult learning centres, town halls and other places that many young offenders have never been and do not consider to be part of their 'normal environment'. In fact, in interviews, many community panel members reported having to drive considerable distances to reach certain community venues, suggesting that they also did not consider these places to be part of their locale. It should be noted that in using such venues, YOTs are not coming any closer to other genuinely community-based practices, such as healing or sentencing circles, for example, which often involve aboriginals living on reserves and which are often held in such reserves (Griffiths and Hamilton 1996). In fact, many other restorative justice practices do not occur 'in the community' – even family group conferences, which are deemed highly restorative, have normally been held in the premises of the Department of Social Welfare (Morris and Maxwell 2000). Besides, using the community as the location for restorative justice programmes, alone, will not automatically translate to an increase in community involvement – indeed, one should bear in mind that several forms of criminal justice activity, such as child curfew orders, parenting orders, probation hostels, after-care for prisoners released on licence, etc., use the community as location but do not involve ordinary members of the community in any aspect of the process (Green 2014; Nelken 1985).

Furthermore, one should bear in mind that panels are usually conducted in the evenings or at weekends so that participants with daytime work, study or other commitments are not precluded from attending. As the anecdote above suggests, community venues may well have restricted opening times or, inversely, be at their busiest during evenings and weekends. As one YOT worker commented, 'It's very easy to say it should happen in the community, but there are all kinds of issues you need to take into account. You're trying to have a serious conversation and next door there's a salsa class taking place!' (YOT5, WORKER1). Altogether, I would argue that the community venues currently being used bring no extra community perspective into play.

The directors, the actors and the spectators

As already argued, youth offender panels do aspire to restorative values – in fact, the legislation, the *Guidance*, and the National Standards for Youth Justice Services (National Standards), all place (and have always placed) emphasis on community involvement, victim participation, dialogue, inclusiveness, among other restorative justice-inspired aspects of the referral order process. Therefore, at panel meetings the young offender should encounter the victim, and both sides should be encouraged to bring their supporters. Indeed, the *Guidance* advises that YOTs 'should ensure that all identifiable victims, and representatives of all corporate victims, are given the opportunity to attend panel meetings' (Home Office 2002: 29; Ministry of Justice 2009: 36). Moreover, according to the legislation, 'any person who appears to the panel to be someone capable of having a good influence on the offender' may also be allowed to attend – that is, in addition to the young person's parents (or 'appropriate person'), friends or schoolteachers, for example, may also be invited to panel meetings.

In practice, however, as will be further discussed in Chapter 7, victims (or representatives of corporate victims) are rarely present. In fact, only five people usually attend panel meetings: two community panel members, one YOT worker, the young offender and her 'appropriate person' (and this is usually the young person's mother, as Table 5.2 shows). This was the picture seen in nearly half (46 per cent) of the meetings observed in this study. In interviews, YOT workers and community panel members confirmed that this was typical. In light of the experience of the pilots, Crawford and Newburn (2003: 122) argued, over a decade ago, that panel meetings were 'significantly less inclusive of young offenders' family members and supporters than family group conferences'. They advised that 'those organising panels should be encouraged to facilitate the attendance of a wider group of people', such as 'extended family members or other people that matter in a young person's life' (Crawford and Newburn 2003: 131–132). Over a decade later, my observations suggest that their recommendations have not been taken on board. Indeed, in over half (54 per cent) of cases observed, the young person attended with only one appropriate person. In a further 29 per cent of panel

Table 5.2 Panel attendance (offender's family members and supporters)

Young person attends	*Number of panels*	*% of panels observed*
Alone	10	29%
With mother	13	37%
With father	2	6%
With brother	1	3%
With stepmother	1	3%
With a carer	2	6%
With sessional worker	1	3%
With two other people*	4	11%
With three other people**	1	3%
Total	35	100%

Notes: *A parent and a social worker. **Mother, stepfather and father.

meetings the young person (all aged 16 years or older) attended alone. This means that in over four fifths (83 per cent) of cases that I have observed the young offender attended either alone or with only one other person. Table 5.2 details the attendance of supporters for the young offender.

With regard to the community members, the *Guidance* considers it 'inappropriate' for them 'to be involved in any case concerning a young offender who is a family member or close acquaintance or with whom they have previously been involved in a different capacity' (Ministry of Justice 2009: 25). My interviews and observations suggest that it is rarely the case that someone in the panel knows the young person or her family. I only witnessed one such case, where a panel member had run judo classes attended by the 17-year-old (and that had been nearly 10 years before). In interviews, I have only been told a few anecdotal stories – for example, one where the panel member had been to school with the young offender's father (but had not seen him since). In any case, when the community members were asked if they would serve on a panel where they already knew the young offender, most of them responded negatively. 'Conflict of interest' and 'impartiality' were key themes that ran throughout many responses:

> No, it would have been a conflict of interest. The same as I have to be careful when carers bring kids, if I know the carer I wouldn't sit then. [This panel member had worked in a care home.]
>
> (YOT4, CPM1)

> Possibly no, not comfortable because then, you see, your feelings can be very biased. You can be very biased about what you give them. I'd rather sit in a panel with someone that I don't know. Ideally. Just because it's

> natural, natural that you feel like OK you want to give this person perhaps a bit, or naturally for me, I'd probably be a bit 'oh, I know his family, I know what he's been through, I know he hasn't had a good start' and stuff like that. So perhaps those feelings would influence my decision and I don't want that. I want to be impartial.
>
> (YOT9, CPM1)

Some people even choose to serve as a panel member in a neighbouring area/town/borough to reduce the chances of knowing the young offenders; as one community panel member commented, 'I chose deliberately to come to [name of the city] because I was too well known in [another city] where I had worked in the schools. I would end up seeing the kids I had worked with who know me. I thought that was not a good idea' (YOT6, CPM1). Clearly, the idea of 'community' in youth offender panels has nothing to do with the bonds of a 'community of care', as would be typical in a family group conference (Morris and Maxwell 2000). The truth is that panel members are generally happy to keep things as they are. This begs the question: to what extent do panel members differ from magistrates? As one YOT worker put it:

> The idea of involving the community is not wrong in principle, but I think there are two problems: one is that the community is already involved, because that's what the magistrates are supposed to be – they are representatives of the community who should decide what happens, and now we've got two sets of representatives of the community (and there's a bit of tension between them anyway); two, they are not representative of the young people's local community – because we deliberately make sure they're not from down the road – so they're actually members of the general public, not members of his or her community.
>
> (YOT4, WORKER1)

It should be noted that the 'principle of impartiality' is 'commonly regarded as indispensable to high-quality restorative practices such as victim-offender mediation, conferencing and circles' (Mesmaecker 2013: 334). So it is not surprising that community panel members, in interviews with me, often emphasised their commitment to 'impartiality' or 'neutrality' – they are trained to believe that this is how things should be done. However, the impartiality set out in international legislation on restorative justice[8] and widely adhered to by restorativists is not the impartiality of community representatives, but the impartiality *of mediators* (for example, in victim–offender mediation programmes) *or facilitators* (for example, in family group conferences) (Mesmaecker 2013). What happens is that youth offender panels fall within that 'hybrid model' of community involvement discussed in Chapter 2, where community panel members are expected to act both as facilitators *and* community representatives – that is, they are themselves parties acting on behalf of the community, but they are also expected to facilitate the communication between the more directly affected parties (offenders, victims and their communities of care). Clearly, this hybridity causes tension: should community panel members be impartial (like magistrates) or not (since they are themselves parties)? Other more genuinely community-based experiments with restorative justice have resisted 'the idea of a solution being crafted by an impartial outsider' (Pali and Pelikan 2014: 152). This is claimed to be the case in the South African Zwelethemba model (see Froestad and Shearing 2013; Shearing and Froestad 2010). Indeed,

> [t]he authority for sorting things out in this model is not an outside authority, who impartially decides what is right and what should be done. Rather, the model insists that resolution comes from inside the community and that it arises as a consequence of deliberation.
>
> (Pali and Pelikan 2014: 152)

In some YOTs, panel meetings are run with three, instead of two, community panel members. This was routine practice in two of the 12 YOTs included in this study. One YOT worker's response, when I asked why there was a third community panel member, was typical: 'With three you've got a more diverse panel, but also, if somebody's sick, you can still run a panel. We cancel very few panels because a panel member can't show up' (YOT2, WORKER1). Although at first glance these arguments are persuasive, during the fieldwork I grew sceptical, as I was not convinced that this translated into more community involvement. Indeed, panel meetings in general, and regardless of the number of community members involved, presented the same pitfalls discussed throughout this and the next chapters. Also, from a young person's point of view, to what extent does adding another adult 'stranger' in the room help the process run more smoothly? How do young offenders differentiate between the three complete strangers at court (the bench of magistrates) and the three complete strangers at a panel meeting?

With regard to staff members, most YOTs I visited run panels with only one YOT panel member. Some YOTs have a fixed 'youth offender panel adviser' (Home Office 2002; Ministry of Justice 2009) – in other words, a certain member of staff is responsible for attending and advising at virtually every panel meeting (typically, the referral order coordinator or someone on the coordinator's behalf). In other areas, wherever possible, the YOT panel member would be the worker who has been assigned to the young person (the 'caseworker' or 'case manager'). Yet some YOTs operated on a rota basis, meaning that the YOT panel member could be any YOT worker (related to the case or not) on duty that particular evening. Finally, in two YOTs I visited, panels are run with an extra YOT member in the room, and they combine some of the aforementioned strategies: with the young offender's caseworker *and* a 'youth offender panel adviser' (based on a rota system) in attendance.

Where the young person fails to attend, provided that there are 'reasonable grounds for the absence (for example, ill health) and a reasonable prospect of attendance in the future' (Ministry of Justice 2009: 38), the meeting may be rearranged. Very importantly, '[i]t is the panel and not the youth offending team that makes the decision to refer a case back to court' (Ministry of Justice 2009: 38). These rules apply both to initial and review panel meetings (for final meetings, as detailed below, special rules apply). I attended a total of 26 initial panel meetings for observation purposes, but in eight cases the young offender did not attend. In all eight cases the panel decided that the meeting should be rearranged, although there were cases where the young person had 'forgotten' about the meeting (and did not wake up on time), or where the young person claimed not to know about the meeting (although she had met with her worker for the referral order interview, and had received a letter). That said, in most cases there appeared to be reasonable grounds for the absence – among them, the young offender was ill; the young person's father died; and 'mum' could not find a babysitter to take care of the offender's siblings while she was at the meeting.

Act one, scene one: a dialogue between actors and spectators

The observation data show that initial panel meetings invariably start with introductions. Most community panel members introduce themselves as follows: 'My name is [first name], I'm a panel member'; or simply 'I'm [first name], I'm going to lead this meeting'. Some add that they are 'volunteers' or, even, 'trained volunteers', and only a very few make use of the word 'community' (e.g. 'I'm a community panel member' or 'we're trained community volunteers'). My interviews with community panel members suggest that not much thought is put into the way they introduce themselves – or, perhaps even more precisely, that when introducing themselves panel members want to focus on the fact that they are there to 'help' the young offender or to 'lead' the meeting, rather than to represent the community (or as members of the community). One YOT worker felt that it was not a good idea to highlight that panel members were people from the community anyway:

> I introduce them as trained community volunteers. I did have a parent a couple of years ago, I phrased it as 'two members of the community' and the mother refused to come to the panel. She was upset because she thought she was going to be judged by two members of *her* community. There was no way that she would have known them – but she thought there was a possibility of that, people from her estate would know about her child's offending. After that I am more careful about the words I choose.
>
> (YOT8, WORKER1)[9]

After the introductions, one of the panel members will go through the ground rules (e.g. phones have to be switched off). More often than not, these ground rules are read out loud from a printout, which makes for a rather formal start. Thereafter, panel members start to facilitate the discussions, following more or less the so-called 'restorative questions' (see Wachtel *et al.* 2010): 'What happened?'; 'What were you thinking about at the time?'; 'What have you thought about since the incident?'; and so on. Perhaps reflecting the fact that victims are rarely present (and their views are rarely brought into the meetings), panel members tend to prioritise the aforementioned questions over the more victim-focused ones (e.g. '*Who* do you think has been affected by your actions?' or '*How* do you think they have been affected?'). After going through the offence and its impacts, community panel members turn to the areas of need and risks presented by the young offender (e.g. poor school attendance or substance misuse). Overall, discussions about the young offender's welfare account for most of the meeting time, at the expense of focusing on the restorative questions or on negotiation of the contract.

Youth offender panels are often said to provide greater informality compared with the courts. On the ground, though, panel meetings are quite formal – as one YOT worker said, 'we try to be formal, but in a slightly informal way' (YOT11, WORKER1). This, I would argue, is precisely what they have been achieving: youth offender panels are formal meetings run in a slightly informal way, albeit the informality is expressed mainly through the use of colloquial language or slang, otherwise they seem quite formal.

Panel members usually enter the room with what looks like court case files – in actuality it is a personal folder containing the report, and sometimes the Guidance and/or the *Panel Matters.* Although most YOTs have adopted the restorative layout (with participants sitting in a circle), I have seen panel meetings being held around a rectangle table, with community members (and all their papers) sitting on one side, and the young people and their parent sitting on the opposite side. I explored this 'layout' in my interviews and the following response from one YOT worker was typical: 'Yes, the panel members like that because they've got their papers. Personally, I prefer a circle, it's a lot more informal, but that's just the way they're run at the moment' (YOT1, WORKER3). The idea of serving tea and/or snacks – often used in other restorative practices as an icebreaker and to stimulate informality – has only been taken on board by two of the 12 YOTs included in this study. Finally, panel members often speak to the young offender as they flip through the report, resembling a magistrate flipping through papers at court. In fact, like one YOT worker said, 'I think sometimes the panel meeting resembles a court room' (YOT1, WORKER3).

Act one, scene two: the contract 'negotiations' and the YOT's 'dessert menu'

Initial panel meetings are ultimately aimed at agreeing a contract with the young offender; the last part of the meeting, then, is focused on deliberations over the contract. While the YOT member may provide any necessary information or advice, community panel members should lead the deliberations (Home Office 2002; Ministry of Justice 2009). In aspiring to restorative values, however, the *Guidance* emphasises that the contract 'should be negotiated with the young people, not imposed on them' (Home Office 2002: 31). That is, deliberations over contracts should be facilitated by the community panel members (not by the YOT member), but led in a way that allows for young offenders (and their parents) to have their say.

My observations of initial panel meetings suggest that rather than *negotiated*, contracts are *explained* – in some instances, very didactically so – to young offenders and their supporters. I have refrained from using the term 'imposed' because community panel members are in general very friendly towards the young people and their family. Moreover, after 'presenting' and explaining the terms of the contract, they *do* ask if the young person agrees. They also read the contract out loud before the young person and her supporter(s) are invited to sign. On the other hand, the use of the term 'negotiated' would also depict a distorted picture. While they 'announce' and explain the terms of the contract, the community panel members do most of the talking – by far. In fact, youth offender panels look nothing like family group conferences, for example, where the young person and her supporters work out a contract proposal (or 'plan' proposal) to be discussed by everyone in the meeting (Morris and Maxwell 2000). Quite the contrary, whereas in family group conferences the 'panel' (facilitators and authorities) normally leaves the room for the young offender and her family to devise a plan, in some YOTs the young offender is asked to leave the room for the panel to set up the contract proposal. One YOT worker criticised this practice, saying:

> Sometimes they [the community panel members] ask the young person to leave the room, because they need to talk about the [reparation] hours. I don't always agree with that because you're talking about them and not talking with them. They're excluded from the discussion. I don't think that's very restorative.
>
> (YOT1, WORKER3)

As mentioned above, more often than not, the young offenders will have heard about the possible (or, in fact, probable) terms of the contract before the initial panel meeting takes place (from their YOT worker, at the 'referral order interview'). In general, thus, they are not surprised by anything that comes up in the meeting, and tend to agree monosyllabically to everything that is being 'announced' by the panel members. I have not observed a single case where the young offender (or her parent) made suggestions for an alternative proposal, and in only a very few cases did the young person or her parent question something that was being proposed – and when that happened, community panel members would explain it again, perhaps more clearly, and insist that it should be done. For example, in one instance the young person said he did not want to write a 'letter of explanation',[10] to which one of the community panel members replied: 'Well, we would love to see the letter anyway, so'. In another case, the young person asked if she really had to go to the Headway Project, to which a community panel member responded, in a rather dismissive way, 'Yes, but there will be preparation and you're not going on your own. Don't worry'. In yet another initial panel, when the young person asked why she would have to attend sessions on alcohol and substance misuse if she was not on drugs, one of the community panel members said 'Because everyone that enters these doors has to go through that'. The following comment from a YOT worker endorses my argument that contracts are 'explained' to, rather than 'negotiated' with, the young people: 'You have to have an idea where you are going, and then explore it with them and *get them to agree with it*' (YOT11, WORKER1, emphasis added).

According to legislation and guidance, the contract should include two main elements: reparation to the victim or to the wider community; and a programme of interventions aimed at preventing reoffending. The latter, to be delivered or organised by the YOT, should include activities that address the key risk factors identified in the ASSET of the young person (Home Office 2002; Ministry of Justice 2009). That might include constructive leisure programmes, anger management, employment or careers advice, victim awareness, drugs or alcohol programmes, and so forth. It means, on the ground, that young offenders have to attend such sessions when they come to the YOT office for their weekly, fortnightly or monthly appointments. As for community reparation,[11] the panel needs first to decide the *amount* of reparation to be undertaken. The *Guidance* provides a guide to the hours of reparation (Table 5.3), which is generally followed by the community panel members. There was only one case where the community panel members departed from the guidelines, and they did so based on the YOT worker's advice that the young person was too young (13) to work so many hours.

Regarding the *nature* of reparation, the *Guidance* presumes that community panel members, 'with their local knowledge', 'may also be able to identify [appropriate] activities and should be encouraged to suggest forms of reparation and interventions for inclusion in contracts that draw on community rather than just youth offending team resources' (Home Office 2002: 33; see

Table 5.3 Guide to the hours of community reparation

Length of order	*Amount of reparation*
3–4 months	3–9 hours
5–7 months	10–19 hours
8–9 months	20–29 hours
10–12 months	30+ hours

Source: Adapted from Home Office 2002.

also Ministry of Justice 2009). In other words, deliberations over contracts should be open to the creative use of community ideas and resources, as opposed to being completely YOT dependent. On the ground, however, contracts tend to replicate the report's recommendations. Table 5.4 contains excerpts from one report and its corresponding contract, and demonstrates how much the latter resembles the former. My observations and documentary analysis indicate that such similitude is the rule.

As one community panel member said, when asked if the report influences the input she has at panel meetings: 'Definitively. There's a point that says "recommendations" and that list of recommendations is the contract, basically' (YOT1, CPM1). Another community panel member responded: 'Quite largely. I wasn't expecting that. I thought we would have more freedom to recommend. But the report suggests anger management, self-confidence training, etc. and we just go along with that' (YOT4, CPM2). One YOT worker, when asked to what extent the terms of the contract were decided before the panel meeting begins, commented:

> About 90 per cent or more – the report has proposals at the end. The panel says what they want and they talk to the young person. If the youth objects we perhaps try and change it, if it is not something crucial. If I know we are going to have a difficult candidate, I try to prepare the panel. You discuss it, and you know how the panel are going to act. They might want to add in Anger Management or whatever. You sometimes reword it to make it more acceptable to panel and/or young person.
>
> (YOT4, WORKER2)

During the course of the pilots, researchers found some imaginative contracts drawing on community resources (Newburn *et al.* 2002). With very few exceptions, which I will come to, my data produced no evidence of that. In practice, contracts resemble reports, and where there is no specific recommendation (for example, over the precise nature of reparation), the vast majority of community panel members appeal to one of the following YOT-based solutions: they either include in the contract terms like 'complete four hours' community reparation *as agreed with the reparation worker*' (see also the case in Table 5.4), leaving it up to the YOT or its partners to decide what sort of reparation will be undertaken; or, alternatively, as one YOT worker put it, 'they basically pick from a dessert menu of activities that we [the YOT] provide' (YOT1, WORKER4). About leaving it for the YOT to decide about reparation, the following comments from community panel members were typical:

Table 5.4 Report vs. contract

	Report	*Contract*
Compulsory elements	In order for YP* to give something useful back to the community he could benefit from completing a set number of indirect reparation.	*Reparation: 14 hours, to be decided.*
	YP could benefit from completing sessions with his case manager and from the Police within the YOS [Youth Offending Service] on consequences of offending and consequential thinking. It could also be beneficial for YP to gain an understanding of his position within the Youth Justice System given that he has received no previous intervention from the YOS.	*To receive sessions on consequences of further offences, and position in the Justice System.*
	YP could benefit from gaining a better understanding of his behaviour and emotions and explore more appropriate ways of dealing with his behaviour, especially when he may find certain situations difficult to deal with.	*To receive sessions on emotional behaviour and how to deal with difficult situations.*
	YP could benefit from gaining an awareness and understanding of how offences of assault can have a detrimental affect upon victim/s involved and it could benefit him to complete victim awareness sessions. This work could also involve YP completing the exercise of writing a letter of explanation.	*To receive victim awareness, to gain an understanding of feelings; to include a letter of explanation.*
	To raise YP's awareness of other types of offences that he needs to avoid becoming involved in it would be beneficial for YP to cover offence awareness sessions with a view to these preventing him from re-offending.	*To be made aware of the type of offences he needs to avoid, to prevent re-offending.*
Voluntary elements	YP could benefit from exploring local activities that are available in the [name of area] area in order to develop wider social networks.	*To explore local activities in the [name of area] area.*
	A referral to YOS Family Support Team would be helpful and offer the family support to address any identified concerns.	*Family Support, if needed, with the YOS Service.*

Note: *YP stands for 'young person'. In the original document, the young person's first name was used.

> Some things depend on the weather. […] I will talk to them about the things they'd like to do, [but] sometimes it is a lot for them to take. [So] we write it into the contract '30 hours' reparation to be decided'.
>
> (YOT11, CPM1)

> In some instances we will say 'a number of hours of community work' but that will be at the discretion of the YOT. They have the problem of arranging it. No good me saying 'five hours' litter picking' when there is no litter picking to be done.
>
> (YOT2, CPM1)

As for the 'dessert menu', YOTs tend to have a rather fixed list of reparation possibilities – with litter picking, painting and carpentry (mainly, making bird boxes) featuring among the most popular. In this context, when asked what community members bring to the panel in terms of ideas and resources, one YOT worker said: 'I think that we're not that romantic, and it's a fairly tried and tested "this is what we know", and the menu is fairly tight' (YOT1, WORKER2). Linked to this idea of being 'tried and tested', the *Guidance* advises: '[t]he case supervisor must ensure that any reparation undertaken by the young person is risk assessed, that there are appropriate health and safety provisions and that it is within the terms of the agreement contained in the contract' (Ministry of Justice 2009: 22). Many YOT workers and community panel members alluded to the limits to creativity imposed by health and safety concerns. The following comment from a community panel member was typical: 'The rules of the YOT are all about health and safety, there's too much red tape' (YOT4, CPM1).

Many YOT workers expressed that they needed to provide a 'menu' in order for panel members to agree workable/relevant contracts. One YOT worker argued: 'Panels look to the YOT for ideas – if we don't bring ideas, they don't have any of their own, often, or they have crazy ones' (YOT4, WORKER1). Regarding 'crazy' ideas, another worker, from another YOT, commented: 'One of my young people who was being done for assault was asked to tidy his bed every day. […] That's like reminding someone to wipe their arse – surely they should be doing that anyway?! Sorry!' (YOT2, WORKER3). In fact, in one of the initial meetings I attended, the panel agreed with the young person that she would: 'Help around the house more – hoovering and walking the dog at least twice a week to show them how sorry you are.' This young person had committed an assault causing actual bodily harm and common assault against two separate victims (from her peer group) in the same incident (at a party). In this context, it is indeed questionable how relevant it is to have the young person agreeing to vacuum the house and walk the dog. Of course, those were not the only terms in the contract – the young person also had to write a letter of apology to the people she had assaulted, visit the Headway Project, complete some sessions on consequential thinking and on alcohol misuse (as she was drunk when committing the offence). However, the point is that while these relevant elements were picked from the YOT's menu, vacuuming the house and walking the dog were the only contract terms that really drew on 'community' (or the community panel members') ideas.

Many community panel members alluded to the YOT's 'dessert menu', also highlighting the benefit of it. In fact, some complained that the YOT could be more informative:

> That's the thing that all of us in the training this year thought was not very good, because we were going through scenarios, but we didn't know what to offer because we didn't know what was available. In each of the rooms there's sometimes a folder, which says what the programmes are, but there's questions as to whether they're up to date.
>
> (YOT5, CPM1)

Among the exceptions to the abovementioned 'menu-driven' practices, perhaps the most interesting examples come from a YOT where the community panel members have adopted what they term 'local-*local* reparation'. The idea evolves around young people doing community reparation in their school or church/mosque/etc. – in their 'individual' community, as explained by one of the panel members. There were a few interesting cases. In one of them, the young person had to help clean the schoolyard and grounds at the end of the school day. In the other, the young person spent her reparation hours helping at her mosque. What is striking, though, is that the community panel members only turned to this 'local-local reparation' approach to compensate for the fact that the YOT had no reparation officer for months and reparation agreements were not being complied with (through no fault of the young people). In fact, while I think of these as the most imaginative and creative reparation agreements that I have seen across all research sites, community panel members there were quite annoyed that they had to come up with the reparation ideas themselves:

> There aren't that many [reparation schemes], they're always difficult to find, and it's not my responsibility as a panel member to decide which activity would be appropriate for the young person.
>
> (YOT7, CPM2)

> I don't think we've got any choice, or else we wouldn't be able to comply with the regulation side of it. For months we had no reparation officer, and there was such a backlog that if someone had a three- or four-month order, they would have finished it before their reparation could start, there were so many other young people waiting to do reparation.
>
> (YOT7, CPM1)

At the very end of the meeting, a panel member reads the contract aloud to the young person to ensure that its contents are fully understood; the consequences for the young person of not complying with the contract are once again highlighted, and then the contract is signed. The young person and the community panel member chairing the meeting should sign it, and it is good practice for parents or guardians to be invited to sign (Home Office 2002). In all panel meetings observed, those accompanying the young person were invited to do so. The contract starts from the date when it is signed (not the court date) and lasts for the time period defined by court in making the referral order. Therefore, the YOT caseworker must ensure that the activities agreed in the contract begin within five working days of the contract being signed (Youth Justice Board 2004, 2009).

The *Guidance* recommends that if a contract is not agreed at the initial panel meeting, a further meeting may be held. If it appears that there is no prospect of a contract being agreed, the young person should be referred back to court. Both scenarios appeared to be equally rare.

5.3 Act two: review and breach panel meetings

After the initial panel meeting, there should be regular contact between the young offender and 'their' caseworker. If a young person is assessed as requiring a standard level of intervention through the Scaled Approach, for example, she will probably have to visit the YOT office once a fortnight. It is during these visits that the young person meets with her caseworker and/or other relevant professionals to undertake the programme of activities included in the contract (for example, sessions on substance misuse, victim awareness work, etc.). As for community reparation, that tends to be carried out at weekends. For example, 10 hours of reparation may involve undertaking two hours of graffiti removal every Saturday morning, for five weeks, on top of the weekly, fortnightly or monthly appointments with their caseworker. Panel members do not normally get involved in any of these activities carried out between panel meetings.

As already mentioned, where a contract is agreed between the young offender and the panel, the panel is expected to hold regular progress meetings – at least once every three months (Youth Justice Board 2004, 2009). In general, YOTs do comply with the guidance. Indeed, sometimes, particularly when the young person receives a four-month referral order, community panel members request that reviews be held every two (instead of three) months. That said, there was one occasion where the young offender had been given a 12-month referral order, and the first review meeting (which I observed) was held some 10 months into the referral order. The YOT panel member justified the delay in convening the review meeting saying that the young person had had many different caseworkers along the way, through no fault of her own. Although the young person clearly cannot be breached for the YOT's inefficiencies, this case suggests that community panel members may have very little (or no) control over when review panel meetings are run.

According to the legislation, at such meetings the panel shall: review the young person's progress; discuss any breach of the terms of the contract; discuss the young offender's wish to vary the terms of the contract; and/or consider whether to accede to any request by the offender that she be referred back to court with a view to the referral order being revoked. In practice, instead of using the term 'progress meetings', YOTs tend to differentiate between regular 'review meetings' (to be conducted at least every three months) and eventual 'breach meetings' (or 'emergency panels', as some YOTs call them, to be conducted where there has been significant non-compliance). Interviewees (YOT workers and community panel members) were unanimous in stating that it is rarely the case that the young offender wishes to seek the panel's agreement to a variation in the terms of the contract, and virtually never the case that she wishes the panel to refer her back to court with a view to the referral order being revoked. In general, young offenders attend progress meetings either because the time for a review has come, or because they are in breach. Many YOT workers, when asked about the most positive aspects of referral orders and youth offender panels, alluded to the review panel meetings. They felt that progress meetings provide the opportunity for community members to keep YOT workers 'on their toes'. One YOT worker commented:

> I think with other orders the reparation stuff can go by the wayside a bit. [...] Sometimes there's a pressure with referral orders, so sometimes I've seen contracts where you'll have to complete 10 hours' reparation by the next panel. And sometimes there's a lot of pressing issues that need to be sorted out, so that you could almost do without having that pressure. They are not in education, they don't have a job, and with other orders that might be what you sort out first. But I think with referral order there's a bit more focus on the reparation side, which is a good thing but sometimes is not necessarily the best thing, depending on the young person's circumstances
>
> (YOT6, WORKER1)

Act two, scene one: review panel meetings

The caseworker should keep a record of the offender's compliance, or non-compliance, with the contract, and is also expected to provide a progress report for discussion at review meetings. Observation of review panel meetings revealed that in all 12 YOTs, panel members received some form of report about the young offender's progress. The routine practice in some YOTs is to provide two reports: a written progress report, where the offender's compliance (or non-compliance) with each of the terms of the contract is commented upon; and a copy of the initial report, so as to remind the panel members about the case (or when the panel members are not the same, to give them a glimpse of the case). In other YOTs, panel members only receive the written progress report. In any case, the caseworker (or the YOT panel member on her behalf) will normally provide a verbal report at the pre-panel meeting.

Wherever possible, according to the *Guidance*, 'it is desirable that at least one community panel member from the initial panel meeting is present at all panel meetings to provide continuity' (Ministry of Justice 2009: 45). With regards to that, the following comment from a YOT worker was typical: 'That's what's supposed to happen, and the majority of the time we try to do it, but it's down to the availability of the panel members. If you have a 12-month order, people's personal circumstances can change, they can get jobs or move away. But the aim is there' (YOT10, WORKER1). This pragmatism has led some YOTs to organise panels mainly on a rota basis, meaning that community members, as a YOT worker put it, 'they'll come in and they'll sit for an evening and whichever kid comes to the door is the kid they'll meet' (YOT2, WORKER1). Having said that, virtually all the interviewees (among YOT workers and community panel members) voiced the opinion that the same panel members *should* follow a case all the way through to completion. They feel that this creates a relationship between the young person and the panel members, whom offenders will not want to 'let down':

> Having those people that come in on day one, form the contract with them, and are there at every review process saying 'it's great that you're doing well' or 'why aren't you doing it, you're letting us and yourself down' is a powerful thing to see. That's why the review process is so important, for me, it's not like a court where you meet them and get a slap on the wrist and never see them again, these people are going to follow you and support you and chivvy you on and do everything they can to get you to the end of that order.
>
> (YOT2, WORKER1)

> It's not always possible, but it is generally that you see someone right through. It's nice for the young person and the panel members, and you get a bit of a relationship with them. You get to see the changes, which are dramatic sometimes.
>
> (YOT6, CPM2)

In general, during a review meeting, the panel will go through the terms of the contract, asking the young person what, by this point, has been undertaken. Of course, from the report and the pre-panel meeting, panel members already know the answers. In this context, the young offender's verbal and non-verbal cues during the review meetings do not appear to be relevant. Indeed, the observation data show that if they are doing well outside panel meetings, even if they do not cooperate with the review meeting, they will be praised and the meeting may take only 5–10 minutes. I have often seen young people claiming that they do not remember anything that they have learned, and based on what the report said, they were praised anyway and the meeting was quickly resumed.

Typically, at the end of a review panel meeting, there are two possible outcomes: community panel members may agree that the components of the existing contract do not need changing; or they may agree to change certain components of the contract, in which case they will specify if the changes are in addition to existing components or a replacement component. In most of the cases observed, contracts remained unaltered.

Act two, scene two: breach panel meetings

According to the *Guidance*, 'if there has been a significant non-compliance and no acceptable reason given for the failure to comply, a youth offender panel meeting must be convened within ten working days' (Ministry of Justice 2009: 45). These are what YOTs call, in practice, 'breach' or 'emergency' panel meetings. Compared with review panels, breach meetings generally take more time. The young offender has to explain the reasons for not complying, and panel members generally challenge the reasons presented. They look very much like court hearings – more than other panel meetings do – as the young people sit like defendants trying to escape punishment (that is, hoping not to get breached). Indeed, while before initial panel meetings, community members are often described by YOT workers as 'nice and friendly people' who 'just want to help you', before breach panels community members are purposely portrayed as 'quasi-magistrates' who have the power to 'sentence' the young person back to court. YOT workers generally enjoy that: 'Sometimes it's a good thing because it takes the pressure off us, it's the panel members' decision to send them back to court' (YOT3, WORKER1).

At the end of a breach panel there are essentially two possible outcomes: 1 'the panel may agree that the contract was too demanding, or that recent changes in circumstances have made it too difficult to comply with, and should consider varying the contract'; or 2 'where the young person is unable to offer any reasonable explanation or justification for the non-compliance, unless there are exceptional circumstances, the panel must refer the offender back to court to consider resentencing' (Ministry of Justice 2009: 45). I have only observed two breach panels, and in both cases, the young people were 'forgiven' and admonished to comply with the contract from then on – that is, they were not sent to court, and the contract remained unaltered.

5.4 Act three: the final panel meeting

The *Guidance* recommends that a final meeting should be held during the last month of the referral order period, the purpose being to review the offender's overall compliance with the contract. There are essentially two possible outcomes here: 1 '[w]here the panel is satisfied that the contract has been fully complied with, the order will be discharged from the end of its period'; and 2 '[i]f the panel is not satisfied that the offender has successfully completed the order, the offender must be referred back to court to consider re-sentencing' (Home Office 2002: 39). In practice, however, I have witnessed situations where the community panel members agreed that the young person had *not* fully complied with the contract, but decided that the referral order should be discharged anyway.

On one of these occasions, the young person had missed six reparation sessions before there were any consequences (no warning letters were sent). It took another few weeks before a breach panel meeting was scheduled, and when that meeting finally happened, there were only three days left of the order. At the meeting, when the panel members asked the reasons for missing so many reparation sessions, the young person responded 'I don't know'. When they asked what had been done during sessions with the caseworker, the young person replied 'we talked about the next session', causing a ripple of amusement around the circle. At the end, community panel members found their hands were tied: on the one hand, they could not request that the young person undertake the remaining reparation hours, as there was no time left; on the other hand, the YOT had failed to establish a breach panel in due course, hindering the opportunity for the young person to 'make up for it', as – in the event – she said she was willing to do. They decided to make that a final, instead of a breach, panel meeting, and to discharge the referral order. They explained to the young person: 'we will sign you off on the comment that you haven't satisfactorily completed the contract'. It is not clear how the young person understood the message, but she was very surprised not to be sent back to court.

On another occasion, the final report read: 'YP has not completed Reparation but this appears due to difficulties in arranging this work which I will investigate further.' The matter was discussed during the final panel meeting, and the community panel members decided to sign the young person off on the grounds that she could not be punished for the YOT's inefficiencies. One of the community panel members, present at that meeting, later commented: 'They know that [reparation is] a really important part, legally binding. But why should they be punished because we've not got our act together?' (YOT7, CPM1). Although I agree that young offenders should not be breached for not doing reparation through no fault of their own, the fact that reparation is not happening in some places – not to the victim or to the 'wider community' – shows that practice does not always follow correct procedure. Many community panel members, from different YOTs, alluded to this in their comments:

> The other issue that I've found [is] that you give them X hours of reparation, but [the YOT] has had little on offer in terms of activities, so many of them haven't done the reparation, through no fault of theirs, but there are not enough staff to organise and supervise it.
>
> (YOT7, CPM3)

> When I came into it five years ago you could set how many hours' reparation a kid had to do, and when they had to do it. [...] You could be flexible about how many hours and there were different things you could send them to. Nowadays they hardly do any reparation because they're short staffed, they haven't got the staff to do the reparation with. [...] Anger management, and stuff like that, that all goes on, while reparation, which is the community element ... I haven't sent anybody on reparation for I don't know how long.
>
> (YOT4, CPM1)

Confirming the latter statement, I have seen some contracts with no element of reparation, such as the following:

> I agree to attend all future Panel meetings arranged by the YOT;
> I agree to keep all my appointments with the YOT worker;
> Peer pressure work, with an emphasis on decision-making;
> Attend [name of an offending behaviour programme];
> Retail Theft Programme;
> Complete a creative piece of work to show the impact of offending on me and others [the young person devised a poster].

Altogether, this suggests that in some YOTs, the programme of activities (e.g. drug misuse programmes) runs at the expense of reparation. In fact, the prioritisation of interventions over reparation suggests that, in some places, the YOT's 'welfare' culture may have taken precedence over referral orders' restorative aspirations.

The non-attendance dilemma: to breach or not to breach?

The decision to discharge the order 'may be taken by the panel even where the young person is unable to attend the meeting, but has otherwise successfully complied with the terms of the contract' (Ministry of Justice 2009: 51). This may be the reason why many young people fail to attend their final panel meeting. Most community panel members, though, consider final meetings to be a very important part of the process:

> The reason that I mention that is because at that point [the YOT] didn't often do final panels, and you're supposed to do them. A number of us had said earlier on that the reward for us in doing this work would've been greater if we had known what had happened to the young people at the end. You knew most of the time if they'd breached because you were asked to send them back to court, but you didn't know if they'd made it.
>
> (YOT7, CPM3)

> If we get a lad say 'I have done well, I am not going to bother to turn up', that I don't accept. It is as important as the others. [...] It gives closure when you say 'well done, put it behind you, move on'.
>
> (YOT12, CPM2)

Accordingly, in most cases observed, where the young person failed to attend the final meeting, panel members asked the YOT staff to rearrange it for another day.

A 'pat on the back' and 'off you go'

The *Guidance* advises that the YOT should provide a 'sign-off' letter or a 'certificate of completion' when the contract is successfully completed (Ministry of Justice 2009: 51). I have only seen this happen in one of the YOTs visited, where the young people receive a certificate at the final panel meeting.[12] On one occasion, both the young person and her mother seemed very proud of it – the mother said 'we're gonna frame this one!', to which the young person added 'and I'll put it on my wall!' This, however, does not appear to be common practice in most YOTs included in this study. On the ground, as one community member described them, final panel meetings tend to be 'a pat on the back' and 'off you go' (YOT9, CPM2). A few community panel members, who were aware of other YOTs providing letters or certificates, regretted that similar practices were not occurring in their area. One of them commented: 'The other interesting thing I've found quite striking in [another YOT] is they have a letter for the young person which says well done [...] That's interesting because [...] it gives the young person a sense of closure, it helps them feel that they've actually completed something [...]' (YOT7, CPM3).

It is worth mentioning that when referral orders and youth offender panels were still being conceived, the idea was that there should be some sort of continuity beyond the period of the contract. In its White Paper *No More Excuses*, the government had suggested: 'Although the formal referral would be for a fixed period of time, the youth panel would be encouraged to identify ways of supporting the young person at the end of the referral through community based schemes such as mentoring, to help prevent further offending' (Home Office 1997: 33). Originally, thus, the plan was for 'youth panels' (as they were termed back then) to 'keep in touch' with the young offender. This is not only acceptable but clearly stimulated in other restorative practices, such as healing and sentencing circles, both of which place a lot of emphasis on the idea of reconnecting offenders to their communities and encouraging new relationships to be formed in the circle (Stuart 1996, 2001). That ideal of continuity espoused in the White Paper, though, is absent from the legislation and all the guidance documents related to referral orders. In fact, community panel members are of the strong opinion that it would be 'inappropriate' to maintain any type of contact with the young people after the completion of their order. When asked if she had ever kept in contact with a young person, one community member responded: 'No, no. That never happens. You're not allowed to, you know, sort of ask any personal details. All we know is their first name; we don't know the surname, their address, and they are the same with us' (YOT1, CPM2). In a similar vein, other community panel members said:

> No. [...] As soon as you've done what you've got to do, and you've got the outcome you wanted, that's the end of it, because there's another one to help.
>
> (YOT4, CPM1)

> I don't think I would be befriending this person outside the YOT kind of thing. Not because of any personal issues, but I think, yeah, we need to learn where to draw that line and keep it professional. [...] I don't see myself, you know, being involved with that young person afterwards.
>
> (YOT9, CPM1)

> Well, [...] the YOS worker says to the young person, at their final review, 'if you're ever in difficulty or want to talk things over, call me' – so that when they leave they don't feel that they're completely abandoned, that the connection has been severed. And I think that it's appropriate that it should be done through YOS. I wouldn't want to give my home telephone number or email to a young person who's come through the system. I don't think it would be appropriate. But, you know, I think it's good that they are left with some sort of notion that the door is open here.
>
> (YOT9, CPM3)

When asked about the possibility of bumping into the young people on the streets, the following comments were typical:

> I think I would not sort of acknowledge them unless they acknowledged me, you know. And if they did, I'd just say 'hi, how are you?' sort of thing. I would never approach them.
>
> (YOT1, CPM2)

> It depends on the situation. I was shopping in Asda. I saw a young person and 'mum' and just said 'hello'. It is ignorant to ignore them. If they were with other people I wouldn't, but they were alone so I felt it was OK.
>
> (YOT6, CPM2)

> There's one mum I see every couple of months and we just say hello as we pass, but that's it. [...] I think probably with a young person I would

> not say anything. Once it's all done and dusted, they are with their mates, it's in the past. I wouldn't speak. It finishes.
>
> (YOT2, CPM2)

And the conviction is spent!

If the contract has been successfully completed, the conviction will be 'spent'. Having a spent conviction means that, with certain exceptions (e.g. when seeking to work with children, within the administration of justice, or where issues of financial probity are in question), the young person does not have to disclose the conviction to others (e.g. employers). It also means that employers cannot refuse to employ (or dismiss) someone because this person has a spent conviction.[13] According to the 2002 *Guidance*, and to the 2009 *Guidance,* the conviction is spent 'in recognition of the fact that referral orders are made on young offenders convicted for the first time and pleading guilty' (Home Office 2002: 11; Ministry of Justice 2009: 18). What is noteworthy is that, as mentioned in Chapter 3, since 2008, a young offender may receive a second referral order – and this is one of the main reasons why new *Guidance* was published in 2009. In other words, since 2008, referral orders are no longer limited to first-time offenders, begging the question as to why the 2009 *Guidance* reproduced, *ipsis verbis*, the abovementioned extract from the 2002 *Guidance.*

Predictably, the idea that referral orders provide a 'last chance' (to avoid a criminal record) continues to be perpetuated. Indeed, when alluding to the most successful aspects of referral orders, YOT workers and community panel members alike would often highlight the benefit of young people not getting a criminal record:

> It is hopefully that last chance, to stop them getting into the system, the conviction being spent. It gives kids a good wake-up call.
>
> (YOT11, WORKER2)

> The fact that it gives young people the opportunity to make a change and they don't come out with a criminal record … it is a bargaining tool to encourage them to make a change.
>
> (YOT3, WORKER1)

> It stops the child getting a criminal record once they've gone through the process, it gives them an opportunity fairly early on in what might be a criminal career to choose a different path.
>
> (YOT5, CPM1)

> The other thing is it's a spent conviction, so they don't have a criminal record.
>
> (YOT7, CPM3)

There are at least two dangers here, the first one being that the wrong message may be conveyed to young people: that they will not get a criminal record upon completion of their referral order. In practice, most community panel members do explain that the young offender will have to disclose the conviction when seeking to work with children or other vulnerable people.[14] Nonetheless, observation of panels revealed that even when community members attempt to explain what is meant by a spent conviction, they often say things like 'this is your last chance or you will have a criminal record'. The second danger is that this 'last chance' discourse, in times when courts are allowed to give multiple referral orders,[15] may discredit the process (and the community panel members, who convey the imprecise message) in the eyes of the young people. Many of my interviewees (among YOT workers and community panel members) shared similar concerns. One YOT worker commented:

> They sell the referral order as a positive, because it's a spent conviction, but it's still a conviction that will always be on someone's record, regardless. It's always going to come up on an enhanced CRB [Criminal Records Bureau] check. A lot of young people do think 'we get it done and then it gets wiped away'. […] I feel in some ways [referral orders are] mis-sold to people.
>
> (YOT10, WORKER1)

In terms of courts being allowed to impose multiple referral orders, another YOT worker commented:

> […] I don't see the point of second referral orders! You say the first time 'last chance, this is like a low end order, you can turn it around, you've got this opportunity to, like, get on with things'. And then they reoffend and then they get another referral order and then you say the same crap. It's pointless. And I think the young people know that as well. […] I worked with a young person who had a second order, and it was a nightmare. She knew the score, what she could get away with. I just think it loses any sort of power when you get a second one. They just think 'it's not a big deal'.
>
> (YOT4, WORKER3)

5.5 Concluding comments

The Home Office research into the introduction of referral orders found that:

> […] during the life of the pilots the community panel members grew into their roles over time and increasingly began to assert a greater independence from the Yot staff rather than being wholly reliant upon them. […]

> Even those community panel members who felt that initially they had played an insufficiently determining role in the panel process believed that, over time, they would take on a more independent role.
>
> (Newburn *et al.* 2002: 33)

Today, over a decade later, I would argue that community panel members are well aware of their central role in the referral order process. In fact, the idea that 'ultimately, it's up to the panel to decide' is well entrenched in both the discourses of community panel members and YOT workers:

> It is community members who say what will happen. We provide background information and some recommendations, but they decide the final outcome.
>
> (YOT12, WORKER1)

> It's heavily influenced by the worker, but at the end of the day, it's the panel members that decide.
>
> (YOT1, WORKER3)

> Their report is for our guidance, we have complete autonomy to put into that contract whatever we want. It doesn't happen very often, but nobody tells me what to do!
>
> (YOT7, CPM2)

> [The report] does definitively influence you because it's there in writing, but of myself personally, I don't worry too much about what's there, you know, because, at the end of the day, it's for us to decide not them.
>
> (YOT1, CPM2)

However, it seems to me that the idea that community panel members 'own' the process, or that they are the ones who determine the direction and outcome of panel meetings, is more rhetorical (or 'theatrical') than real. Over a decade ago, when referral orders were introduced, this may have been due to a lack of confidence on the part of community panel members, a resistance among YOT workers to give up a certain amount of control, or a combination of the two. Today I would argue that, in the best scenario, the professionalisation of panel members, some of whom have been sitting on panels for 10 years,[16] has contributed to a 'blended' YOT panel culture shared by all, YOT workers and panel members. In this vein, one community panel commented: 'What I like is when you're reading through [the report], you're making notes about what you'd like to include in the contract, and then when you get to the recommendations, what they've got there is what you were going to put down anyway' (YOT11, CPM1). In the worst scenario, community panel members remain playing an insufficiently determining role in the panel process – indeed, as fictional characters in a play.

In other models of restorative justice, such as conferencing or victim–offender mediation, the facilitator(s) also uses a 'script'. This script, however, 'is made up of series of "restorative questions", which structure the conference and guide the participants throughout a restorative process' (Chapman 2012: 65). That is, it does not foresee the outcomes. With youth offender panels it seems to be different: in a process that supposedly promotes greater community involvement, community members are actually just voicing what is in the report; young people are made to believe that they are taking part in the decision, but in actuality they are being told what to do; contracts are only remotely about reparation, while referral orders may be discharged without any type of reparation (to the victim or to the community) being undertaken.

The aim of this chapter was to provide an understanding of how youth offender panels operate on the ground. Now that the process of the referral order is theoretically (Chapter 3) and empirically explained, I shall turn to a more critical interrogation of the data. The professionalisation of community panel members, the limits to genuine community involvement, the representativeness of community panel members, the 'restorativeness' of youth offender panels, among other themes that have been touched upon at various points throughout this narrative, will be given central attention in the following chapters.

Notes

1 The fact that panel members are not representative of the local community was a key theme that ran throughout many interviews. This will be discussed at length in the next chapter.

2 At the time of the research, both training programmes could be downloaded from the Ministry of Justice website at: www.justice.gov.uk/youth-justice/workforce-development/working-with-volunteers/training-forvolunteers. Nowadays, YOT staff and volunteers are provided with a code to access the Youth Justice Interactive Learning Space (YJILS), 'an online interactive learning environment where the youth justice workforce can get access to a range of online learning resources and tools' (see yjils.justice.gov.uk/login/index.php), and there they can view all of the training material.

3 Towards the end of the fieldwork period, the 'Revised Restorative Justice Panel Matters' training was launched on YJILS. Nevertheless, panel members had not yet been retrained in line with this new training package.

4 In October 2014, a new assessment tool, called 'AssetPlus', was launched. More (up-to-date) information on the assessment and planning framework for the youth justice system of England and Wales can be found here: www.gov.uk/government/publications/assetplus-assessment-and-planning-in-the-youth-justice-system.

5 YP here stands for 'young person'. In the original documents, the young people were either referred to as 'X', by their actual initials, or had their family names omitted.

6 Headway is a charity providing specialist services and support to people with acquired brain injuries. It operates in many areas across England and Wales. When the young person is charged with an offence that could have caused a brain injury (e.g. assault), they tend to be asked as part of their referral order to visit Headway.

The aim is for them to learn about the impact of assaults on victims and, it is hoped, prevent them from going on to commit further violent offences.
7 An inexperienced panel member, who was in training.
8 For example, the United Nations Basic Principles on the use of restorative justice programmes in criminal matters.
9 I shall come back to this case in Chapter 7, when discussing the distrust that permeates social relations in urban, 'late modern' contexts.
10 It is perhaps worth mentioning that the victim had not even been contacted yet regarding her willingness to participate in the process. That is, chances were that the letter would not even be sent to the victim.
11 In only one instance did a panel meeting involve a victim (the young person's mother); therefore, I do not have sound empirical data on reparations to victims. For this reason, and given that the present study is on the role of community, I shall for the main part focus on reparation to the community. My reflections upon victim involvement, though, will be included in Chapter 7.
12 The certificate is signed by the referral order coordinator, and states: 'This certificate is presented to [young person's name] in recognition of the fact that the holder has now completed all work set out in the contract between them and the [name of the area] Youth Offender Panel'.
13 See the Rehabilitation of Offenders Act 1974 for more details.
14 This is the primary, if not the only, example used – giving the impression, one could argue, that the list of exceptions is smaller than it actually is.
15 As explained in Chapter 3, since 2012, a young person may receive multiple referral orders.
16 From the beginning (2002 *Guidance*), the recommendation was that community panel members should not serve on panels for more than six years. According to the 2009 *Guidance*: 'Volunteers are normally encouraged to serve on youth offender panels for terms of up to three years. Towards the end of any period of three years['] service, there will be a full performance review by the YOT and subject to satisfactory performance, the period of panel service may be extended by a further term of up to three years, at the discretion of the YOT manager and dependent on the needs of the panel and the availability of the volunteer' (Ministry of Justice 2009: 24). In this respect, YOTs have clearly departed from the guidance. Nearly 25 per cent of panel members interviewed were serving for more than six years, and a handful of them were there from the very first youth offender panel.

References

Chapman, T. (2012) 'Facilitating Restorative Conferences', in E. Zinsstag and I. Vanfraechem (eds), *Conferencing and Restorative Justice*, Oxford: Oxford University Press.

Crawford, A. and Burden, T. (2005) *Integrating Victims in Restorative Youth Justice*, Bristol: The Policy Press.

Crawford, A. and Newburn, T. (2003) *Youth Offending and Restorative Justice: Implementing Reform in Youth Justice*, Cullompton: Willan Publishing.

Froestad, J. and Shearing, C. (2013) 'Meditative Reflections on Nils Christie's "Words on Words", Through an African Lens', *Restorative Justice: An International Journal*, 1(1): 31–47.

Green, S. (2014) *Crime, Community and Morality*, Abingdon: Routledge.

Greene, D. (2013) 'Repeat Performance: Is Restorative Justice Another Good Reform Gone Bad?', *Contemporary Justice Review*, 16(3): 359–390.

Griffiths, C.T. and Hamilton, R. (1996) 'Sanctioning and Healing: Restorative Justice in Canadian Aboriginal Communities', in B. Galaway and J. Hudson (eds), *Restorative Justice: International Perspectives*, Monsey, NY: Criminal Justice Press.

Hallett, C., Murray, C., Jamieson, J. and Veitch, B. (1998) *The Evaluation of Children's Hearings in Scotland, Volume 1*, Edinburgh: The Scottish Office Central Research Unit.

Home Office (1997) *No More Excuses: A New Approach to Tackling Youth Crime in England and Wales*, London: Home Office.

Home Office (2002) *Referral Orders and Youth Offender Panels: Guidance for Courts, Youth Offending Teams and Youth Offender Panels*, London: Home Office/Lord Chancellor's Department/Youth Justice Board.

Mesmaecker, V.D. (2013) 'Victim-Offender Mediation Participants' Opinions on the Restorative Justice Values of Confidentiality, Impartiality and Voluntariness', *Restorative Justice: An International Journal*, 1(3): 334–361.

Ministry of Justice (2009) *Referral Order Guidance*, London: Ministry of Justice/Department for Children, Schools and Families/Youth Justice Board.

Morris, A. and Maxwell, G. (2000) 'The Practice of Family Group Conferences in New Zealand: Assessing the Place, Potential and Pitfalls of Restorative Justice', in A. Crawford and J. Goodey (eds), *Integrating a Victim Perspective within Criminal Justice: International Debates*, Aldershot: Ashgate Publishing.

Nelken, D. (1985) 'Community Involvement in Crime Control', *Current Legal Problems*, 38: 239–267.

Newburn, T., Crawford, A., Earle, R., Goldie, S., Hale, C., Hallam, A., Masters, G., Netten, A., Saunders, R., Sharpe, K. and Uglow, S. (2002) *The Introduction of Referral Orders into the Youth Justice System: Final Report*, Home Office Research Study 242, London: Home Office.

Pali, B. and Pelikan, C. (2014) 'Con-texting Restorative Justice and Abolitionism: Exploring the Potential and Limits of Restorative Justice as an Alternative Discourse to Criminal Justice', *Restorative Justice: An International Journal*, 2(2): 142.

Shearing, C. and Froestad, J. (2010) 'Nodal Governance and the Zwelethemba Model', in H. Quirk, T. Seddon and G. Smith (eds), *Regulation and Criminal Justice: Innovations in Policy and Research*, Cambridge: Cambridge University Press.

Stuart, B. (1996) 'Circle Sentencing: Turning Swords into Ploughshares', in B. Galaway and J. Hudson (eds), *Restorative Justice: International Perspectives*, Monsey, NY: Criminal Justice Press.

Stuart, B. (2001) 'Guiding Principles for Peacemaking Circles', in G. Bazemore and M. Schiff (eds), *Restorative Community Justice: Repairing Harm and Transforming Communities*, Cincinnati, OH: Anderson Publishing.

Wachtel, T., O'Connell, T. and Wachtel, B. (2010) *Restorative Justice Conferencing: Real Justice and the Conferencing Handbook*, Pipersville, PA: The Piper's Press.

Youth Justice Board (2004) *National Standards for Youth Justice Services*, London: Youth Justice Board.

Youth Justice Board (2009) *National Standards for Youth Justice Services*, London: Youth Justice Board.

Youth Justice Board (2010a), *Case Management Guidance*, London: Youth Justice Board.

Youth Justice Board (2010b), *Youth Justice: The Scaled Approach – A Framework for Assessment and Interventions*, London: Youth Justice Board.

6 The role of community in youth offender panels

In Chapter 2 I discussed how the notion of community involvement has been conceived and operationalised throughout time and across different contexts of restorative justice. I argued that there are at least four typical ways of involving members of the community in restorative processes:

1 In some programmes (e.g. most victim–offender mediation schemes) community participation is limited to the involvement of lay (but trained) volunteers serving as mediators (e.g. McCold 2004).
2 In practices such as family group conferences, community participation is sought through the involvement of the so-called 'community of care' of both offenders and victims (e.g. Morris and Maxwell 2000).
3 Other restorative justice experiments have broadened the notion of community to include a much larger number and wider range of community members; restorative circles, for example, are virtually open to any resident of the locale where the crime has occurred (e.g. Umbreit and Armour 2011).
4 Finally, some restorative programmes, such as the reparative boards in the USA (see Karp and Drakulich 2004), include features of the other three models. So, like mediators in victim–offender mediation programmes, community members in reparative boards are chosen from a pool of volunteers who are trained to perform that role. As in circles, they are themselves parties, actively involved in the decision-making process. As in family group conferences, the community of care also (normally) participates and helps to shape the restorative plan.

As earlier chapters indicate (particularly Chapters 3 and 5), youth offender panels in England and Wales, at least in theory, fall within this latter hybrid model. First, the community panel members are lay volunteers who are trained to perform that role. Second, they must be 'representative of the local community' (Ministry of Justice 2009: 9). Finally, while representing the locale where crime has occurred, and instead of acting as a neutral party, they are statutorily supposed to take the lead in the panel meeting and in the drawing up of the contract. However, the question of how, in practice, the idea of community involvement has been 'manipulated' by youth offender panels deserves a closer, more careful look. Drawing on the findings presented in Chapter 5 and on further empirical data, this chapter aims to provide this closer scrutiny.

6.1 The idea of 'community involvement' in youth offender panels

On the whole, YOT workers and community panel members appeared quite positive about the involvement of the community in the referral order process. For example, respondents often celebrated the fact that community members bring to panel meetings 'life experience' instead of 'professional knowledge'. Indeed, the importance of *lay* involvement was a key theme that ran throughout many interviews. Likewise, a common theme for many respondents was the fact that community panel members are *volunteers*. Respondents often argued that young offenders are pleasantly surprised to see that panel members 'are not being paid to be there'. At the same time, as will be argued throughout this chapter, young people appeared quite indifferent to community panel members. While the particular values of lay participation will be dealt with in greater detail later, the following sections are an attempt to depict an overall image that respondents have of 'community' and of 'community panel members'. That is, what follows is aimed at answering two key questions: on the ground, and in the context of youth offender panels, what does 'community' mean, and who are the 'community members'?

Community and community members in the views of YOT workers

When I asked YOT workers what they thought about the involvement of the community in youth offender panels, the following responses were typical:

> I think it's a great idea. It allows different views to come into play.
> (YOT6, WORKER2)

> I guess the value of the panel members is they bring their own experience, whatever that might happen to be.
> (YOT1, WORKER2)

> The reality? People bring their life experience, who they are. Rather than 'community', they bring individual experiences, they bring their own personality to the table.
> (YOT11, WORKER1)

In fact, YOT workers often held the perception that community involvement is about piecing together the mosaic of different attitudes and opinions of the 'general public'. To put it differently, they often felt that involving the community meant bringing together a group of different people, with different backgrounds and perspectives, or a rich 'blend of experiences', through which the 'general public' should be represented.

When asked, YOT workers often agreed that community panel members do bring a 'community perspective' to panels. When probed further about what they thought a 'community perspective' was, the majority of the respondents referred to the 'ripple effect' of crime on the community and the need for panel members to represent the 'victimised community'. The following comment from one YOT worker was typical:

> When a young person offends, it does have that ripple effect, it does also affect the community. So the referral panel is designed to repair the harm that has not only been caused to a victim but also to the community. So incorporating panel members is almost like providing a representative from that community, and they can have an input around what type of work that young person needs to do to repair those relationships.
>
> (YOT6, WORKER2)

In any case, it is important to note that YOT workers tend to speak of 'community' as a 'place' and, thus, of 'community members' as 'people who live in that place'. In fact, when they referred to the 'victimised community', they often meant the whole town, borough, or indeed, the whole 'YOT area'; by 'general public', they usually meant the people residing in that very YOT area:

> You're not listening to your parents at that age, so sometimes it takes someone to say 'I'm a member of the community, and you did this *in the same town* as I live, and I'm the one who has to walk past that every day'.
>
> (YOT3, WORKER1, emphasis added)

> [Community panel members] live in the community, they experience things that everyone *who lives in [name of YOT area]* would experience, so they can bring that perspective.
>
> (YOT7, WORKER1, emphasis added)

Community panel members' self-perception

I have explored community panel members' views of themselves – or of their role in the referral order process – through a series of questions, ranging from more general ones (e.g. *Why were you interested in becoming a community panel member?*) to more specific ones (e.g. *In your opinion, what is the purpose of community involvement in youth offender panels?*). I shall start by analysing their reasons for becoming panel members, as this should help to contextualise their responses to more straightforward questions.

Gill and Mawby (1990), in their study of volunteers in the criminal justice system, asked people volunteering in the probation service, the police (as special constables) and representatives from victim support schemes what had attracted them to voluntary work and why they had chosen that particular agency. They then coded the replies into six different categories – *self-directed, career-directed, agency-directed, religious-based, other-directed*, and *drift* – some of which have proven useful in analysing my own data. As in their study, most of the volunteers whom I interviewed became panel members for *self-directed* reasons, for example, 'to meet other people', 'to escape from doing nothing at home', 'to learn new skills', and so on. Among them, a large number cited a more specific type of self-directed motive: they became panel members for *career-directed* reasons. Indeed, as discussed in Chapter 5, many of my respondents saw their work in youth offender panels 'as a step on the ladder towards paid employment' (Gill and Mawby 1990: 46).

Fewer community panel members gave answers that were *agency-directed* (or YOT-directed), and the few who did, revealed their hope to become a YOT worker in the future:

> I'm really interested in working with young people and families and the youth justice arena, so this was kind of … this was ideal really. I mean, one day, you never know, if there's any more money in it, there might even be an opportunity … I understand several volunteers have actually moved over to employment within the YOT. It's just a particular interest I've got, really.
>
> (YOT2, CPM2)

Yet fewer of my respondents mentioned other-directed reasons, such as their desire to 'give something back to the community' or 'to help young people', but these respondents appeared driven by philanthropic motives rather than by intentions to voice the 'community' in decision-making processes dealing with young offenders:

> I just think children get a raw deal and I thought I could do something to help, even if in a tiny little way.
>
> (YOT6, CPM2)

> I didn't really know what it would involve. I think it was about thinking then that maybe I could play a role in helping young people get back on a clean path after their problems.
>
> (YOT7, CPM3)

Finally, as Gill and Mawby (1990: 47) found, I interviewed a small number of panel members who simply drifted into voluntary work, instead of making a conscious decision to volunteer. For example, one of them commented: 'There was an advertisement in our local paper. I didn't know anything about it. A friend fancied going to the Open Day, I went to accompany her. She didn't carry on with it, I did' (YOT2, CPM3).

Overall, those panel members I interviewed did not become panel members out of a sense of representing the 'general public' or the 'victimised community' in restorative justice processes. In fact, more often than not, their reasons for becoming panel members – whether 'self-directed', 'career-directed', 'other-directed' or 'agency-directed' (Gill and Mawby 1990) – are better understood as reasons for undertaking voluntary work. That is, most community members whom I interviewed became involved in *panel* work out of a desire to do *any voluntary* work (or any voluntary work *with young people*):

> I sat next to a lady at a function and said I was looking for voluntary work and she gave me the phone number. Purely chance meeting. Before I moved here I had worked with people with learning disabilities. I wanted to do something completely different and with young people.
>
> (YOT12, CPM2)

> I was a nursery nurse in the local infants school. I finished when my son was born, and never went back. When he went to Uni, the information from youth offending came to me and I was interested. I felt I had knowledge of teenagers, and I wanted to do something for me as well. It's easy to sit there and do nothing. I wanted to help the young people and do something for myself.
>
> (YOT11, CPM1)

> In all my work as a counsellor/psychotherapist, I was in the NHS [National Health Service], but the youngest I saw were aged about 17, and I was interested in working with young people. And I wanted to carry on being useful. I wanted to contribute to society. It was a natural life stage, my own children grown up, retirement…
>
> (YOT4, CPM2)

The notion of being a voice for the 'victimised community' comes later with the training. Indeed, as part of their training, community panel members are instilled with a sense that 'crime not only affects the individual victim, but also the community', and that 'volunteers are selected to represent the community' (see *Panel Matters*). In fact, besides having analysed their training programmes (as mentioned in Chapter 5), I also had the opportunity to observe a few training sessions in one particular YOT, and there was a big emphasis placed on the 'ripple effect' of crime and on the need to explain this to the young people. Unsurprisingly, when asked what they thought the purpose of community involvement in youth offender panels was, most community panel members repeated the 'official' YOT discourse:

> I think it's about showing how the community is affected by the young person committing an offence [...] And as the community, then, we can sort of say, 'well, I don't like seeing graffiti up a wall', you know.
>
> (YOT1, CPM1)

> To me it's the fact that you've offended against the community and, one way or another, it's right that the community should have some say in what happens to you and how you make reparation for the damage you've caused. [...] It's the community that has to suffer the hoodies on the streets and all these things they perceive that are happening, and it's right that they have a voice through the panel to try and deal with some of those things, so that the young people can hear what the community feels about their actions.
>
> (YOT5, CPM2)

Some, however, were more critical of this notion. For example, when asked if she thought that panel members brought a 'community perspective' to panels, one community panel member commented: 'I'm not sure because you are a member of the community, but you are not representative of the community. You put yourself forward to do this. You are not nominated. You're not "speaking on behalf of". I don't represent [YOT area]. I am just an ordinary person' (YOT2, CPM4). Another respondent said: 'It's not channelled, you're not the voice of the community, there isn't a process where the community can say what they want you to say on their behalf' (YOT5, CPM2). In this context, some volunteers shared with YOT workers the opinion that community panel members come to panels as individuals, representing their own views, opinions and experiences, rather than carrying a mandate from the community:

> I bring 'me', but that is affected and shaped by all the other roles I have played in my life already.
>
> (YOT4, CPM2)

> I think I bring the mum more than I bring the community. I think I bring an effective parent – a lot of these [young] people have very ineffective parents.
>
> (YOT7, CPM1)

In fact, on the whole, panel members' views of themselves are largely similar to YOT workers' views of them. The fact that community panel members come from 'all walks of life', for example, was also a common theme for many panel members. Indeed, when prompted to evaluate the benefits of community involvement, panel members often referred to their different backgrounds and life experiences:

> We are a disparate group, we all bring something different – old, younger, different areas of work, different life skills.
>
> (YOT6, CPM1)

> It could be done another way, but I don't think it would work as well as it does, with us all coming from different walks of life.
>
> (YOT4, CPM1)

Finally, it should be noted that community panel members, like YOT workers, also refer to community as a place:

> We'll tell the young people that we live in [YOT area]. But I don't live in [particular neighbourhood within this YOT area], so if a young person lives there I can't necessarily relate to their lifestyle. I can only bring the perspective in terms of living in [YOT area]. [...] But what I do say as well is we all live in the same city, we all have to rub along together and respect each other.
>
> (YOT7, CPM1)

> I would know this area [referring to the YOT area]. [...] I might not know every street, but I know this community and it is important to me.
>
> (YOT8, CPM1)

> Well, I suppose it's that thing of this is my environment as well as your environment kind of thing. And the mere fact that I'm saying that I live here [...], I think that's saying I'm in your place and you're in my place. I don't think that if I said I was from [another YOT area] and I was coming here by train or whatever, it would feel the same.
>
> (YOT9, CPM3)

Usually, the place to which they refer is the YOT area, as a community panel member from one of the London YOTs states:

> Well, I suppose it's that thing of living in London, I have to say I love London, I like the notion of doing something which I think of being for London. Now London, as you know, is a big city. So to get that sense, I suppose, I thought more of my local patch, and I live in [YOT area]. And it is that feeling that I am doing something for my locality, if you like.

The 'panel people' as they are seen by the young people

When I asked young people if they thought it was important to have two members of the community in the meeting, they often replied with questions such as: '*Who do you mean?*', '*You mean the granny looking woman and the other one?*', '*You mean the panel people?*', '*You mean the two ladies?*' It became obvious during my interviews with young people that they are not familiar with the expression '*community* panel members'; in fact, their views of community panel members are quite blurred. This may be because most volunteers do not use the word 'community' to introduce themselves to young people (see Chapter 5), but it also probably reflects the fact that, prior to panel meetings, YOT workers do not tend to explain to the young people that the 'panel members' are members of the community. Instead, they tend to highlight that the 'panellists' with whom the young person will be meeting are 'friendly people who only want to help'. Indeed, the following comments exemplify how YOT workers typically explain to young people who the panel members are:

> You explain that the panellists are volunteers, and that the court has given them permission to work with you.
>
> (YOT9, CPM1)

> You would say, 'they're people that are there to help you, they're not there to judge you'.
>
> (YOT5, WORKER1)

On a more critical note, one YOT worker commented:

> I don't always think that young people understand why we've got volunteers here – they might just think we pull them in off the street half an hour before the panel, for all I know! I don't know how well it's explained to the young person beforehand, or if we ever tell them why we use volunteers.
>
> (YOT5, WORKER1)

Once they were clear about to whom I was referring, the majority of young people I interviewed were not sure whether they found it important to have the two (or three) members of the community in the meeting: 'don't know' and 'not sure' were the most typical replies. Only four out of the 25 respondents replied affirmatively:

> Yes, because they are less strict.
>
> (YOT1, YP1)

> Yeah, there's not as much pressure [as in court].
>
> (YOT2, YP2)

> Yeah, they bring a different point of view.
>
> (YOT4, YP2)

> Yeah, it does make a difference actually. At the start I didn't really like it, you know, coz I thought this is awkward, you know, what you say when there's something new. But at the end, like my last one [i.e. her final panel meeting], I actually enjoyed it, you know. Like, they made me see, yeah, how much I've done. I was glad with that really. Yeah … they show you the progress you've done.
>
> (YOT12, YP3)[1]

Then, when asked why they thought community members were there, most young people answered 'to help', probably reproducing the explanations that they get from 'their' YOT worker. There were, however, a couple of interesting exceptions to this rule. For example, one young person commented: 'I don't see a difference between them and [name of her YOT worker]' (YOT10, YP2). Another one guessed: 'They're two representatives of the court?' These two examples suggest that young people do not fully understand the role of community panel members in the referral order process. What is more, they suggest that young people might not perceive (or feel) the 'informalising' and 'deprofessionalising' intentions of youth offender panels – something to which I shall return when discussing the values of lay participation. Even if one considers the majority who thought panel members were there to help, they too do not seem to understand where these 'panel people' come from. In fact, I did ask in a few interviews where they thought the community panel members came from. Two responses will stand for all the other examples that could be given:

> Random people. They don't know me. They only sit there once or twice.
>
> (YOT5, YP1)

> Just people from the streets?
>
> (YOT9, YP4)

I also asked young people if they thought the meeting would have been the same without the community panel members. Again, most said they did not know – and 'I don't know' was a typical answer even amongst those who had earlier cited that 'panel people' were there 'to help you'. However, the following comment expressed a typical opinion among those who had one: 'It'd be the same. They [community members and YOT workers] basically say the same stuff' (YOT4, YP2). Again, this suggests that young people are uncertain about the role of community panel members vis-à-vis that of YOT workers. This will be further explored in later sections, but for the time being it suffices to say that young people appeared quite indifferent to the involvement of community members in youth offender panels. Indeed, if anything, community panel members are seen by young people as 'friendly *kinda* people' (YOT10, YP1), who are there 'to help you out' (YOT9, YP1), but then, even if there were no community panel members, YOT workers are already there to help them out anyway.

Community is 'a place' and community panel members are 'the public'

According to Clear and Karp (1999: 130), three dimensions ought to be considered when defining 'community': *geography, interdependency* and *identity.* Although their focus is on the community justice ideal, I found their three-dimensional approach to community particularly useful in the process of theorising about community involvement in youth offender panels.

They start off by recognising the importance of 'place' (see also Clear *et al.* 2011). The *geographic conception of community,* they argue, is advantageous 'because social relations are often more extensive and intensive with proximity' (Clear and Karp 1999: 130). Their reasoning sits comfortably with a more general shift in criminological concern from people to places. As Crawford (1997: 156–157) puts it, '[s]pace, rightly, has come to be recognized as a critical variable in understanding and mapping the incidence of crime, together with its prevention'. However, the problem is that 'these boundaries are often arbitrary – imposed by the constraints of funding or political niceties – and often mean little in human terms' (Crawford 1997: 157).

Clear and Karp (1999: 26) agree that places are often defined by political boundaries and that 'from the point of view of community life, these legal perimeters are often without meaning'. Hence, they suggest that community justice schemes should operate at the neighbourhood level, as a means of responding to specific (local) problems 'in a comprehensive, context-specific manner' (Clear and Karp 1999: 27):

> The focus of community justice is not individuals or individual criminal incidents. Nor is the focus on a city-, state-, or nationwide crime problem. Community justice is explicitly concerned with a pattern of relations and institutions that effectively operate at the level of the neighbourhood.

They acknowledge, however, 'the importance of intimate ties' and note that these 'extend well beyond neighbourhood boundary lines' (Clear and Karp 1999: 131). In this vein, they suggest a second conception of community: *the interdependency of individuals.* According to this dimension, community is better described by social networks than by the determinism of space (Wellman and Leighton 1979), and thus, the focus is turned from the neighbourhood to the importance of family links, friendship and other social ties, which Clear and Karp (1999: 131) remind, 'are now more diffused than concentrated'.

The last dimension is *identity,* which according to Clear and Karp (1999: 132), 'is a dimension of community that reflects the degree to which members share similar demographic traits' such as 'membership in the same church, race, profession, or other social organization or category'. They acknowledge that geography and identity often overlap, as they do in ethnic enclaves, but argue that 'shared identity may be a stronger factor than geography in sustaining the community' (Clear and Karp 1999: 132; see also Firey 1945; and Suttles 1968).

All in all, Clear and Karp's (1999) three-dimensional approach to community could be summarised as follows: 1 they promote a focus on the neighbourhood because they realise both the importance (or inevitability) of place and the need for the place to be meaningful; 2 they accept the importance of place while acknowledging that meaningful social relations (or 'interdependency') are not constrained to postcode areas; and finally, 3 they consider the importance of similar social traits and identities (such as ethnicity) in conceptualising the idea of community.[2] While enhancing all three dimensions of community is the ideal, *their bottom-line argument is that one dimension may compensate for another's deficit*. Indeed, according to them, 'community building strategies compensate for a weakness in one dimension by developing the others' (Clear and Karp 1999: 132).

What I found was that despite their rhetorical appeals, youth offender panels do *not* explore or develop any of the three dimensions of community. To start with, while it is clear that YOT workers and community panel members see community as a 'place', they often mean the whole 'YOT area', and youth offender panels, therefore, tend to operate at the 'YOT area' level. The problem is that YOT areas can be geographically huge and diverse, and therefore, as meaningless as criminal law jurisdictions or any other 'places' that have their boundaries politically defined (e.g. states, municipalities and governments). This only strengthens my argument, in Chapter 5, that having panel meetings at 'community venues' does not currently add any extra value to the process compared with holding them in YOT premises: both places are equally not part of the participants' locale. Very few respondents provided a view on this, but a few did help to make my point:

> No they don't represent the community. We have people driving from the other side of the county. [...] We have a motor intervention programme – all young people who commit a motoring offence are eligible – but if you live in [certain part of the YOT area], the programme is in [another part of the YOT area]. It's a two- or three-day programme, and you spend over an hour being transported to it. So for one person it's a two-hour programme, for another its four hours.
>
> (YOT4, WORKER4)

> Community perspective must be from the same neighbourhood, and restorative justice or 'this is the effect on us' talk needs to be localised. It doesn't work so well if the panel members are from far away. If you live there you can relate to the effect of the offence.
>
> (YOT4, WORKER5)

Indeed, panels do not operate at the neighbourhood level. This comes as no surprise if one considers that, more often than not, community panel members do not live in the same neighbourhood as the young people: 'No, they're all from quite affluent areas. [...] I don't think we have any from the council estates or the areas where the young people live. I think that's something we need to work on [...]' (YOT1, WORKER1).

On the other hand, in panels, the importance of family links, friendship and other social ties is largely overlooked. As described in Chapter 5, young people tend to come to panels alone or with only one other person (usually 'mum'), and they are not supposed to know the community members or stay in contact with them. Indeed, there are no affective attachments between community panel members and the young people. It comes as no surprise, then, that young people struggle to differentiate community panel members from YOT workers or (friendly) 'representatives of the court'. One YOT worker commented:

> I think you need to look at what's important to that young person, what influences them? Do they go to a church? Would it be better to get someone from that church, someone they care about, someone that influences them? [...] There are lots of different communities within [name of YOT area]. The [YOT area] as a whole isn't a community.
>
> (YOT9, WORKER2)

In fact, Clear and Karp's (1999) second conception of community, the interdependency of individuals, speaks a great dealt to the idea of a 'community of care' – that is, to the importance of involving in restorative justice processes people who care for the young offenders and, very importantly, *for whom they care* (Harris *et al.* 2004). This does not happen in the context of youth offender panels. Although community panel members generally care for the young people, and are often sitting on panels out of a desire to help them, and despite the fact that young people often describe community panel members as people who are there to help, the truth remains that young people are indifferent to the involvement of community panel members in youth offender panels.

Finally, as regards the third dimension of community – *identity* – community panel members and young people are more often than not from completely different socio-economic worlds. All in all, 'community', in the context of panels, is a place, but a place without much meaning – the (whole) city, borough or, indeed, the whole YOT area. 'Community members' are the people living in these diverse places – or, indeed, members of 'the public' who have no personal attachment to the individual young people. In addition, in terms of identity, young people and community panel members do not often share socio-demographic traits, and this brings us to the next section, on the representativeness of community panel members.

6.2 The representativeness of community panel members

I have explored the representativeness of community panel members in interviews with all three types of respondents. For example, volunteers were asked if they thought they were at the panels to represent the community, and if so, which community they thought they represented. In turn, YOT workers were asked if they thought community panel members represented the local community and/or the same community to which the young offenders belonged. Finally, questions to the young people included '*Do you think you belong to the same community as those community members present at the meeting?*' Beside interviews, my observational field notes include information regarding the age, gender and ethnicity of those participating in panel meetings. Moreover, seven YOTs provided me with a table showing the socio-demographic profile (age, gender and ethnicity) of their panel members. Analysis of these different sets of data forms the basis of the following discussions.

The socio-demographic profile of community panel members

Community panel members are typically white, British, middle aged (or older), middle class and mostly female. This description mirrors the population that I have interviewed, as well as respondents' accounts of the population that they see in panels:

> We've got very few ethnic minority panellists, more women, less men, probably more middle-class than working-class people, most of them reasonably well educated.
>
> (YOT10, WORKER2)

> My only concern is that the group of people we have – I can stereotype them, middle class, predominantly women, retired, or business owners – they are the ones with the time to give.
>
> (YOT4, WORKER6)

> How representative we are is questionable. [...] We are probably older than we should be, perhaps because we have more free time.
>
> (YOT2, CPM1)

> I would say that most of the people I trained with were either middle class or young professional academics who were doing this because they could see a way into the criminal justice system. Only a couple of people were truly working-class background.
>
> (YOT5, CPM1)

The analysis of YOT records from seven YOTs suggests the same overall picture. Figure 6.1, for example, shows the socio-demographic characteristics of community panel members in YOT11.

In terms of age and ethnic origin, it was only in a couple of (London) YOTs that a different pattern prevailed, but in both sites the female predominance remained evident. Figure 6.2 shows the socio-demographic profile of community panel members in a London YOT, which appears to have the most diverse pool of volunteers among all the YOTs that I have visited. It should be noted, however, that when I began my fieldwork in this site, there were only six community panel members there, and a new referral order coordinator had just been appointed. Towards the end of my fieldwork period, when the new coordinator had already been working there for a year, I asked her if she thought panel members represented the community, to which she replied: 'They do now. When I started here, we had a lot of white, middle-class, older panel members that didn't represent the community of [YOT area], but now we're a lot more diverse' (WORKER2). Despite the obvious improvements, and the fact that this indeed turned out to be the research site with the most diverse group of volunteers, other people working there still felt that community panel members were not sufficiently representative:

> It's unfortunate that most panel members are retired and most are white. There are a few students who are doing it for experience, but there's a lack of ethnic minority panel members, which is a weakness, because [YOT area] is a multi ethnic community, and most offenders are from

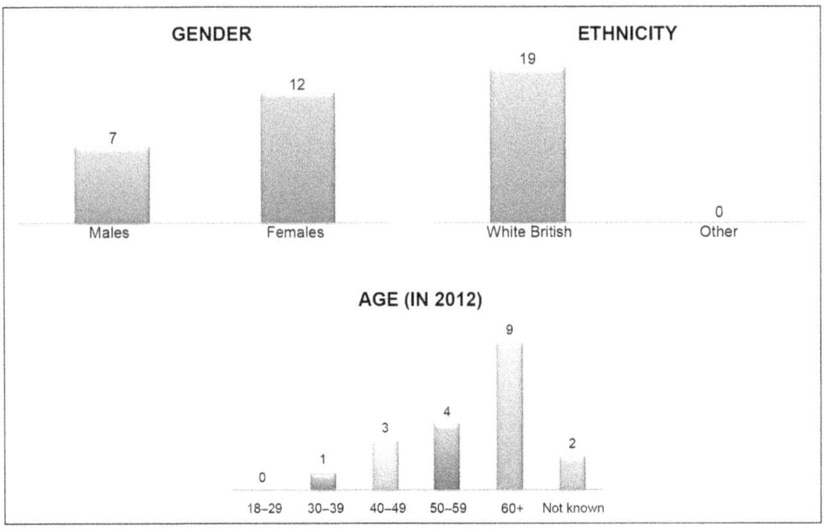

Figure 6.1 The socio-demographics of community panel members in YOT11
Source: YOT11's official records.

> BME [black and minority ethnic] communities. [...] For example, many of our young people are from Somalia, but we don't have any Somali panel members.
>
> (WORKER3)

This is not news. During the pilot period, for example, Newburn and his colleagues (Newburn *et al.* 2002: 9) found that most community panel members were white (91 per cent), female (69 per cent), and over 40 years of age (68 per cent). Moreover, other 'non-restorative justice' initiatives that have sought to engage the community are also confronted with the problem of unrepresentative community members. For example, it is a common complaint that community policing projects 'are made up of middle-class, middle-aged, white, pro-police individuals' (Green 2014: 20). In fact, within the volunteer literature, it is often lamented that only certain types of people offer services as volunteers (e.g. Aves 1969; Jackson 1985; Musick and Wilson 2008). However, Gill and Mawby (1990) go beyond lamenting that volunteers are unrepresentative of the general public, and make an important point, to which I would like to draw attention: 'the almost widespread comment about the typical volunteer has not included discussions about the role of agency policies in perpetuating those biases' (Gill and Mawby 1990: 112).

Gill and Mawby (1990) found that in areas where it was relatively easy to recruit volunteers, agencies commonly relied on word of mouth. While recognising the well-established use of such informal recruitment strategies, they criticise the over-reliance on word of mouth by asking a fundamental

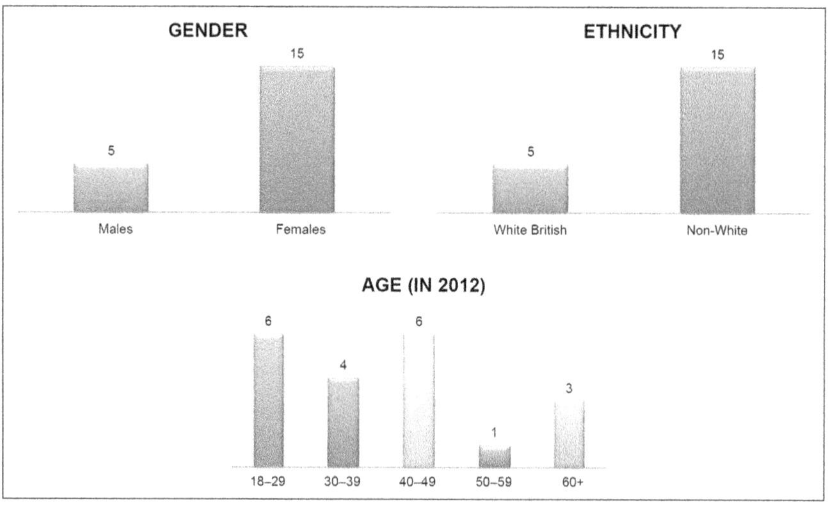

Figure 6.2 The socio-demographics of community panel members in a London YOT
Source: YOT official records.

question: 'Whose mouth?' (Gill and Mawby 1990: 113). They suggest that where methods such as word of mouth are used, 'homogeneity of *some* sort among volunteers is likely' (Gill and Mawby 1990: 83). Indeed, my findings provide support for this. As noted in Chapter 5, YOTs often celebrate the fact that word of mouth is sufficient to sustain a waiting list of volunteers. One YOT manager, for example, was proud to say: 'We've only ever had to advertise once' (YOT7, WORKER2). Likewise, a year into the implementation of referral orders, Newburn and his colleagues (2002: 10) found that 'experienced community panel members speaking to friends and colleagues about the work of panels' was regarded as successful, 'particularly for attracting the interest of ethnic minority groups'. Nonetheless, over 10 years later, I have found that although YOTs continue to regard word of mouth as a successful recruitment strategy, they still struggle to recruit community panel members who are male, younger and/or from minority ethnic groups. What is more, I have come across a handful of volunteers who drifted into working as a panel member because they heard about it from a sister, a daughter, a neighbour and so on, and it should be noted that those were white, middle-class women who became panel members following the advice of their white, middle-class sister, daughter or neighbour.

I would argue that YOTs could do more to attract a more diverse group of volunteers. First and foremost, word of mouth, as a recruitment strategy, should be used with caution. The question of 'whose mouth?' provides a useful check for bias. Other strategies, such as advertising in ethnic minority newspapers and specific ethnic minority centres appear more relevant than word of mouth for attracting the interest of ethnic minority groups. The more creative advertising methods mentioned in Chapter 5 – for example, YOT workers giving talks at universities – should also stand out as examples of what further can be done. As Gill and Mawby (1990: 113) suggest, 'more emphasis could be placed on recruiting volunteers through advertisements in shop windows and libraries'. Moreover, while YOTs have been rather critical about recruiting students, attracting people who volunteer for 'career-directed' reasons may well lead to a more diverse group of community panel members. It may well be the case, as suggested by the coordinator of a victim–offender mediation service, that we would get more diversity if volunteers were going to be able to move on to paid work (see Crawford 1997: 187). Indeed, while equal opportunity laws apply to paid work, they clearly do not to unpaid – but what if unpaid work were used as a route to paid opportunities? In any case, the fact that YOTs have a role in determining who gets selected should not be overlooked.

Examining the edges between diversity and representativeness

Clearly, the concepts of diversity and representativeness go hand in hand, inasmuch as diversity is not an end in itself but an important 'enabling condition' (Phillips 1995) for addressing the problem of representativeness. In this vein, the idea among respondents that community panel members are not sufficiently diverse in terms of ethnicity, age, gender and class almost always led them to the conclusion that panel members do not represent the community.

It is important to note, however, that increasing the numbers of a particular group in panels does not automatically translate to an increase in community panel members' representativeness. Mere numbers – or 'descriptive representation', in Pitkin's (1967) terms – are a necessary but insufficient condition for meaningful or 'substantive representation'. As Crawford (1997: 185) suggests in the context of victim–offender mediation schemes, it is important to reflect on 'which forms of social identity constitute a significant group within a locality', such that it should be represented among panel members. Or, indeed, 'what criteria denote significance' (Crawford 1997: 185). Is it age, gender, class and/or ethnicity? Is it really a matter of accurate correspondence between the socio-demographic characteristics of young people and community panel members, or do common histories or experiences denote more significance? When expressing their opinion about the representativeness of panel members, respondents often focused on one particular aspect that they thought was lacking more than others. Very often, this was 'class':

> My feeling is a community representative would have a real inside out understanding of all levels of the make-up of the young people's community and for most of these young people – here in [YOT area], they are from one of three estates – our panel members have no idea of the challenges, family, socially, of these young people. They are very distant, and it makes for difficulties in the process.
>
> (YOT4, WORKER4)

> I'd say I represent a middle-class community, and the children who have a referral order are generally lower class … so it's kind of a different level.
>
> (YOT4, CPM3)

Due to the lack of a truly diverse pool of volunteers, some YOTs I visited are careful in selecting, for each panel meeting, community members who 'match' the young person and her family. For example, if the young person is black, some YOTs will avoid having a completely white panel, even if most of their community panel members are white. YOT workers explain:

> For example, the offender might be a young black man, and his mum is a single parent. We might not have a black single parent there, but we might have a white single parent. We try to have some kind of balance, but we might not always get the match.
>
> (YOT9, WORKER1)

> When we arrange panels I encourage them to mix people up so we've got a mix of younger, older, male, female, experienced and less experienced.
>
> (YOT5, WORKER1)

This may well be 'better than nothing', as one YOT worker said. However, with the 'mix and match' strategy, YOTs are going around the problem, not through it. Indeed, most young people whom I interviewed felt that they did not belong to the same community as the panel members, and this was true even in YOTs where the 'mix and match' strategy was used. When asked '*Do you think you belong to the same community as those community members present at the meeting?*', answers such as 'Got nothing to do with 'em!' (YOT5, YP1), and 'No, they're a bit higher, you know, from a higher class' (YOT5, YP2) were the most typical responses among those who did not simply say 'no'. Moreover, the 'mix and match' strategy may have unintended side effects such as that of YOTs having a large pool of volunteers from which only a small number of panel members is over-used.[3]

Perhaps the 'solution' to this representativeness problem requires a completely different take on the concept of diversity and a rearrangement of our expectations in relation to community involvement. A worker based at one of the London YOTs commented: 'It's a delusion that community is involved. In this borough there are more than 200,000 people, and only 20 are involved, so how can you draw the conclusion that community is involved?' Perhaps she is right. For centuries, the magistrates' courts in England and Wales have shared the same aims (of community representativeness), and the same problems (of not being able to attract lay magistrates who represent the community). In fact, as argued by Pitkin (1967: 240), representation 'is a continuing tension between ideal and achievement', and far beyond the remit of youth offender panels, this is a struggle for democratic representation in general. As Sampson *et al.* (1988: 489) note, 'each locality is made up of many different and invariably conflicting interest groups, including isolated and often unrepresented people', so no one 'can properly lay claim to speak for "the community" in its entirety'. In fact, 'those who are active in community politics [...] are by their very nature unrepresentative of the larger body of people who prefer to leave politics to other people for most of the time' (Sampson *et al.* 1988: 489). Now, one important difference between the magistrates' court and youth offender panels – or indeed, between the traditional criminal/youth justice structure and restorative justice processes – is that within youth offender panels the concept of diversity can be more easily (and creatively) transformed or adapted. One YOT worker commented:

> In theory, it is a great idea to have people that are not involved with the criminal justice system and have them be representative of the local community. But in practice, I am not sure how much it works, opening up to the community. I think if it worked, it would be a panel of

> ex-offenders who have turned themselves round, and want to divert young people from that kind of lifestyle. The young people would be able to relate and identify with panel members. At the moment the young person comes in and sees three middle-class panel members, in their 50s, and automatically thinks 'what do you know about the kind of life I live?' – it creates distance. In terms of motivation, the young person is unable to relate to the panel – 'you have never been in my situation, how can you understand?'
>
> (YOT8, WORKER2)

With the exception of sexual offences, offences against children or a criminal conviction within the last two years (see Ministry of Justice 2009, 2012), there are no legal constraints preventing YOTs from recruiting ex-offenders as panel members. In fact, according to the *Guidance*, and with the above exceptions, 'where the applicant can demonstrate that he or she does not present a reoffending risk, previous offending need not necessarily be a bar to recruitment and is a matter for the YOT manager's discretion' (Ministry of Justice 2009: 24; Ministry of Justice 2012: 20). I would like to argue that bringing in ex-offenders, ex-drug addicts or any people who may not share the same socio-demographic characteristics with young people, but who may share with them similar past experiences, should also be considered an important form of diversity. When analysing the Vermont Reparative Boards, Boyes-Watson (2004) arrived at similar conclusions. She made a special case for the involvement of ex-offenders who themselves had previously come through the restorative process:

> Ex-offenders have valuable and constructive information to impart within the restorative process, and their participation sends a clear message that reintegration is not lip service. Their presence is often pivotal in breaking through patterns of denial, offering a role model for the offender and a unique source of on-going support.
>
> (Boyes-Watson 2004: 690)[4]

Similarly, in their evaluation of the Northern Ireland Youth Conferencing Service (YCS), Maruna *et al.* (2007: 64) suggest that:

> [...] there might also be a role for working with ex-participants of YCS conferences, drawn from the same neighbourhoods and same age groups as the young person referred to the conference. Such individuals could act as a mentor or guide through all stages of the conferencing process. [...] [I]t is conceivable that their involvement would substantially increase the perceived legitimacy of an intervention that can appear very middle-class, very professional and very 'adult' despite being more informal and comfortable than the traditional court system.

Although they appeared ideologically open to this idea (see Chapter 5), the YOTs I visited do not seem to be targeting recruits from these groups.

All in all, what seemed to be a problem of implementation that YOTs were keen to work on – and were better at dealing with than the magistrates' court, as panel members have been found to be more representative than lay magistrates (Biermann and Moulton 2003; Crawford 2004) – the representativeness of community panel members is still a big issue within the remit of youth offender panels. During the pilot period, Newburn *et al.* (2002: 61) found that 'difficulties were experienced in attempting to recruit a "representative" body of panel members', but that YOTs were 'developing strategies for broadening the base from which they recruit'. Eight months after the national implementation of referral orders, Biermann and Moulton (2003) found that 'YOS managers remained keen to attract a greater number of people from ethnic minority backgrounds and younger people, notably, young men'. Over 10 years later, YOT workers and panel members have reported to me that they think they need a more representative sample, and that they are working on it. Clearly, intentions and discourses have not changed, but apparently neither has the problem of unrepresentative panel members.

The 'invisibility' of community panel members

Discussions about representativeness must include reflections on the legitimacy of those who are supposed to be representing the community (see Ashworth 2001). In fact, as London (2011: 216) argues:

> In the conventional criminal justice system, the public is represented by a prosecutor whose position is attained through the political process and who is ultimately accountable to the electorate. By contrast, the process of selecting community representatives is without any public mandate or public accountability.

Indeed, according to Crawford (2002: 116):

> […] it is rarely clear exactly what […] the lines of legitimacy, accountability or representation, particular community members have. […] On whose behalf do they speak? […] If one is not involved as a state representative or as a representative of one of the immediate parties, then what is their mandate?

We cannot fully discuss the representativeness of community panel members, or the legitimacy of their 'mandate', if the community that they represent is not even aware of them. One of Clear and Karp's (1999: 155–156) questions to confirm the presence of a 'community justice ideal' appears particularly relevant here: Do community members know about and generally agree with the work of youth offender panels? Or indeed, how well is the work of the panels communicated to community members who might otherwise not know about it? I do not have concrete answers to these questions, as this would require tailored public opinion research. Nonetheless, I do have reason to assume that people who are not in any way involved with YOTs do not know what youth offender panels are and what work they do – let alone that their views are supposedly being represented by community panel members. If the community is unaware of their existence, it would seem odd that panels are supposed to represent the community.

Although this topic was not explored in my interviews, some community panel members have suggested (*en passant* and usually whilst trying to make another point) that people around them (e.g. extended family members and neighbours) do not know what they do. One community panel member commented: 'I don't know if anyone knows I do it? My friends and family know ... I live in a small village, but people don't say "Oh [her name] works for the youth offender panel". It's not as if you are a councillor' (YOT11, CPM2). Some YOT workers also commented, *en passant*, that they thought the work done by YOTs and youth offender panels is largely unknown, but that they hoped community panel members would 'spread the word'. For example, when asked about the purpose of involving community members in the process, one YOT worker replied: 'I think some people don't know what the YOS does, so linking it with panel members from the community strengthens the information' (YOT11, WORKER3).

In all possibility, people know too little about YOTs and the works of youth offender panels. In the first national, representative survey of public attitudes to youth crime and youth justice in England and Wales, Hough and Roberts (2004) found that three-quarters of the sample (76 per cent) had not heard about YOTs, and only one in eight correctly identified their purpose. According to Hough and Roberts (2004: 24), 'If this relatively high profile initiative is so poorly understood, a greater effort needs to be made to educate the public regarding recent criminal justice reforms in the area of youth justice'. Although the survey has not been replicated since – so we do not know if the creation of YOTs and the introduction of referral orders remain 'unnoticed reforms' (Hough and Roberts 2004) – my interviews suggest that the involvement of community members in youth offender panels does not necessarily result in them 'spreading the word' in the community. Therefore, the role of YOTs in promoting themselves and youth offender panels is crucial, and while in one of the YOTs I visited they mentioned doing 'open days' to promote the YOT and its activities in the local area, I have not heard of any similar initiative from any other YOT.

Although the question of how we are to know that community panel members are truly representative is likely to remain unanswered in a process where they are not elected (Ashworth 2001), a greater effort to educate the public about the work carried out by YOTs could, at the least, assist in the recruitment of a more diverse pool of volunteers. Discussing why they were not able to recruit ethnic minority young men, one YOT worker speculated:

> I don't know if it's because people don't know about it – that you're not a magistrate, that you're not tied for time as much as in the court, that you could come in once a month and do it for two or three hours. When I've spoken to my friends, they didn't know about that. I think in the younger generation they just don't know about it. It seems to have stuck with the older, white, middle-class women, and I don't know why.
>
> (YOT7, WORKER2)

6.3 Community panel members' participation in the referral order process, and ownership of youth offender panels

In the previous chapter, it was suggested that the idea that community panel members 'own' the process, or the idea that they are the ones who determine the directions and outcomes of panel meetings, is more rhetorical (or 'theatrical') than real. Now, let us dig deeper into the questions of *who the decision makers are, what the community members bring to the process in terms of ideas and resources*, and *who supports the young people during the course of the contract*. The answers to these key questions should lead us to a more critical understanding of community panel members' participation in, and ownership of, youth offender panels.

Who are the decision makers?

Despite a few more critical accounts, the majority of YOT workers and panel members whom I interviewed expressed views that 'at the end of the day, it is up to the community panel members to decide'. If anything, community panel members would admit to sharing decision making with YOT workers, but only on rare occasions would they suggest that YOT workers were taking over or exerting direct control over the process (see Chapter 5 for the few examples). They were generally more open, however, to admitting that young people do not have a real say about what goes into the contract. The following exchange suggests this:

> We used to get the report seven days before, which was a better way because you could study it and get your contract together before you got here. But now, with the data protection, you have to read it here and all the names are blanked out. Now we have to come half an hour earlier, and you only get half an hour before the kid turns up.
>
> *[And do you have a pre-panel meeting or a chance to meet with the YOT worker and ask questions?]*
>
> They'll bring us the report, we'll have a read and the caseworker will

> come in and discuss anything you want to talk about. We'll try to agree a contract between the three of us.
> *[So the contract is decided before the kid comes in?]*
> Yes.
>
> (YOT4, CPM1)

The same can be said of YOT workers: only a very few admit that the decision-making process happens outside panel meetings, and without the involvement of community members (also see Chapter 5 for the few examples). Yet far fewer openly admitted exerting direct control over the process:

> I think as a worker I'm able to say to the panel, 'I've met this kid, trust my instincts, this is what I'm suggesting', and they'll go for that. I've been in situations where a kid hasn't turned up for two initial panels, and the panel have wanted to breach them, and I've been able to say, 'don't do that, my gut feeling is there's something there, I can't tell you what it is, but there's a reason, and it's not because they can't be bothered'. When they met that young person, they felt that was the best thing to do.
>
> (YOT9, WORKER1)

> They [the community members] put it together with the young people – they are to be advised by us, not dictated. But I also believe intervention is assessment-led, and a thorough assessment of where the risks are, what are the factors impacting further offending, that leads to everything you put in the report. It is about being smart, presenting it in a compelling way that leads them to their conclusions for the contract.
>
> (YOT4, WORKER4)

As community panel members, YOT workers also spoke more openly about young people not having a real say:

> In practice it's always decided before the panel meeting, between YOT officers and panel members ... Yes, and the young person *is made* to agree with the terms of the contract.
>
> (YOT7, WORKER3, emphasis added)

> I'd say about 70 per cent of the time the contract's decided before the panel have set eyes on the young person. I think the other times is when something has come about from when the report was written, and it might have been some time from when the report was written until the initial panel. The longer the wait, the more likely the contract is changed in the panel.
>
> (YOT7, WORKER2)

On the other hand, although nearly all the young people I interviewed replied 'yes' when asked if they had been given a chance to speak and explain their side of things, their more general comments suggested that they did not feel as if they had a role to play in the decision-making process. For example, when asked '*If a friend of yours had to attend a panel meeting, what would you tell him/her about it?*', one young person replied: 'Shut up and listen' (YOT9, YP2). Another one answered: 'Sit in the room, and they just explain' (YOT10, YP2).

All in all, whereas young people are more clearly excluded from the decision-making process, community members' ownership of youth offender panels is more difficult to assess (or challenge) as interviewees spoke less openly (or critically) about this. Nonetheless, it became clear to me that community panel members do not truly decide anything apart from the amount of reparation to be undertaken by the young person and, perhaps,[5] who will play which roles in the script (that is, which community member is going to lead the meeting, which one is going to discuss school-related issues, and so on). Indeed, as if the narrative provided in Chapter 5 were not enough, there is further evidence of the 'theatrical'[6] nature of community members' control over panels.

In a couple of cases observed, for example, the YOT worker had already written the contract before the initial panel. She explained to me that the only reasons for doing so were to 'save time' and to 'avoid awkward silence' during the meeting, and highlighted that panel members were free to amend the pre-typed contract as they wished. Although I have no reason to doubt what she was saying, in both cases observed, community panel members said they had nothing to add or change – they just signed the contract as it was. It should be stressed that this is by no means widespread practice. In the vast majority of cases observed, across all 12 YOTs, contracts were written – or completed, when they took the format of a form – during panel meetings, and usually by community panel members themselves. But however exceptional, pre-typed contracts provide proof of a process that is not always committed to deliberation.

There are further examples of 'aberrations' occurring in other YOTs, which only strengthen my arguments. For instance, let us return to the library case described in the previous chapter – the case where everyone had to leave the panel meeting, before a contract could be discussed, because the library was closing. After we all left the library, the YOT worker drove me to the train station, which allowed us time to talk about what had happened and what would be done about it. What happened was that the YOT worker collected the community panel members' signatures, and she told me that sometime soon she would arrange to meet with the young person and her mother 'to explain the contract better and to get them to sign it'. That is, she would 'get the young person to sign the contract' during another meeting, at which the community panel members would *not* be present. Again, I have only seen this happen once. Nonetheless, such aberrations, in what is supposed to be a deliberative process, are only possible (and remain unchallenged) because, on the ground, community panel members still play an insufficiently determinative role in the panel process. The truth is that despite panel members' great theatrical performances, the decision makers are the YOT workers, not the community panel members – let alone the offender, her family or the never-present victim.

What do community members bring to the process in terms of ideas and resources?

As mentioned in Chapter 5, in theory, community panel members should bring ideas of activities for inclusion in contracts 'that draw on community rather than just youth offending team resources' (Home Office 2002: 7; Ministry of Justice 2009: 11). In practice, however, the whole referral order process is heavily – if not exclusively – based on YOT ideas and YOT resources. Although most of my respondents (among YOT workers and volunteers) maintained that community panel members bring a 'fresh view' to the process – because they come from 'all walks of life' and/or because they are not (YOT) professionals – I witnessed something very different on the ground.

First, as documented in Chapter 5, contracts tend to replicate the report's recommendations – that is, the idea of which activities should be included in contracts often comes from YOT workers, not from community panel members. Second, the recommendations that tend to become the very terms of the contract are all YOT-based activities and interventions, and when the recommendations give community panel members a certain amount of choice, the volunteers tend to 'pick' from the YOT's 'dessert menu' of pre-existing programmes. One YOT worker suggested another analogy: 'We tell them all about what we offer, and it's like a supermarket, they pick the one that's best for the young person, but that takes a bit of the creativity away from what they think the young person could benefit from' (YOT5, WORKER2). Finally, on the rare occasions when community members divert from YOT recommendations and pre-existing programmes, their 'creative' ideas tend to get tied up in the 'red tape' imposed by under-staffed YOTs and/or health and safety issues:

> We only have one full-time worker for the whole county, split between two people. So we don't have a great team working on reparation, and the ideas the panels have cannot happen. We are struggling with councils and health and safety and everything. Everything has to be risk assessed. Not criticising the system, but you have community volunteers trying to work within a very cumbersome bureaucratic system and it does not work in the way it was intended.
>
> (YOT4, WORKER2)

> Some [community panel members] are a bit elaborate and they will come up with suggestions to go and do this and that, and we do have to jump in there because, you know, it's not manageable, and we've got to remember that it's whether we've got the resources to meet some of their suggestions, and health and safety, and all sorts.
>
> (YOT6, WORKER2)

> I think probably a lot of panel members are quite frustrated because when they have raised ideas, the reality is, in terms of reparation activities, it's more complex because it should be linked to the offence, and it has to be available when the young person's free, and we have to do a risk assessment, and find someone to supervise it. Sometimes the YOT can come off like a parent, always saying 'you can't do that!'
>
> (YOT4, WORKER6)

As a result, all contracts tend to look very much the same, and it is not clear what community panel members actually bring to the process in terms of ideas and resources:

> To my knowledge I don't think [community panel members] offer a great deal. You talk about bringing in resourcefulness and ideas, but I don't see a lot of variety in terms of the contracts that are handed back to me – and as such, I don't believe they bring a lot more to it.
>
> (YOT2, WORKER3)

Who supports the young people during the course of the contract?

As mentioned in the previous chapter, community panel members do not normally get involved in any of the activities carried out in the period between panel meetings. Young people meet regularly with their worker (and with other service providers, such as the nurse, the 'drugs and alcohol' worker, and so forth), but they only tend to meet with the community members at panel meetings. Volunteers do not necessarily follow a case all the way through to completion either, meaning that young people often meet individual community members only once. In this context, one community panel member commented:

> Kids are the same […], they do stupid things just the same, and you have to try and remember that although we're panel members, we don't do very much. We talk to them for an hour maybe, and may not see them again for three months or not at all, so our job is to get them to accept a contract between the YOT and them. It's the people here that carry out that work, and if they are going to stop them reoffending, it's them [the YOT workers], not us [the community panel members].
>
> (YOT5, CPM2)

Likewise, in a one-off group interview, carried out in one particular YOT, mentioned in Chapter 4, all the respondents agreed with the following statement made by one of the community panel members: 'The success is down to the worker and not the panel members; that's not down to us. We do a good job, but it's down to the YOS worker' (YOT3, group interview). In fact, 'YOT workers' would be the short answer to the question of who supports the young people during the course of the contract.

Having said that, there are a few community panel members who, in addition to serving on panel meetings, also serve as mentors, supervising young people as they undertake reparation activities. It should be noted, however, that they will not supervise the same young people whom they see in panels. YOT workers and community members feel that there would be a conflict of interest otherwise:

> If she did end up mentoring the same young person, […] we'd take her off the panel and get somebody else. You can't be the judge and the jury.
>
> (YOT9, WORKER3)

> The panel, you have to understand, is a formal meeting in a way, whereas the mentoring is more quite laid back. And you don't wanna kind of give that mixed message that in the panel I was pretty much like 'you will have to attend your reparation meetings every Saturday!', and then if he doesn't turn up on Saturday, then you're 'OK, it's alright, don't worry'. […] So you need to keep that structure. […] As a mentor, […] you're trying to be their buddies in a way. […] Whereas in the panel, we are not allowed that luxury. It's like being a police officer on the streets and, at the same time, kind of trying to be friends with the criminals. You have to be one or the other. Because at the end of the day, where do you draw that line? 'Oh, Miss, I saw you last weekend in carpentry, and we were all good, and now you're telling me that just because I've missed one appointment, you're gonna send me back to court? Oh, come on, don't do that!' And then do you switch to [with a tough tone of voice] 'yeah, but I told you that you have to'?
>
> (YOT9, CPM1, who serves both as a panel member and as a mentor)

On the whole, community members often expressed in interviews that they felt 'under-used' – that they were willing to do more to support young people during the course of the contract, but that their participation was largely, if not exclusively, limited to panel meetings. Indeed, when I asked community members if they contributed to panels as much as they would like to, the following replies were typical and indicated frustrations that their time and enthusiasm, as well as good ideas, were not sufficiently drawn on:

> Sometimes I get frustrated because I have a lot of experience I could bring to a panel but I can't because it's not in the job description. There

> was a kid a couple of weeks back I would have loved to have gone and met his parents. He was a good kid, just had one offence, a stupid prank, but you could see from the way he's talking that his parents wouldn't move along with the times. […] I would have loved to have gone to the parents and tried to explain that society's changed from when we were kids, and you've got to let them have a bit more room, because of the experience of such a fast-moving society that they're having. […] I'm frustrated that I can't go the extra mile […]
>
> (YOT4, CPM1)

> I'd like to do more. The timetable came through and I was in for two [panel meetings] in the next three months, which doesn't seem like a lot. The longer periods we have in between, the harder it is to come back and do it again. I was supposed to be in one, two or three weeks ago, and now my next meeting is not until next week, so that's a five week wait, and then I've not got one until November, December, January [she was interviewed in August]. You've just got everything in your head, you know what you're going to do, and then you've got five weeks' wait again. It is a long time, especially when you've got work, family life … you can soon push it to the back of your head. It would be good to do more, but it's just when you're needed.
>
> (YOT5, CPM3)

The under-utilisation of volunteers has long been discussed within the volunteer literature (Gill and Mawby 1990; Hill 1981; Riddick 1984; Stockdale 1985). As Gill and Mawby (1990) suggest, and as the last of the above quotations supports, the provision of work is key to volunteer morale and commitment. Indeed, '[s]ince volunteers forsake financial rewards, they require alternative forms of recompense, and the provision of work is a minimum requirement' (Gill and Mawby 1990: 116–117). Although the under-use of panel members may reflect an 'oversupply' of volunteers, more likely it suggests poor management. YOTs should be rethinking the 'mix and match' strategy that I described earlier, and their over-reliance on a core of more experienced panel members that I will discuss in further detail later. Besides, they should be reflecting on how community members could be more widely 'used'. Establishing a dialogue about this with the panel members themselves may be the way forward to create more opportunities for community involvement. For example, in interview, one community panel member shared an interesting idea:

> There is one area where I'd like to give more of my time and that's to get some kind of victim inclusion system set up where panel members can go and talk to the victim and hear how it was for them, and then bring their understanding of the victim's experience into the room.
>
> (YOT7, CPM2)

YOT workers hardly ever spoke about the need to address the under-utilisation of panel members, but one YOT worker stood out among others, with the following innovative idea:

> They're starting to get involved in writing letters of explanation and apology. We've recently brought [...] a victim awareness programme that's run in a group work programme, four weeks of group work and then in the final week they write a letter of explanation or apology. [...] So what we're looking at are volunteers in some areas co-facilitating those sessions, and in some areas helping the young person to write their letters in the final week. That will involve them being properly trained; we're going to pilot it and review it.
>
> (YOT5, WORKER1)

During the pilot period, it was found that panels only took advantage of a small part of the potential contribution of volunteers (Crawford 2004). Again, it is over 10 years since youth offender panels were piloted, and the scenario remains largely unaltered: community panel members still want to give more, and YOTs have still not been able to do much about this.

A passive conception of community involvement and community members' rhetorical ownership of the process

According to Crawford (1997: 166), 'in the "double-speak" of criminal justice rhetoric, the notion of "community ownership" frequently translates into "the community must mobilize its own resources"'. He continues:

> The 'responsibilities' and 'obligations' to which politicians refer as the hallmarks of 'community' membership, are the human and material costs of crime prevention. *However, the conception of 'community involvement' implicit within most crime prevention project* [sic] *is a passive one, which casts the community in the role of recipient of a set of mechanisms.*
>
> (Crawford 1997: 166, emphasis added)

Although Crawford's focus was on crime prevention initiatives (such as community policing), the idea of a passive conception of community involvement is equally valid to the case of youth offender panels. Indeed, let us recapitulate:

1 The terms of the contract are discussed between young people and 'their' YOT workers before initial panel meetings take place.
2 YOT workers write rather comprehensive reports, which include specific recommendations regarding the content of the contract.
3 Contracts tend to be a 'copy and paste' of the YOT workers' recommendations as they are laid out in the report.
4 Reparation schemes are largely, if not exclusively, YOT based.

5 Most of the process happens outside panel meetings, and regardless of community panel members.

On the ground, community panel members only participate in a very small part of the referral order process – panel meetings – and do not have true 'ownership' of youth offender panels. If anything, the conception of 'community involvement' implicit in referral orders and youth offender panels is, indeed, a passive one – so much so that some volunteers feel their value has lessened in a process heavily dominated by YOT workers, or even question the utility of them being part of the process:

> They [YOT workers] now recommend more of the contract so they are more in the driving seat. Our role has diminished; theirs has increased. So our value is less and I think some of them feel that and I understand it. It's a bit extreme but … we do not play as major a part as we used to.
>
> (YOT4, CPM4)

> We get a report before initials. If anything, we probably get too much information, some of them are like a book! […] That's one drawback to the setup – if people who work for the youth offending service put all their recommendations in the report, why do you need us? All you need to do is write the report and the contract and we're sitting there talking to somebody who will end up with the same thing on the paper as their suggestion. It does seem sometimes like a waste of our time.
>
> (YOT5, CPM4)

These more critical accounts, however, were rare. As mentioned before, most YOT workers and community panel members I interviewed shared the discourse that the latter 'own' the process, and that 'at the end of the day, it's up to the panel members to decide'. Indeed, the discrepancy between rhetoric and practice was clear.

One possible reason for this is panel members' perception that they are more involved in the process when they know more about the young person and her life/offending circumstances. For example, a community panel member who also serves as a mentor commented that she felt more involved in the referral order process by doing panels than by supervising young people while they do their reparation: 'I'd say panels, because I'm able to read the report, get a good idea of what services we can suggest that will make a difference to their lives' (YOT9, CPM3). Clearly, the efforts to bridge the gap between rhetoric and practice will need to be sustained for most of my (adult) respondents appeared genuine in their belief that community panel members have true ownership of youth offender panels.

6.4 The meaning and value of lay involvement

At the time referral orders were introduced, lay involvement was celebrated as one of the most important changes to the youth justice system in England and Wales (see, for example, Crawford 2004; Crawford and Newburn 2003; Newburn *et al.* 2002). Those conducting research during the pilot period or shortly after the introduction of referral orders and youth offender panels were quite optimistic. For example, Crawford (2004) saw in lay involvement a drive against overly technical, bureaucratic and managerial proceedings. According to him, the participation of ordinary citizens in criminal justice proceedings:

> [...] can facilitate the 'opening up' of otherwise introspective professional values [...] It can help break down inward-looking cultures and paternalistic attitudes held by professionals and, in their place, encourage responsiveness to the concerns articulated by citizens.
>
> (Crawford 2004: 695)

The empirical study that is the basis of Crawford's arguments was conducted over 10 years ago (Newburn *et al.* 2002), when the shortcomings of lay involvement in referral order processes could still be overlooked as a problem of implementation, which YOTs were keen to work on. The problem is that, over a decade later, these expectations around the benefits of lay involvement remain as yet unrealised expectations.

Respondents' views about lay involvement

The value of lay involvement was a common theme for many YOT workers and community panel members. As referred to in the first section of this chapter, respondents often commented that, as 'outsiders', community panel members were able to 'think outside the box' and bring an alternative perspective to that of YOT workers. What is more, they often held the perception that because the community panel members are *not* professionals – and, therefore, are *not* in a position of authority, are *not* working to targets, and are *not* using professional jargon (but *lay* language) – young people see them differently and are more likely to engage in the process:

> I think it works having volunteers doing it, and I think it would be different if it was all professionals. It would feel more formal, maybe, and a lot of professionals would come with their own agenda and their own expectations of what that young person needs.
>
> (YOT5, WORKER1)

> The young people see it differently. They are sceptical of social workers, magistrates, whoever. I always make it clear that I am not in

> authority, that I am not a professional, with no legal training. They see us differently, we can talk to them in ways the professionals can't.
> (YOT4, CPM5)

By contrast, my interviews with young people suggest that they are more likely to engage in conversations (or 'open up') with 'their' YOT worker than with community panel members. In fact, I often found in my interviews and observations that young people have a more 'professional' (or 'detached' and 'disinterested') relationship with community panel members than volunteers and YOT workers are ready to admit. In this vein, when I asked whether she felt that the meeting would have been the same if the community panel members were not present, one young person replied: 'It made it a bit more professional, because me and [name of her YOT worker], we are always joking around' (YOT8, YP1). Another young person seemed to have no opinion about panel meetings, but when I probed further, asking about the regular appointments she had with her YOT worker, she commented: 'Oh, that helps me more! I mean, it's like I can talk to [name of her YOT worker] about anything. It helps a lot' (YOT12, YP3). Yet another young person, when asked '*If a friend of yours was asked to attend a panel meeting, what would you tell him/her about it?*', replied: 'Do it. The panels are the least important' (YOT5, YP1).

This should not come as a surprise. One should bear in mind that young people spend far more time with their YOT workers than with community panel members, whom they may only meet once during their referral order. Additionally, the decision to return young people to court (for a breach) lies in the hands of community panel members, and this, as mentioned in Chapter 5, is made very clear to young people. What is more, as documented in Chapter 5, while panel meetings often resemble courtrooms full of adult strangers, sessions with 'their' YOT workers usually happen on a one-to-one basis and in a much more relaxed and informal environment. Taken together, to the eyes of young people, community panel members appear more formal and professional than YOT workers – or, indeed, it was often clear to me that young people tend to see YOT workers as 'on their side' and community panel members as 'sitting in judgement'.

The meaning of lay involvement

> I have spent my life doing it at work, you see. I was with PricewaterhouseCoopers, a big consulting accounting firm, and latterly I led all the financial services teams in the City. I'd be in Tokyo, New York, the City, all the time. These problems come to you all the time from the clients and they can never articulate the problem, all they can tell you is the symptoms. So you have to sit down and work out the underlying causes, what you can do about it. You have to be very structured to do that and

> I know I am too structured for the panels, I know that. That's why I don't get cross – its my problem, not theirs.
>
> (YOT11, CPM3)

The above quotation reminds us that *lay* members of the community do not necessarily come to panels devoid of professional backgrounds and cultures. In fact, as warned by Santos (1982: 258):

> [...] one characteristic of informal dispute processing is that the third party (judge, mediator, or arbitrator) is not a jurist or legal professional. We therefore refer to such third party as a 'layperson'. But he or she may still be a professional and be employed in some other state bureaucracy. And since all state bureaucracies are structurally homologous and have the same operational logic, the latter may filter down into the argumentative discourse in the informal setting.

Further to Santos's concerns, later empirical studies have revealed that 'lay' members of the community may in fact have a *legal* background and/or experience with the criminal justice system. For example, Olson and Dzur (2003: 69) found that two of the three community members volunteering in one restorative justice programme (in the USA) had some sort of experience with the criminal justice system, 'one as an advocate for prison reform and the other as a former counsellor for young offenders in the division of youth corrections'.

In the present study, community panel members often reported that they were retired schoolteachers and/or had spent their whole professional lives working with children. Moreover, a couple of community panel members whom I interviewed had been magistrates, and another interviewee said she currently works in the police (at the DNA unit). Clearly, the idea that lay people do not see children through professional lenses, and even criminal justice lenses, is flawed. They may be vastly experienced in dealing with young people, or even in working with the youth (or criminal) justice system. Unravelling the actual benefits of lay involvement entails establishing what being a layperson actually means. My interviews and observations suggest that, on the ground and within the remit of youth offender panels, being a 'lay' person means '*not* being a YOT worker', and thus, hiding behind the 'community member mask' there may well be various other professional cultures.

The value of lay involvement

If community panel members often come to panels carrying their own professional attitudes and biases, what then is the value of lay involvement? As mentioned in Chapter 2, a common answer to this is that as members of the community, lay people have better 'local knowledge' than professionals (Dzur and Olson 2004). One YOT worker commented:

> They [the community panel members] know what goes on in their areas, they know the problems in their areas, they know many people within their areas [...] I think you lose a sense of a local library of knowledge if you get rid of them, because they know the areas, they walk the streets, they know areas young people talk about. They can talk about the places that the kids go to, they know what they do and how people see it.
>
> (YOT11, WORKER4)

On the whole, however, my interviews and observations do not provide support for assumptions of this kind. In fact, contrary to that, I found that YOT workers themselves usually have better local knowledge than community panel members. For example, in one of the few training sessions I observed, when the YOT worker was listing the places where young people could go for constructive leisure, one panel-member-to-be commented out loud: 'Are you serious? There's a youth centre on this street? That's the street I live on, how come I've never noticed?!' The comment caused a ripple of amusement around the room, and the YOT worker used the opportunity to say that through their involvement in panels, community members would learn a lot about their local area. Moreover, when I asked community panel members what they expected from YOT workers throughout a panel meeting, the following was a typical reply:

> Support, really. The YOT member of staff is there obviously to give advice if we don't know anything [...] I mean, sometimes, I can ask one of the kids a question and they can answer it and I can just sit there thinking 'what does that mean?' you know. Then I can ask a member of staff. For example the young person mentions the name of a youth club that I have never heard of, but the YOT worker will know about that club.
>
> (YOT1, CPM3)

In effect, '[i]t must also be remembered that criminal justice practitioners are also members of the community' (Clear and Karp 1999: 2), and in the context of referral orders, with the considerable amount of anti-social hours that the work entails, this appears even truer:

> [...] in a previous YOT I'd been reparation coordinator and court officer, and they did a pilot on referral orders there and I got really fascinated by it and became involved in the victim/offender mediation group that was beginning to emerge. [...] I got really involved in this new concept of restorative justice. Then I realised that if I was going to be working those kinds of irregular hours I wanted to be somewhere near my home, because you don't want to be travelling at 9pm, and then the job came up in [this YOT area].
>
> (YOT9, WORKER3)

All in all, the experience of youth offender panels suggests that we need to lessen (or adjust) our expectations regarding the values of lay involvement – a topic that I shall explore further in the next chapter, when discussing what lessons restorative justice programmes more generally can draw from the English and Welsh experience. For now, I shall keep youth offender panels under the spotlight, while turning the focus to another important and connected theme: the value of being a volunteer.

6.5 The value of being a volunteer

The value of 'being a volunteer' is inextricably linked to that of 'being a layperson' – so much so that, when commenting on community involvement, scholars often refer to both values interchangeably (see, for example, Crawford 2004). They should both be seen (and analysed) in connection and not in isolation. Having said that, I have purposely dwelt separately upon the two values in order to highlight one particular aspect of 'being a volunteer': the fact that volunteers *are not paid* for what they do. This was a key theme across interviews with YOT workers and community panel members, and one that I have explored with the young people too.

How adults view the voluntary status of community panel members

When Gill and Mawby (1990) were researching the role of volunteers in the criminal justice system, they asked respondents to indicate the two greatest advantages of having volunteers. 'The two most commonly expressed categories of replies', they report, 'centred around the particular advantages of having non-professionals, ordinary members of the community, involved in the service' (Gill and Mawby 1990: 38). In my case it went quite the other way around: when I asked YOT workers and panel members about the advantages of having ordinary members of the community involved in the referral order process, the most common replies centred around the particular advantage of them being *unpaid* volunteers. Indeed, for most of my adult respondents, the fact that panel members are 'not paid' has a positive impact on the young person. The following comments were typical of others:

> I think the use of community is one of the things that makes panels work, because it would be easy to replicate panels with a bunch of professionals, in terms of the process. But for me, one of the things that continues to strike young people when they sit there is these people are volunteering, they're not being paid to be there, or have any desire to be there other than to see that justice is done, and the young person moves on with their life and stops offending.
>
> (YOT2, WORKER1)

> In my introduction I say 'I'm sitting here, I'm a member of the community, and I'm not paid for sitting on this chair'. And you can see their mouth drop, because they're so used with teachers and social workers and so on. And, indeed, people from YOS all being professionals, telling them what to do. And here's somebody saying 'I'm doing this for free, just because I care about what happens to you'.
>
> (YOT9, CPM3)

Only rarely did YOT workers and community panel members divert from the opinion of the kind quoted above:

> I've never come across a young person saying it was more valuable for them because they're not being paid. The magistrates, it's the same for them, they're not being paid, they get paid expenses, same as panel members, but I don't suppose the young people even know that, and if they did, I don't suppose it would make a difference for them.
>
> (YOT11, WORKER5)

> I don't think it would make a difference to them if we were being paid or unpaid. I don't think it would probably enter their heads to think about that. I mean, I'm not even aware if the young people know that we're volunteers or not. I don't know if it's explained to them.
>
> (YOT1, CPM2)

As I shall argue in turn, such critical views are probably more accurate than the widespread idea that young offenders are pleasantly surprised to see that community panel members are not paid to sit on panels.

How young people view community panel members' voluntary role

On the whole, young people did not appear impressed by the fact that community panel members are volunteers. In fact, to start with, when I asked if they knew that panel members were not paid to be there, most of the young people I interviewed said they did not know – although, in some of these cases, I had observed their panel meetings, and I knew this had been mentioned (e.g. community members had introduced themselves as 'volunteers' or 'trained volunteers'). In his analysis of the pilot sites, Crawford (2004) found that community members at panel meetings would often both highlight their sincerity in their concern for the welfare of the young person and mention their own status as volunteers, '*implying something unique and important about the voluntary participation of local citizens*' (Crawford 2004: 699, emphasis added).

My observations suggest a rather different scenario: while community panel members clearly emphasise their sincerity in their concern for the welfare of the young person, they do not often explore the fact that they are volunteers. In fact, at panels, the reference to their own status as volunteers tends to be done in an *en passant* fashion – so much so that, as suggested above, some young people even 'miss' this information.

In turn, when I asked if the fact that panel members were not paid made a difference to them, only four out of the 25 young people I interviewed replied affirmatively:

> Yeah, shows respect.
>
> (YOT3, YP1)

> I had more respect for them.
>
> (YOT4, YP2)

> Yeah, they're giving up their time.
>
> (YOT10, YP1)

> Little bit, because they're just wasting their time.
>
> (YOT10, YP2)

All the others felt it did not make a difference, with only a couple of them giving more elaborate answers (than 'no' or 'doesn't make a difference'):

> No. It's how they come across that makes the difference.
>
> (YOT1, YP1)

> They're here to help me. Doesn't matter if they're paid or not paid.
>
> (YOT9, YP2)

All in all, there appears to be a gap between how adults think young people see community panel members and how young people actually see them. In fact, this study suggests that, on the whole, young people do not value community members *more* because they are volunteering. If anything, it is the panel members' willingness to help that they perceive as valuable; but then again, in their view, YOT workers are already there 'to help'.

The value of voluntarism

If it does not matter to young people whether community panel members are paid or not paid, what then may be the benefits of 'being a volunteer'? In 1949, Beveridge and Wells wrote about the importance of a voluntary sector for increasing civic participation in political life. Indeed, voluntarism has long been seen as an essential ingredient for participatory democracy. It has also often been tied up with the notion of 'the good society' inasmuch as it reinforces the values of mutuality and solidarity (Etzioni 1996). In fact, various claims have been made with regard to the benefits of volunteering, although it is worth stating that 'much of the work on volunteering and voluntary agency has been carried out by its disciples' (Gill and Mawby 1990: 22).

One typical claim is that volunteers are more likely to expose and criticise malpractice than paid employees because they are not dependent upon income (Morris 1969). In this vein, one of the community panel members commented: 'I think it is quite good, because as a complete outsider you are not restricted by the same rules. If I disagree I can say so. It does not affect my job, promotion, bonus, whatever. I am independent' (YOT12, CPM2). Some YOT workers also referred to the 'independence' of community panel members; they felt that through review panel meetings, volunteers were able to keep YOT workers 'on their toes':

> It could be [run just with YOT workers] – but it would be totally different. The community members bring neutrality, and they hold us to account. As part of the panels we have kids coming in to set contracts and to be reviewed. Panel members have a report. The front sheet is 'what you agreed to do'; the next two sheets are 'what is the progress'. So it will say 'Johnny met with a police officer to talk about the consequences of offending and he engaged well (or not)' or 'Johnny hasn't started his reparation yet'. And then the panel member will turn to me and say, 'It has been six weeks – why not?!' They are not afraid to say that. They know their role, neutral members of the community, holding the young person and us to account.
>
> (YOT11, WORKER1)

When analysing the Vermont Reparative Boards, Boyes-Watson (2004: 688) also drew attention to the possibility of public scrutiny of staff conduct, which from the outset appears to be one of the greatest values of volunteer involvement.

The 'independence' of panel members, however, is not as straightforward as some might think. In fact, examples such as that where the first review meeting was held some 10 months into the referral order (see Chapter 5) remind us that panel members do not even have control over when panel meetings take place. What is more, with training and experience, community panel members are likely to 'blend in' with YOT workers. I will discuss the professionalisation of community panel members in the next and last section of this chapter, but the following comment from a YOT worker summarises the point that I now want to make:

> There's a risk that panel members almost become quite staid in the role. Also a risk that if you haven't got a large pool of members, there's a risk they become more attached to the service, more attached to the YOT rather than maintaining their independence as community members. I hope we achieve that quite well. But a number have been there for a number of years, and then for me that begs the question of ... you know,

> their alliances are more with the YOT. They have built up relationships with us, so it's about whether they're able to challenge, whether they'd feel confortable to challenge me if I were presenting the report. Or whether, because of the positive relationship that we may have, whether it becomes a little bit collusive?
>
> (YOT11, WORKER2)

At the end of the day, perhaps the rather amorphous claim that voluntary work is an essential ingredient of 'the good society' is still the best way to go about explaining the value of *voluntary* community panel members. One community panel member commented:

> As an adult, knowing that people are still taking the time to help young people of today is the biggest thing that could ever happen [...] For people to give a couple of hours a week to say 'yeah, I'll help' is what we need as a society. The select few who think 'I can make a difference', rather than moaning and doing nothing about it.
>
> (YOT5, CPM3)

As Iris Young (1990: 168) reminds us, '[t]he city is a place of endless possibilities and stimulation but it is also a place where there is a social withdrawal and disengagement which can easily boil over into hostility. There is both an acute sense of difference and an indifference in the urban experience.' In this vein, I agree with the above-quoted community panel member: for me, it is the drive against indifference embedded in voluntary work that best explains the value of community panel members 'being volunteers'. Even if it does not matter to young people whether community panel members are paid or not paid (and my empirical experience suggests that it does *not*), I would argue that the participation of volunteers in youth offender panels is a message against indifference. But then, however persuasive, the claim that voluntary work is an essential ingredient of 'the good society' is 'practically impossible to test in any quantitative [and I would add qualitative] way' (Gill and Mawby 1990: 23).

6.6 The professionalisation of community panel members

Another limitation to the enthusiasm for lay participation and the involvement of volunteers in the process of youth offender panels is the professionalisation of community panel members. Indeed, as paradoxical as it may sound, while YOT workers and volunteers place great hope or expectation on the fact that community members do not wear a 'professional hat', a new (semi-)profession of community panel members may well be emerging.

'We need to keep it professional'

Commenting on the early days of youth offender panels in England and Wales, Crawford (2004: 700) drew attention to the fact that 'a core group of panel members are increasingly relied on for much of the work', and that, as a result, 'panel members may begin to look and behave more like quasi-professionals than ordinary lay people'. There is evidence of this (still) occurring today. For example, when providing me with the socio-demographics of their panellists, one YOT worker warned me that despite the list of 15 volunteers, they had only six 'hard-core panel members' whom they always 'use'.

In all YOTs I visited, the 'hard-core community panel members' tended to be those serving the longest – typically, the handful of volunteers who were there 'from Day 1' (i.e. from the very first youth offender panel), or who came shortly after that. In fact, the longest-serving panel members invariably had more experience sitting through panels than the referral order coordinators themselves. As experienced panel members, they usually have a higher 'status' among the pool of volunteers. The following comment from one YOT worker was typical of others: 'If I know I've got a particularly difficult young person with lots of different issues, I'll ask for an experienced panel member' (YOT3, WORKER1). In one of the 12 YOTs I visited, one of their longest-serving panel members even had a security keycard to get into the YOT office, just as any member of staff. When I asked one of her fellow panel members if she felt that YOT staff valued her work, the reply was: 'I don't even have a card to get into the office! [The other panel member] does, but I have to knock and wait for people to come and open doors for me, and I've been coming here for years. So no, they definitively don't' (YOT7, CPM1).

My interviews suggest, however, that it is not only a core group of experienced panel members who behave in a professional way (or gain a semi-professional status). Some panel members adopt a 'professional' attitude from the start. For example, I had the opportunity to interview a panel member before she did her first panel meeting, and when I asked about panel members staying in touch with the young people, she did not agree with the idea, adding that 'we need to learn where to draw that line and *keep it professional*' (YOT9, CPM1, emphasis added). The truth is that, whether among more or less experienced panel members, the 'professional boundaries' approach was common:

> There is only one reception area [in the YOT office], so sometimes you meet up in there [with the young person], which isn't good. *It isn't professional.*
>
> (YOT8, CPM1, emphasis added)

> Obviously a personal opinion – the danger is falling into sentiment. As soon as it gets sentimental, I see the boys' faces blank out. You have to

> keep it keep business-like. Much better like a Mafia deal. He's done that, we do this, you do that, it's a deal. No commotion: break the deal, prison; keep the deal, no record. There's a terrible temptation to tell them off, 'you shouldn't do that', 'you've done a bad thing' – they don't care if some old fool like myself says that. There's a deal on the table, 'take it or leave it'. The downside [of youth offender panels] is that challenge to stop my colleagues from slipping into sympathy or psychoanalysing.
>
> (YOT11, CPM4)

This comes as no surprise if taken in the context of their training programmes. For example, within the Foundation Programme,[7] volunteers have a whole session on 'professional boundaries' which includes the following guidelines:

> Stay in the professional. This does not mean be aloof and unfriendly. [...] But you are not a friend. You are there in a professional capacity to effect or support some sort of positive change. So make sure the boundaries do not blur. Avoid 'blurred' involvement – it is fine to accept a cup of tea, but is it professional to accept an invitation to dinner?

In fact, during interviews, my respondents would often refer to their training: 'When I trained, we were told we were to put things in place, but not get close to the young person. That is not our role' (YOT4, CPM4). While analysing victim–offender mediation schemes over a decade ago, Crawford (1997: 188) commented that:

> The proliferation of guidelines on training and standards of 'good practice' has led some commentators to the perception that we are witnessing a reformalization and reprofessionalization of mediation, which runs counter to the informalizing and deprofessionalizing declarations of many schemes and aspirations of early proponents.

I fear this may also be the case for youth offender panels. Nevertheless, in my opinion, it is important to distinguish between different types of training. I have found that apart from their initial training, panel members also receive 'top-up' training sessions, normally once or twice a year. What is interesting to note, however, is that these sessions tend to cover very professional (or 'technical') topics – for example, 'speech and language problems', 'child protection', 'drug awareness', 'gang culture', 'child and young adult mental health first aid', were some of the themes mentioned throughout my interviews. Indeed, except for the more recent push by the YJB to increase the restorative justice training given to YOT staff and community panel members (see Conclusions), top-up training does not focus on restorative justice work or panel work, but on YOT work. Community panel members appeared to enjoy this sort of training as they felt it helped them to 'be more professional' at panels.

The 'danger of professionalisation', it seems to me, is embedded in the type (and content) of training. I agree with Walgrave (2012) that facilitating a conference is not like organising a party with neighbours: skills are needed and, therefore, training to acquire those skills is also necessary, but if the aim is to have lay members of the public using a restorative approach to youth crime, the focus of initial and 'top-up' training should be on 'working restoratively'. Refresher training on the values of restorative justice from time to time is more appropriate than, for example, sessions on 'gang culture'.

The 'blended' YOT culture

> It's always challenging to ensure diversity, and I think one of the problems is that people come in diverse, but through their experiences of panel, they become more like YOT members, because their knowledge levels increase, their understanding of young people's issues increase. So if they come in and are quite hawkish in their approach, they tend to mellow because they start to understand more about what's behind the behaviour, and they start to empathise more with young people and young people's issues. So it is difficult to keep that diversity.
>
> (YOT2, WORKER1)

This comment from a YOT worker raises an important issue that has long been a crucial point of discussion within the volunteer literature: training and experience not only make volunteers more akin to the professional, but also communicate the organisation's ideology and values (e.g. Aves 1969; Gill and Mawby 1990). Indeed, the professionalisation of community panel members, apart from enhancing their skills and knowledge, also facilitates their assimilation of the YOT's culture.

This is particularly problematic in the context of YOTs and youth offender panels. While it may be short sighted to talk of a shared or unified 'YOT culture',[8] my interviews and observations suggest that YOTs are rather 'welfarist' oriented or, indeed, that YOT workers are very much offender focused in their approach to youth crime. By contrast, as argued in Chapter 3, youth offender panels are supposed to operate on restorative justice principles and values, and this includes operating in a way that allows for increased victim, as well as community, participation and ownership. The problem is rooted in the fact that through this process of 'professionalisation' and consequent 'culture assimilation', community panel members end up very much offender focused in their approach to panel work. The following comments exemplify the widespread idea among community panel members that their role is to help the young offender:

> I mean my job, inverted commas being job, is to support the offender. That's my role. I'm not here as a support for the victim.
>
> (YOT2, CPM4)

> You're purely there to help the young person.
>
> (YOT4, CPM1)

> The short answer to that is no, I don't think I'm there to represent the community, I think I'm here because I have the skills to persuade young people to engage in appropriate interventions so they won't reoffend. My focus is always on the young person [...]
>
> (YOT7, CPM2)

The dangers of professionalisation

The professionalisation of volunteers is not just a virtual or rhetorical possibility; it has happened in the past, including with the creation of new formal professions. The probation role in England and Wales, for example, was a voluntary one until 1907, when local authorities were permitted to employ probation officers: 'a clause made compulsory by the 1925 Criminal Justice Act' (Gill and Mawby 1990: 30). However, apart from the assimilation of an offender-focused 'YOT culture' – a problem that speaks to the restorativeness of YOTs and youth offender panels, and to which I shall return in Chapter 7 – what is so problematic about the professionalisation of community panel members?

According to Abel (1982: 304), '[t]he result will be yet another layer of professionals – relatively unthreatening to the existing constellation, eager to handle (and ultimately to monopolize) cases the latter do not want – who increase the dependence of citizens on occupational specialists'. Indeed, if lay members of the community are gradually turning into quasi-professionals, most of the arguments around lay involvement being better than professional 'intrusion' lose their strength. In this vein, it is hard to understand why restorative justice practices should seek to curtail the role of criminal justice professionals (Crawford 2002) and yet create a new class of 'professionals' (or quasi-professionals, as it were). If there is no such thing as genuine lay involvement, how can the involvement of community members be justified on the grounds of laypeople being better than professionals at certain tasks?

What is more, in the early days of referral orders and youth offender panels, it was hoped that the involvement of the community would militate against the managerialist pressures on youth justice (Burnett and Appleton 2004; Crawford 2004). With the professionalisation of community panel members, however, the creativity of practice tends to take a pragmatic and managerial form. Indeed, my interviews and observations suggest that when panel members were creative, this tended to be about 'getting through the day's business' (Crawford 1997: 135) rather than pursuing restorative goals. This was clear in the case, reported in Chapter 5, where community panel members appeared annoyed that they had to come up with the reparation ideas themselves. Their 'local-*local* reparation' ideas of young people helping out in their local school or church were some of the most imaginative and creative reparation agreements that I have seen across all research sites. However, it was about 'getting through the day's business', as community panel members only turned to this creative practice because that particular YOT was short on reparation schemes, for months had no reparation officer and the community panel members were not happy about this.

Ultimately, the professionalisation of community panel members – or, indeed, the creation of a new profession or 'semi-profession' (Etzioni 1996) – is not 'bad' (or 'dangerous') in itself, but it goes against the 'informalising' and 'deprofessionalising' ideals of community involvement in youth offender panels. It is, ultimately, a rejection of that diversity of backgrounds and perspectives so celebrated in making the case for lay participation and volunteer involvement in youth offender panels.

6.7 Concluding comments

With the development of pluralistic societies, the aim to define community as a uniformity or homogeneity of culture and identity becomes less feasible and desirable. Yet, in order to involve the 'community', restorative justice programmes need to be clear about what is meant by 'community involvement'. In youth offender panels, the involvement of the community is attached to the concepts of informalism, of lay involvement, of voluntarism (voluntary work), and of localism (or 'place'). In this chapter I have analysed these concepts in light of my empirical data so as to depict an overall picture of the role of the community in youth offender panels. I return to consider the implications of these insights for an understanding of the role of community in restorative justice in Chapter 7.

Notes

1 This is from one of the couple of interviews with young people that I recorded, hence the precision of the quotation.
2 Clear and Karp's three-dimensional notion of community resembles that of other scholars. According to Willmott (1987: 2, emphasis in the original), for example: 'A useful distinction can be made between the *territorial community*, defined by geography and meaning the people who live in a particular area; the *interest community*, a set of people with something in common other than just territory (the black community, the Jewish community, the gay community); and the *attachment community*, where there is the kind of attachment to people or place which gives rise to a "sense of community".'
3 Later in this chapter, I discuss some evidence that YOTs tend to have a small group of over-used panel members.
4 Boyes-Watson (2004) quotes are reproduced with kind permission from the American Society of Criminology.

5 In a couple of YOTs I visited, community panel members do not even decide who takes the lead: when informed about the day and time of a panel, they are also informed of who will be the leading panel member.
6 As Chapter 5 makes clear, I use the term 'theatrical' to suggest that the role of community panel members in the referral order process is more 'rhetorical' (or 'artificial') than real. It should be clear that by 'theatrical' I do *not* mean 'overly dramatic'.
7 See Chapter 5 for more details about the existing training packages for volunteers, including information on where these documents are made available.
8 For more in-depth analysis of organisational cultures in the inter-agency working of YOTs, see Burnett and Appleton 2004; and Souhami 2007.

References

Abel, R.L. (ed.) (1982) *The Politics of Informal Justice*, New York: Academic Press.

Ashworth, A. (2001) 'Is Restorative Justice the Way Forward for Criminal Justice?', *Current Legal Problems*, 54(1): 347–376.

Aves, G. (1969) *Voluntary Workers in the Social Services*, London: Allen and Unwin/BASW.

Beveridge, W.H. and Wells, A.F. (1949) *The Evidence for Voluntary Action*, London: George Allen and Unwin.

Biermann, F. and Moulton, A. (2003) *Youth Offender Panel Volunteers in England and Wales*, Online Report 34/03, London: Home Office.

Boyes-Watson, C. (2004) 'The Value of Citizen Participation in Restorative/Community Justice: Lessons from Vermont', *Criminology & Public Policy*, 3(4): 687–692.

Burnett, R. and Appleton, C. (2004) 'Joined-up Services to Tackle Youth Crime', *British Journal of Criminology*, 44(1): 34–54.

Clear, T.R., Hamilton Jr, J.R. and Cadora, E. (2011) *Community Justice*, 2nd edn, New York: Routledge.

Clear, T.R. and Karp, D.R. (1999) *The Community Justice Ideal: Preventing Crime and Achieving Justice*, Boulder, CO: Westview Press.

Crawford, A. (1997) *The Local Governance of Crime: Appeals to Community and Partnerships*, Oxford: Oxford University Press.

Crawford, A. (2002) 'The State, Community and Restorative Justice: Heresy, Nostalgia and Butterfly Collecting', in L. Walgrave (ed.), *Restorative Justice and the Law*, Cullompton: Willan Publishing.

Crawford, A. (2004) 'Involving Lay People in Criminal Justice', *Criminology & Public Policy*, 3(4): 693–702.

Crawford, A. and Newburn, T. (2003) *Youth Offending and Restorative Justice: Implementing Reform in Youth Justice*, Cullompton: Willan Publishing.

Dzur, A.W. and Olson, S.M. (2004) 'The Value of Community Participation in Restorative Justice', *Journal of Social Philosophy*, 35(1): 91–107.

Etzioni, A. (1996) *The New Golden Rule: Community and Morality in a Democratic Society*, New York: Basic Books.

Firey, W. (1945) 'Sentiment and Symbolism as Ecological Variables', *American Sociological Review*, 10(2): 140–148.

Gill, M. and Mawby, R. (1990) *Volunteers in the Criminal Justice System: A Comparative Study of Probation, Police, and Victim Support*, Maidenhead: Open University Press.

Green, S. (2014) *Crime, Community and Morality*, Abingdon: Routledge.
Harris, N., Walgrave, L. and Braithwaite, J. (2004) 'Emotional Dynamics in Restorative Conferences', *Theoretical Criminology*, 8(2): 191–210.
Hill, J. (1981) *The Use of Volunteers by the West Midlands Probation and After Care Service*, Birmingham: West Midlands Probation and After Care Service.
Home Office (2002) *Referral Orders and Youth Offender Panels: Guidance for Courts, Youth Offending Teams and Youth Offender Panels*, London: Home Office/Lord Chancellor's Department/Youth Justice Board.
Hough, M. and Roberts, J.V. (2004) *Youth Crime and Youth Justice: Public Opinion in England and Wales*, Bristol: The Policy Press.
Jackson, H. (1985) *Recruiting Volunteers*, London: HMSO (HORPU paper 31).
Karp, D. and Drakulich, K. (2004) 'Minor Crime in a Quaint Setting: Practices, Outcomes, and Limits of Vermont Reparative Probation Boards', *Criminology & Public Policy*, 3(4): 655–686.
London, R. (2011) *Crime, Punishment, and Restorative Justice: From the Margins to the Mainstream*, London: First Forum Press.
Maruna, S., Wright, S., Brown, J., Marle, F.v., Devlin, R. and Liddle, M. (2007) *Youth Conferencing as Shame Management: Results of a Long-term Follow-up Study*, Belfast: Youth Conferencing Service.
McCold, P. (2004) 'What is the Role of Community in Restorative Justice Theory and Practice?', in H. Zehr and B. Toews (eds), *Critical Issues in Restorative Justice*, Monsey, NY: Criminal Justice Press.
Ministry of Justice (2009) *Referral Order Guidance*, London: Ministry of Justice/ Department for Children, Schools and Families/Youth Justice Board.
Ministry of Justice (2012) *Referral Order Guidance*, London: Ministry of Justice/Youth Justice Board.
Morris, A. and Maxwell, G. (2000) 'The Practice of Family Group Conferences in New Zealand: Assessing the Place, Potential and Pitfalls of Restorative Justice', in A. Crawford and J. Goodey (eds), *Integrating a Victim Perspective within Criminal Justice: International Debates*, Aldershot: Ashgate Publishing.
Morris, M. (1969) *Voluntary Work in the Welfare State*, London: Routledge & Kegan Paul.
Musick, M.A. and Wilson, J. (2008) *Volunteers: A Social Profile*, Bloomington: Indiana University Press.
Newburn, T., Crawford, A., Earle, R., Goldie, S., Hale, C., Hallam, A., Masters, G., Netten, A., Saunders, R., Sharpe, K. and Uglow, S. (2002) *The Introduction of Referral Orders into the Youth Justice System: Final Report*, Home Office Research Study 242, London: Home Office.
Olson, S.M. and Dzur, A.W. (2003) 'Reconstructing Professional Roles in Restorative Justice Programs', *Utah Law Review*, 57(1): 57–89.
Phillips, A. (1995) *The Politics of Presence*, Oxford: Oxford University Press.
Pitkin, H.F. (1967) *The Concept of Representation*, Berkeley: University of California Press.
Riddick, M. (1984) 'A Voluntary Associate in the Probation Service', in G. Darvill and B. Munday (eds), *Volunteers in the Personal Social Services*, London: Tavistock.
Sampson, A., Stubbs, P., Smith, D., Pearson, G. and Blagg, H. (1988) 'Crime Localities and the Multi-Agency Approach', *British Journal of Criminology*, 28(4): 478–493.

Santos, B.d.S. (1982) 'Law and Community: The Changing Nature of State Power in Later Capitalism', in R. Abel (ed.), *The Politics of Informal Justice*, New York: Academic Press.

Souhami, A. (2007) *Transforming Youth Justice: Occupational Identity and Cultural Change*, Abingdon: Routledge.

Stockdale, E. (1985) *The Probation Volunteer*, Berkhamsted: Volunteer Centre.

Suttles, G. (1968) *The Social Order of the Slum*, Chicago, IL: University of Chicago Press.

Umbreit, M.S. and Armour, M.P. (2011) *Restorative Justice Dialogue: An Essential Guide for Research and Practice*, New York: Springer.

Walgrave, L. (2012) 'The Need for Clarity about Restorative Justice Conferences', in E. Zinsstag and I. Vanfraechem (eds), *Conferencing and Restorative Justice: International Practices and Perspectives*, Oxford: Oxford University Press.

Wellman, B. and Leighton, B. (1979) 'Networks, Neighborhoods, and Communities: Approaches to the Study of the Community Question', *Urban Affairs Quarterly*, 14 (3): 363–390.

Willmott, P. (1987) 'Introduction', in P. Willmott (ed.), *Policing and the Community*, London: Policy Studies Institute.

Young, I.M. (1990) *Justice and the Politics of Difference*, Princeton, NJ: Princeton University Press.

7 Towards a coherent framework for operationalising community involvement in restorative justice programmes

Having presented the empirical data and teased out some of the discrepancies between the theory and practice of youth offender panels, I now draw on the wider sociological literature so as to revisit restorative justice's problematic appeals to community introduced in Chapter 2. By doing so, I shall arrive at an answer to the central question motivating this chapter: what lessons can be learned from the English and Welsh experience?

As has been made clear from the start, this study was not intended as an empirical evaluation of whether restorative justice *works* or, more precisely, of whether community involvement *works*. My focus has been on what 'community involvement' means and what work it does in restorative justice – that is, on the question of '*how* does it work?' rather than 'does it work?' In this vein, I did not enter the field with the intention to examine the restorativeness of youth offender panels. I wanted solely to understand *why* (or, *for what purposes*) and *how* (or, *within what limits and under which conditions*) the community is involved in the referral order process.

Having said that, as I began to reflect on what lessons could be learned from the English and Welsh experience, assessing the restorativeness of youth offender panels became an inevitable development. Indeed, I have found this to be an important point, which one necessarily needs to go through before drawing inferences towards a coherent framework for community involvement in restorative justice. Therefore, the first part of this chapter is organised around what has turned out to be an essay on the restorativeness of youth offender panels – but one that is particularly focused on issues related to community involvement.

7.1 Are youth offender panels inclusive, informal and empowering?

> We get the report. I read it. We have a pre-meeting. We decide before the young person comes in how many hours' reparation, how many hours' consequential thinking, letters of empathy, and all that. Then once we have had the discussion [with the young person], we key in parents, etc., and then I close the meeting by saying, 'this is what we think you should do and why'. I always say 'why'.
>
> (YOT11, CPM5)

As argued in Chapter 1, to the maximal possible extent, restorative justice processes should be inclusive, informal and empowering. In restorative justice processes, *all* participants help to define the harm and develop a plan to repair it. They all feel free to 'talk things out' in an informal atmosphere where dialogue and genuine exchange can occur. Moreover, instead of having offenders 'taking' punishment 'given' by professionals, restorative justice processes empower offenders to 'own' their offending behaviour and to seek reintegration into their communities by taking every opportunity they can to put right the wrongs they have caused. In light of all this, and of the more detailed discussions in Chapter 1, the quotation above sums up the reasons why I would like to maintain that panels are *not* the inclusive, informal and empowering process that they were set up to be – or that many YOT workers and community panel members believe they are.

Decisions being made before the young person comes in, as well as contracts being explained *to* them rather than discussed *with* them, are not characteristics of an inclusive and empowering process. Having the process all organised and ready, to the point of contracts replicating report recommendations and all participants knowing the exact outcomes in advance, works against the aims of inclusiveness and informality. In fact, such practices replace the idea of a flexible and culturally appropriate process with a 'tick box' managerialist approach to justice (Shearar and Maxwell 2012). While explaining 'why' to the young people is an important step (see quotation above), it is still not the same as empowering parties to voice their concerns and to work towards restoration. Hence, the quick answer to the title of this section is 'no, generally speaking, youth offender panels are not inclusive, informal or empowering'. Nonetheless, the topic deserves a more careful treatment than that, and one which avoids simply repeating the discussions in previous chapters. In this vein, let us widen the focus of our discussion from youth offender panels (and the interactions between young people and community panel members) to the referral order process as a whole (and the interactions between young people and 'their' YOT workers).

It is important to note that '"formality" and "informality" are not "all or nothing" concepts' (Crawford 1997: 143). Within the 'sociology of organizations', for example, 'a good deal of attention has been given to the observation that [...] "informal" interaction was not just to be found occurring within "formal" organizations, but seemed to be quite crucial for the practical achievement of "formal" organizational goals' (Atkinson 1982: 86–87). The experience of youth offender panels suggests that the opposite may also be true: 'formal' interactions at some point in the restorative justice process may play an important role in the practical achievement of 'informal' restorative goals. Indeed, as described in Chapter 6, YOT workers and young people appeared to enjoy a rather informal relationship. In fact, young people often felt that their relationship with community panel members was more 'professional' than with their YOT worker, with whom they could 'joke around'. Perhaps, in a process where, ultimately, young people *have to* comply with the terms of a contract, the 'formality' of youth offender panels facilitates (or enables) their 'joking around' with YOT workers. One community panel member commented: 'The other aspect is that we can also be used as the sort of "bad guys", such as "If you don't turn up, the panel members might say something where you end up back in court"' (YOT4, CPM5). Similarly, one YOT worker commented:

> But I think the panel is quite nice, actually, because it's kind of like an extra layer, so it's not just me. [...] In terms of enforcement it does [make a difference] because we can say 'we will return you to the panel and you'll have to explain that to the panel'. And I think it just adds an extra layer before they get to court. A lot of young people view the panel as quite a serious thing, really, so from that point of view it's quite good and quite useful for caseworkers to be able to say 'well, it's not up to me; I have a process to follow'. [...] It can help our relationships with them, I think.
>
> (YOT6, WORKER1)

This is not to suggest that youth offender panels should remain formal, or that professionals are better able to build informal relationships than lay members of the community, but to say that the correlation between 'informal' and 'formal' actions is less straightforward than it might initially appear. As discussed in Chapter 1, a certain degree of formality in restorative encounters is always necessary to allow for all participants to have their say and to mitigate power imbalances (Quill and Wynne 1993). In this context, community panel members might not bring informality with them, but by being the 'bad guys' (see quotation above) or those who can return the young person back to court, they might unwittingly help to facilitate a 'buddy-type' relationship between the young person and her YOT worker – one that makes the whole process indeed less formal than other youth justice processes. Put differently, it may well be the case that young people have more of a say in the process of referral orders than was discernible given that I have not observed any of the one-to-one meetings between them and their YOT worker.

7.2 Are youth offender panels aimed at reparation?

> Take reparation. I've got a kid who's got mental health issues, I know he can't work in a group, he can do individual, but my most important thing is for him to keep appointments with me, see the drug workers, and stop reoffending. So you have to prioritise, and you know if they're giving him 20 hours of reparation, he's not going to manage that. The contract is not there to set them up; it's about balancing justice against the welfare need of the young person.
>
> (YOT9, WORKER1)

As argued in Chapter 1, restorative justice cannot be limited to a process. Intentions and outcomes are also important in determining the restorativeness of a given programme – and among all restorative justice's goals, reparation is deemed the most important. Indeed, the primary goal of any restorative justice initiative should be to encourage appropriate forms of reparation by offenders towards their victims and/or the wider (victimised) community. In line with this, as already mentioned, the stated purpose of youth offender panels is to 'operate on the restorative principles of responsibility, *reparation* and reintegration' (Home Office 2002: 5, emphasis added). In practice, however, the whole referral order process tends to focus on the programmes of intervention – and, thus, on a fourth 'R', that of 'rehabilitation' – at the expense of reparation. Indeed, the quotation above, which summarises many others transcribed in Chapters 5 and 6, suggests that, on the ground, youth offender panels are *not* primarily aimed at reparation.

As mentioned in Chapter 1, different kinds of actions can be considered reparation. For example, the offender can agree to make financial restitution to the victim, or to fix the window that she has broken, or to write a letter of apology. Reparations can also be made to the 'victimised community', which is usually achieved symbolically through community service. In any case, as also discussed in Chapter 1, the nature of reparation should be determined, as much as possible, by those affected by crime. Besides, imposed 'generic' solutions (or 'blanket-reparation' programmes) should never take precedence over more 'personalised' solutions (or individually tailored reparation packages). That is, to the extent possible, reparation activities should take into account the type of offence committed and the needs of the victim and/or the victimised community.

As will be discussed in the next session, victims rarely attend panel meetings and most of them do not get involved in the process in any other way, either because they do not want to or because they have not been contacted by the YOT. In turn, my data suggest that, in the context of youth offender panels, the most common form of reparation was 'community reparation'. As mentioned in previous chapters, however, these tend to be blanket-reparation programmes – that is, regardless of the crime committed, the young person involved, and the harms caused, YOTs tend to have a 'set menu' of reparation activities from which the young people may choose (or their YOT workers choose for them). This only confirms previous research. In a national evaluation of restorative justice programmes, for example, Wilcox and Hoyle (2002) found that most young people took part in 'community reparation' or 'victim awareness training'; in fact, they 'uncovered a marked tendency for restorative interventions to *over-rely* on community reparation' (Gray 2005: 951, emphasis added). Crawford and Burden (2005: 84), in their study of the Leeds YOT, found that 'it was often unclear how the reparation activity related to the offending behaviour itself and that it was more likely to be conditioned by the availability of specific schemes of community reparation combined with the young person's interests and preferences'.

What is more, in line with Crawford and Burden's (2005: 86) findings, my data also suggest that 'distinctions between reparative activities and activities aimed at addressing the young person's offending behaviour are neither self-evident nor clear for all concerned'. In fact, my respondents often described as 'reparation' those activities that are, in fact, aimed at addressing the young person's offending behaviour (e.g. visit to the Headway Project).[1] In this vein, one YOT worker commented:

> In terms of reparation, we've got a menu, but we have had panel members make suggestions. We had a panel member who worked at the BBC, who invited a young person to come and see what they do and write about it. So it's a different kind of ... this young person had never had that kind of opportunity.
>
> (YOT9, WORKER1)

Although there is nothing wrong with this type of interaction between young people and community panel members – in fact, it shows the possibility of community panel members acting as role models for the young people – this can 'send confused messages both to victims and offenders about the value and role of reparation within referral orders' (Crawford and Burden 2005). All in all, youth offender panels need to give more consideration to reparation.

7.3 Are youth offender panels victim aware?

> I'm very bitter about it, sorry! There is never, in the last 10 years, I have never seen a victim liaison officer in the YOT. And that is one of the major components of referral orders, that you bring in the victim's views to be included in the referral order, or at least discussed. But if you don't have a victim liaison officer, who's going to contact the victim? Victims are continually being let down by the system. I think in this process they are being re-victimised.
>
> (YOT7, WORKER3)

As discussed in Chapter 1, because they are inclusive, informal, empowering and committed to reparation, restorative justice processes are 'naturally' victim aware. Victims should be given the opportunity to participate in restorative justice programmes, if and to the extent they wish. As with offenders, they too should be empowered to have a say in how they think their own case should be dealt with. Also, as the most directly harmed parties, victims should be at the top of the list of 'reparation-receivers'. In this context, the quotation above draws attention to what is possibly one of the biggest flaws of youth offender panels: they have failed, for over 10 years now, to involve the victim. In fact, on the whole, if anything, they are only *slightly* victim aware.

Before I move on to present my criticisms, however, it should be highlighted that an in-depth analysis of victim involvement in referral orders is beyond the scope of this book.[2] The present study is about the role of *community* in youth offender panels – that is, in the field, my focus was not on victim attendance rates or on victim awareness strategies. The debate that follows, thus, is limited to an analysis of victim issues that are closely related to the role of community panel members. It should also be highlighted that, instead of making use of a narrow conception of restorative justice as 'victim-centred', I have preferred the notion that restorative justice processes are 'victim aware'. In fact, as discussed in Chapter 1, one of restorative justice's impulses is to move away from the 'zero-sum game assumption' whereby any enhancement in the rights or interests of the offender is assumed to be at the expense of the victim (Garland 2001; Hudson 2003; Strang 2002; Strang and Sherman 2003). What is more, by adopting a conception of restorative justice as 'victim aware' instead of 'victim centred', I have also recognised the need to move beyond the victim–offender labels towards exploring 'the multiple layers of harms done by the offending behaviour' (Hoyle, in Cunneen and Hoyle 2010: 10), including the harms done to the offenders themselves and their families. On balance, I agree that restorative justice 'should pay equal heed to victims, offenders, and the wider community' (Hoyle and Young 2002: 534). Hence, the criticisms that follow are not directed at YOTs' preoccupation with offenders per se, but at youth offender panels' almost complete disregard for victims.

The rate of victim attendance in restorative justice processes varies a great deal across different schemes, justice systems and offence types, and many are the reasons for victim non-attendance (Dignan 2005; Hoyle 2012; Strang 2002). Hence, any hurried generalisation about victims' involvement with restorative justice could lead to inaccurate conclusions. Having said that, several studies have found that victim attendance rates are low. For example, in their evaluation of the Thames Valley Police initiative in restorative cautioning, Hoyle *et al.* (2002) found a victim attendance rate of 14 per cent. In South Australia there has been a steady drop in the percentage of victims attending restorative conferences: between 2000 and 2007, for example, 'the rate of victim *non*-attendance has climbed from 50% to around 70%' (O'Connell and Hayes 2012: 313, emphasis added). And 'a substantial number of early restorative justice programmes, including the seminal Victim-Offender Reconciliation Program, focused on corporate rather than individual victims' (Richards 2014: 132). Such low rates suggest that more work needs to be done to close the gap between ideal and practice as regards victim involvement in restorative justice programmes (Karp and Drakulich 2004). This is definitely the case with referral orders and youth offender panels: as with many other restorative practices, victims hardly ever come to panel meetings.

In their evaluation of the 11 pilot sites, Newburn and colleagues (2002) found a victim attendance rate of 13 per cent. A few years later, in their study of the Leeds YOT, Crawford and Burden (2005) found an even lower average of 9 per cent. In the present study, I have only observed one panel meeting where the victim was present: the young person had physically assaulted her mother, and they came together to the initial panel meeting. My impression, though, was that 'mum' was invited to the meeting more as a 'community of care' for the young person than as a victim. The only difference between this meeting and all the other 38 that I have observed was that before the young person came in, the panel had a quick five-minute chat with 'mum' to ask her how she was feeling. The victim said that things were fine at home, praised her daughter and regretted that the case had reached the YOT (the young person's sister had called the police, but had no idea that this could lead to court hearings and a formal criminal justice disposal). It followed that the whole panel meeting was very much focused on the well-being of the young person: the reasons for her anger, her school attendance rates, the need for her participation in constructive leisure time, and so on.

In this context, some scholars have raised a concern that in the practice of restorative justice, 'there can be a tension between community involvement and victim participation' (Crawford and Newburn 2003: 241; see also Crawford 2004; Dignan 2005; Karp and Drakulich 2004). According to Crawford and Newburn (2003: 241):

> The community, it may be felt, is capable of bringing a victim perspective through its own role as an indirect or secondary victim of the crime. This expanded notion of victim feeds into restorative justice models of harm, but may limit the involvement of actual victims.

To put it differently, some scholars have raised a concern that in criminal justice settings still so resistant to victim participation, the 'involvement of community representatives [may] serve to side-line or operate at the expense of direct victim input' (Crawford 2004: 695). This, clearly, remains a legitimate concern. In fact, although referral orders have been operational for over a decade since the evaluation of the pilot sites, the truth remains that in the victim's absence, it is generally expected that the community panel members will bring a 'victim perspective' into the panel meeting. This is problematic.

First, community panel members often bring very limited 'victim perspectives'. As a YOT manager said, they tend to operate 'like any member of the public with their own perceptions of what the victim would feel like, but not with an awful lot of experience of talking to victims and hearing from victims' (YOT1, WORKER2). Indeed, community panel members often say 'this is how I would feel if it happened to me'; however, my observations suggest that, in the eyes of the young offenders, such guesses are not meaningful in terms of empowering them to empathise with the victim. Although there have been some well-intentioned attempts to better represent the absent victim, it is doubtful how much victim awareness young offenders gain from community panel members' symbolic reference to the direct victim. For example, in one of the YOTs I visited, community panel members use an empty chair in the room as a means of representing the victim throughout the panel meeting. A community panel member reported that once she was explaining the meaning of the chair to a young person – 'this empty chair is to remind us of someone that isn't in this room but has also been affected by your behaviour' (YOT4, CPM6) – and the young person giggled dismissively: 'Yeah … right!'

It is also perhaps worth mentioning that, in some of the cases observed, the young person had been given a referral order for possession of cannabis. In such cases, while stretching to identify a victim or the harm caused by drug possession, community panel members tended to make long, moralising speeches on how the community is severely damaged by drugs, and the young people appeared quite annoyed at having to hear this (probably, all over again). As Greene (2013: 383) did in her analysis of a restorative panel in the USA, 'I observed that the panelists were relentlessly adamant on this point and used a hysterical tone reminiscent of the public political discourse ballyhooing the so-called scourge that is "illegal" drugs'.[3] This, of course, is not a shortcoming specific to referral orders or youth offender panels (or community involvement therein), but speaks to more fundamental questions central to the restorative justice movement itself – for example, it reminds us that although restorative justice is often referred to as a completely new criminal justice paradigm where crime is seen as an act that causes harm to people (as opposed to a mere violation of criminal law), in practice it has been unable to question whether certain offences ought to be viewed as criminal (Pavlich 2005). As Greene (2013: 383) rather neatly puts it:

> All presently criminalized behavior retains its status as an offense. […] Rather than question whether an act is actually harmful, participants weave creative stories to explain where the pre-prescribed harm lies.

This, it seems to me, adds nuance to the artificiality of the role of community in restorative justice initiatives.

Moreover, community panel members have very mixed views about whether they should bring a 'victim perspective' or not. For example, as mentioned in the previous chapter, one community panel member commented: 'Not particularly, no. I mean, my job – inverted commas being job – is to support the offender. That's my role. I'm not here as a support for the victim' (YOT2, CPM4). To the same question, another replied: 'I think, as a panel member, I'm just myself. I'm neither for the victim nor for the offender. As a community panel member, I have to be objective' (YOT9, CPM1). A third one said: 'I like to believe that we can also advocate for that victim that is not there' (YOT1, CPM1). In turn, because community panel members have limited victim perspectives and do not necessarily agree that they should bring these to panels, the focus of the meeting quickly reaches the stage where full attention is drawn to the young person's needs.

In their study of restorative justice policing in the Thames Valley, Hoyle and Young (2002: 115) found that 'benefits to victims are most likely to be achieved when they attend restorative sessions', and that therefore 'the most crucial role the facilitator plays is to provide all potential participants with an adequate explanation of the restorative process to enable them to make an informed choice about whether or not to attend the session'. In the context of referral orders, community panel members are *not* trained to contact victims or prepare them for panels, and thus, unless the victim attends a panel meeting, they do not have any involvement with panel members. All the 'victim work' has to be carried out by a YOT worker.[4] Nonetheless, most YOTs I visited do not have a full-time victim liaison officer; instead, contacting/preparing the victim adds to the workload of busy YOT staff who are already grappling with their existing tasks of attending court, writing reports, attending panel meetings and recording all their work onto databases. Unsurprisingly, the task of contacting the victim is often neglected.

Hoyle and Young (2002: 116) remind us that even if victims are provided with sufficient information to make informed choices about attending meetings, some will decide not to attend, 'and then the facilitator needs to explore with the victim the alternative ways of participating: most obviously by making a statement and by receiving feedback after the session'. On only two occasions have I witnessed a victim statement being read at a panel meeting, and in both cases the YOT had a victim liaison officer. On the whole, youth offender panels' victim awareness efforts were quite limited: the panel tends to ask the young people to write a letter of apology and/or to attend victim-awareness sessions with the YOT worker as part of their contract. What is noteworthy, though, is that, according to my respondents, letters of apology are often not sent out to victims, either because the victim has chosen not to take part in the process or simply because the YOT has not been able to contact her. This was also apparent in other research studies. For example, in their evaluation of the Plymouth Restorative Justice Programme, Gray *et al.* (2003) found that 'these letters were never sent to victims and thus were no more than an exercise in "responsibilisation" rather than "restoration"' (Gray 2005: 951). On the other hand, it should be noted that there is still no robust evidence to support the effectiveness of victim awareness interventions. In fact, a victim awareness session with a victim worker is not itself considered to be a restorative intervention, although many YOTs seem to believe they are, and there is still no evidence about whether such sessions increase offenders' awareness of victims or only their ability to pay lip service to the victim at an eventual restorative meeting (Adler and Mir 2012). All in all, I would argue that youth offender panels are only *slightly* victim aware.

7.4 Are youth offender panels community based?

Drawing together the many points made in the previous two chapters provides a quick answer to the above question: no, if anything, youth offender panels are clearly *YOT* based, as opposed to *community* based. Panel meetings happen in places that are not meaningful to any of the participants; community members do not truly 'own' the process; reparation to the community is *not* a priority, and when it happens, community panel members are largely side-lined in the discussions about it; and so forth. Clearly, the process is not rooted in or focused on the community. Or, to use Nelken's (1985) types of community involvement, youth offender panels are not run *by* the community (*community as agent*), do not happen *in* the community (*community as locus*) and are not taken as *for* the community's benefit (*community as beneficiary*). However, restorative justice cannot assume a pre-existing community on which to base the restorative justice process; restorative justice processes should allow for broken communities to be restored and/or for new communities to be built (McCold and Wachtel 2003; Pranis 2003; Zehr 2002). This raises an important question: Do youth offender panels restore or build communities?

As introduced in Chapter 1, the 'fully restorative' (McCold 2000) model envisages a process from which people leave connected to one another, more committed to the common good, and more capable of resolving together problems and conflicts in their own community. Youth offender panels do not live up to this model. There are normally no prior social bonds to be strengthened or reaffirmed in the course of a referral order process, as community panel members do not tend to sit on panels involving young people (or supporters) who they are already acquainted with or who come from the same social milieu. Further, community panel members and young people (or their supporters) do *not* stay in contact with each other after the referral order process has finished. In fact, nearly every community panel member and YOT worker I interviewed deemed this inappropriate. When community members serve both as panel members and reparation mentors, they do not supervise the same young people whom they see in panels: as mentioned in Chapter 6, according to YOT workers and community panel members, there would be a 'conflict of interest' otherwise.

Interactions between community panel members and young people are restricted to panel meetings. They do not meet before the first meeting, during the course of the referral order process (except for panel meetings), or after the last meeting. If they bump into each other on the streets, community panel members tend not to acknowledge the young people. Hence, at most – that is, when panel members follow the same case all the way through – they will meet the young person perhaps three times in their lives, including quick review meetings, which may only last for five minutes. Clearly, youth offender panels build only 'aesthetic communities', as Bauman (2001: 71–72) terms them:

> [...] the common feature of aesthetic communities is the superficial and perfunctory, as well as transient, nature of the bonds emerging between their participants. The bonds are friable and short-lived. [...] One thing which the aesthetic community emphatically does not do is weave between its adherents a web of ethical responsibilities, and so of long-term commitments. [...] Like the attraction on offer in theme parks, the bonds of aesthetic communities are to be 'experienced', and to be

> experienced on the spot – not taken home and consumed in the humdrum routine of day after day.[5]

The 'bonds' between community members and young offenders are superficial and perfunctory, as well as transient; they are to be 'experienced' at the panel meetings, not taken home with a view to 'building' a better community. As one community panel member commented:

> For me, community isn't how you read it in the books. Maybe 50 years ago, but now, community is … I don't get on with my neighbour; they've got a dog barking all night. Where I live, I live in a tiny cul-de-sac, and I don't know half of the people that live there. I say hello, and they'll just walk past and ignore you, because they don't want to know their neighbours.
>
> (YOT5, CPM3)

Clearly, the involvement of community members in youth offender panels does nothing to change the kind of disconnected neighbourhood in which many live.

Having reflected upon the restorativeness of youth offender panels, the remainder of this chapter is devoted to considering the implications of the English and Welsh experience for development of a more coherent framework for operationalising community in restorative justice practices in general.

7.5 What lessons can be learned from the English and Welsh experience?

As described in Chapters 1 and 2, restorative justice is based on a philosophy that goes *against* professionalisation, standardisation, bureaucratisation, centralisation and formalisation. The involvement of the community in restorative justice programmes should work as an important enabler of these 'informalising' and 'deprofessionalising' goals. Nonetheless, despite the great theoretical emphasis placed on community involvement in youth offender panels, I have found that, on the ground, they appeared quite professional, standardised, bureaucratic and formal. That is, first and foremost, the English and Welsh experience shows that community involvement does not automatically translate into a community-based or community-focused process. Restorative justice programmes need to find ways of making community involvement more concrete than 'theatrical'. They need to lessen their expectations of lay involvement, while recognising the important role that remains to be played by professionals. Moreover, the experience of youth offender panels invites other programmes to rethink the benefits to community of its involvement in restorative justice initiatives. Finally, while embarking on the ambitious plan of moving 'from the margins to the mainstream' (London 2011), restorative justice initiatives should be prepared to struggle with the paradox of being a community-based process implemented within the formal and managerial justice system apparatus.

The danger of falling into 'theatrical productions'

> If I wanted to save money in youth justice today, I would scrap referral orders. While it is very well intentioned – I understand why it was put onto the statute books, and why we do it – but I don't actually think pound for pound, it is effectively reducing offending, or that young people value the process, meeting these independent community panel members. That's not how young people see it. I don't think that part of it is meaningful to them. We don't live in cosy little village communities anymore, we don't have tribes and elders … we don't have that remit. You can understand how the panel way of dealing with the naughty child might be appropriate – but we don't live like that anymore. In a sense, the young people have already appeared before a community panel in terms of the magistrate's bench, and they really, really hate being questioned about the offence again.
>
> (YOT9, WORKER3)

Through its stated purpose to operate according to restorative justice principles – that is, *as any other restorative justice-inspired initiative* – youth offender panels are committed to establishing more concrete and meaningful ways of involving the community in mainstream youth justice practice. However, because they borrow much from restorative justice's appeals to community, youth offender panels have also imported a rather 'romantic' idea of community. Indeed, as introduced in Chapter 2, the restorative justice discourse is often infused with an implicit, and sometimes explicit, communitarian nostalgia that emphasises community as a locale of like-minded and well-acquainted people – or as an 'urban village' of consensus and conformity (Young 1990, 1999). On top of that, as mentioned in Chapter 3, New Labour's criminal justice and penal strategies have been heavily influenced by Etzioni's (1995, 1996) communitarian perspective (Taylor 2011). That is, in one way or another, lurking in the background of youth offender panels is Etzioni's normative vision of what communities ought to look like. According to Etzioni (1995, 1996), we have overemphasised individual rights and liberties at the expense of responsibilities – or, put differently, 'individualism has gained too much ground' (Etzioni 1996: 40). His belief is that 'we have become preoccupied with our individual entitlement, the cost of which is the loss of a shared moral voice that provides both social control and a sense of community' (Green 2014: 77). This leads Etzioni (1996: 59) to advocate 'a regeneration of the moral order in societies that have lost it'. That is, to redress the excesses of individualism, he points to the need for *more* community in (American) society. One can accordingly identify in communitarian discourses of this kind, all at once, 'a romantic view of the past, a pessimistic one of the present and an optimistic view of our future capacity to influence patterns of human behaviour' (Hughes 1996: 25). The problem is that the communitarian ideology progressed by Etzioni:

> [...] underplays the nature and character of community structures and arguably fails to engage with contemporary conditions that foster particular forms of social relations. [...] [B]y failing to engage with current social conditions, the communitarian ideology is either potentially unworkable or potentially incompatible with the way people [now] live their lives.
>
> (Green 2014: 152)

Altogether, the hopes for youth offender panels were high. In times of late modernity, when diversity is essential and individualism is inevitable, panels were expected to realise the idea of a unitary community capable of dealing with its own problems. In fact, as suggested by the above-quoted YOT worker, youth offender panels are based on an ill-conceived and inadequate notion of community that disregards the late modern world around them, and which does little to make the involvement of the community more concrete than in other criminal justice initiatives (such as the magistrate's court). The result is a well-orchestrated theatrical production that pays lip service to restorative justice values, and where YOT workers take care of nearly everything; a group of white, middle-class volunteers *play* their part as 'community members', but do not make for meaningful community involvement; and the young people 'don't get it'. To avoid falling into such theatrical traps, restorative justice programmes need to start from a more concrete and up-to-date notion of community than youth offender panels have – or, to put it differently, they need to make community involvement more contemporary and real.

In this way, to start with, restorative justice programmes need to avoid the romantic vein in communitarian thought that seeks to restore the kind of community that featured in pre-modern societies. In their pursuit of a 'bygone golden age where no one had to lock their doors and everybody got on', communitarians have largely ignored 'the wider social, technological and cultural transformations that were brought about by the onset of modernity and which signalled the beginning-of-the-end for traditional forms of community life' (Green 2014: 5). Indeed, 'as a result of romanticised visions of the past, there exists an unconscious consensus that believes we can reintroduce social conditions typical of one hundred years ago to combat an entirely new set of social problems in an entirely new set of social conditions' (Green 2014: 131). As Frazer and Lacey (1993: 200) suggest, 'we have moved on from the small, homogeneous, stable communities [...], and any return to them seems not only unrealistically romantic but also powerfully unattractive given the repressive implications of life in unitary value-generating communities'. Indeed, the representation of a pre-modern world of relative simplicity and homogeneity is only possible, for example, if one ignores the exclusion of women or slaves from citizenship (Frazer and Lacey 1993). Or, as Kymlicka (2002: 259) puts it,

> [...] the problem of the exclusion of historically marginalized groups seems endemic to the communitarian project. As Hirsch notes, 'any "renewal" or strengthening of community sentiment will accomplish nothing for these groups'. On the contrary, our historical sentiments and traditions are 'part of the problem, not part of the solution' (Hirsch 1986: 424).

So, while in the popular imagination 'the past is subject of a selective nostalgia, of golden ages lost through industrialisation and post-industrialisation', the extent to which such harmonious communities ever existed is, of course, a matter of debate (Forrest 2009: 129). In fact, 'a bygone era of strong community and inclusionary citizenship is fictional' (Green 2014: 191). What is more, while appeals to 'lost community' (Bauman 2001) are often anti-urban, 'city life' exerts a powerful attraction that cannot be overlooked by restorative justice programmes.[6] In other words, restorative justice programmes need to acknowledge that we not only do not live in close-knit communities anymore, but also that this Arcadian ideal of community is the very opposite of what is attractive in the urban life experience. Indeed, we enjoy urban life, among other things, because cities are places 'where people stand and sit together, interact and mingle, or simply witness one another, *without becoming unified in a community of shared final ends*' (Young 1990: 240, emphasis added).

In this 'late modern' world, restorative justice programmes are likely to involve participants who have *never* met each other before, and who will *not* stay in contact after the process. This is not just typical of youth offender panels. In her analysis of victim–offender mediation schemes in Belgium and Spain, for example, Bolívar (2013: 208) found that 'while unknown-offender victims would more likely opt for direct mediation, known-offender victims would opt for indirect mediation'. According to her, this finding helps to explain 'why other *researchers have detected a majority of unknown-offender victims among direct-mediation participants*, contradicting the high proportion of known-offender victims described in victimisation studies' (Bolívar 2013: 208, emphasis added). That is, restorative justice meetings in general, and not just youth offender panels, more often than not involve people who are not acquainted with each other and who will not mutually befriend each other. In this context, the goal of restoring relationships (among them) or building communities (around them) does not make sense. The real challenge, in such contexts, is how to make these meetings *between strangers* a meaningful experience for all. In this vein, restorative justice programmes need to find the right balance between, on the one hand, supposing that participants will want to mutually befriend each other and, on the other hand, deeming inappropriate any 'beyond-office' relations among them. While restorative justice initiatives should not hinder the possibility of new relationships emerging – or discourage this, as happens with youth offender panels – in times of 'late modernity' and 'aesthetic communities', they should also not expect that participants will *want* to keep (or benefit from keeping) in touch. That is, restorative justice processes should run more *organically* and not be so prescriptive or restrictive.

One of the YOTs I visited, a few days before I left the field, told me about an interesting project that they are working on, one which may well achieve this balance between an Arcadian ideal of community and more meaningful community involvement. It is a mentoring project where, if they wish, young people will be allowed to stay in touch with one of 'their' community panel members[7] after the referral order is finished, with whom they will be able to work on CV writing, to receive advice for job interviews, to have someone to help them out with maths or English or whatever subjects they need help with for their GCSE[8] exams. From the outset, this idea makes community involvement more contemporary and real. Indeed, participants are not forced into a 'fake' ideal of homogeneous community, but they are given the opportunity to interact in a way that other criminal justice institutions, such as the magistrates' court, do not allow. Such a mentoring project could ultimately lead to the building of a new type of 'community of care' – a community of people who, before the restorative intervention, were *not* acquainted with the young offender, but who, after the restorative process, still 'care'. In Vermont, 'restorative re-entry programmes' have been designed to harness communities' capacities for reintegrating medium- to high-risk offenders (often sex offenders) (Fox 2012, 2014). Soon-to-be-released offenders are referred to programmes such as 'Circles of Support and Accountability' (CoSAs), which use a group of community volunteers to meet regularly and informally with the offender and serve as social supports. According to Fox (2012: 100), '[b]eing socially supportive could entail offering concrete assistance, but the crux of the program was an ongoing relationship within the context of the offender's everyday life'. Although these programmes are referred to with a certain enthusiasm (see Fox 2012, 2014), it remains to be seen whether this idea takes off, and whether such programmes could be coupled with other restorative justice-inspired initiatives (such as reparative boards or, indeed, youth offender panels).

Another lesson that the English and Welsh experience illustrates is that restorative justice programmes need to recognise the importance of 'place'. The idea of community as a 'place' may sound out-dated at first, but one needs to bear in mind that the restorative justice 'ethos' is heavily based on face-to-face interactions, and therefore restorative justice programmes will always have a geographic dimension attached to them; in a way, they will always be localised. What is more, there is evidence available through community studies 'that show the continued importance of place-based solidarities built around the idea of "community"' (Crow 2002: 5). So restorative justice programmes need to work out a 'late modern' notion of community, but at the same time, they cannot disregard the community's geographic dimension.

Now, some initiatives appear truly (and meaningfully) localised, such as healing or sentencing circles, which often involve aboriginals living on reserves and which are often held in those reserves (Griffiths and Hamilton 1996). Others are less meaningfully and more politically localised, as happens with youth offender panels. As discussed in Chapter 6, YOT areas (and criminal law jurisdictions alike) are defined by political boundaries, and 'from the point of view of community life, these legal perimeters are often without meaning' (Clear and Karp 1999: 26). Having said that, '[a]n ideal can inspire action for social change only if it arises from possibilities suggested by actual experience' (Young 1990: 241). In this vein, if we are to mainstream restorative justice – that is, if we are to accept restorative justice as a new paradigm of criminal justice, and not just an addendum at its margins – the likelihood is that we will have to work within such politically defined, meaningless places. That is, we will have to work from (or around?) the idea of 'postcode justice', as it is currently organised. The challenge, then, is not how to get rid of the concept of community as a place, but how to make it meaningful outside the 'restorative justice oasis' of restorative circles. This is of paramount importance, for example, if one considers the significant residential segregation by race, class and ethnicity (Boyes-Watson 2004: 689). One of the YOTs I visited is trying to make their panels more localised, as the manager explains:

> There is a rather curious cultural divide in this city which goes back longer than I've been here, which is simply there's an east and west divide in the city. [...] There were two football teams, one which is east, and west. And people identify themselves in east or west. So if you talk to [YOT area] people, they'll tell you they're east [YOT area] people or west [YOT area] people. [...] So I think that when they first set up this east and west [YOT area] stuff, it was an attempt to try and make a connection between the panel members and the young people. I think it was also trying to cut down the amount of travelling that the kids did around the city. But for me it hasn't gone far enough to make, you know, a really genuinely connect with communities. [YOT area] is now beginning to divide its delivery public services into three localities, which will be north, east and west. And my intention is to try and mirror the recruitment of more volunteers into our panels, and to try and get a much tighter connect between what I've just been describing.
>
> (YOT1, WORKER2)

Fennell (1997: 90) reminds us that Sheldon (1948), in a study of elderly people after the Second World War, 'defined a close relative as someone who lived within five minutes' walking distance, being a measure of the distance a hot meal could be carried from one dwelling to another without reheating'. The example serves to show to what extent the idea of 'community as a place' may be archaic. Indeed, the task of balancing a 'late modern' concept of community against its geographic dimension is a difficult one. In this context, while recognising the importance of place, restorative justice programmes need also to consider that, in our times, people's sense of belonging (or 'collective identity') is often de-localised (Thompson 1996). Restorative justice programmes should not overlook the importance of family links, friendship and other intimate ties 'that extend well beyond neighbourhood boundary lines' (Clear and Karp 1999: 131). In this context, the experience of youth offender panels shows that their emphasis on community involvement 'through lay (but trained) members of the community' has side-lined the importance of involving the offender's 'community of care'. In other restorative justice practices, such as family group conferences, the community of care is always involved and has to take on some of the responsibility, and this is one of the reasons why they have been considered the most fully restorative of all restorative justice programmes (McCold 2000; Zinsstag 2012).

If we are to keep away from romanticised visions of the past – that is, if restorative justice programmes are serious about making community involvement more contemporary and real – our notions of this community of intimates cannot be confined to traditional family arrangements. Indeed, one must bear in mind that scattered throughout much of the communitarian literature – which, as mentioned already, heavily influences restorativists' perception of community – is a lament for the breakdown of traditional two-parent families (see, for example, Etzioni 1995, 1996, 1998). Nevertheless, in the world we now inhabit, 'the family structure has evolved in response to important changes in the political, social and cultural landscape' (Green 2014: 157). Indeed, in times of 'late modernity', 'divorce and single-parent families, homosexuality and same-sex relationships; choosing to live alone for longer or indefinitely became more socially tolerated and legally available' (Green 2014: 158). That is, the family structure is increasingly more fluid and restorative justice programmes need to be sensitive to this diversity. What I am saying is that inviting 'mum' and 'dad' will not always be the best or only option to ensure the involvement of the young offender's (or the victim's) 'community of care'.

In fact, in times where the internet (and other communication technologies) 'increasingly disconnects the individual from the constraints of birth, family or environment', the task, crucially, becomes one of 'understanding how belonging [or social connectedness] is experienced in contemporary society' (Green 2014: 136). In his attempt to do so, Pahl (2000: 12) suggests that friendship (and not family links) 'is sure to grow in social and political importance as traditional forms of social glue decline or are modified'. According to him, on the one hand, while family and kin links get geographically dispersed, '[local] friends may be taking over various social tasks, duties and functions from family and kin, simply out of practical necessity' (Pahl 2000: 8). On the other hand, for him, the meaning of friendship vis-à-vis that of family links has changed: nowadays, 'we are even prepared to judge the quality of our relationships with kin on the basis of some higher ideal of whether we can be closer to them as friends' (Pahl 2000: 8). Despite all this, in both restorative justice theory and practice, the notion of a community of care for the victim or the offender has been tied too closely to the ideal of *family* involvement, perhaps because the role of the community of care is more insistently discussed in the context of *family* group conferences. Be that as it may, in the practice of restorative justice, particularly when restorative justice is used with young offenders, the assumption has been that the involvement of their parents is desirable. Although this may well be true (for the majority of cases, even), young people need to be heard about whom they consider to be their 'significant others'. It may not always be their parents, but a friend, a school teacher, a cousin, a boyfriend or girlfriend, a roommate or a flatmate. Accordingly, in other practices, facilitators are trained to brainstorm together with the parties about whose presence would be useful. For example, in their *Handbook for Facilitating Peacemaking Circles*, Fellegi and Szegó (2013) suggest that circle keepers should:

- discuss the list of the possible participants with the legally concerned parties (i.e. with the victim and the offender); [...]
- encourage the parties to suggest people as supporters, community members and professionals by explaining the possible advantages of involving extra people (e.g. they can add extra resources, knowledge, new perspectives, can help 'bridging' the opposing sides, can raise empathy and understanding towards each other and the underlying issues, etc.);
- give priority to suggestions coming from the parties about the persons they propose to invite; [...]

This is overlooked in the process of referral orders, which, as already mentioned (see Chapter 3), may include a court *order* for 'mum' (or another 'appropriate person') to attend panel meetings.

Finally, while Boyes-Watson (2004: 688) argues that 'meaningful and substantial citizen participation in restorative justice programmes requires policies that support volunteer participation', the experience of youth offender panels suggests that it is not enough to recruit a significant volunteer presence within the system.[9] Volunteers have to be deployed, and not as actors performing a script produced and directed by professionals. They need a true degree of autonomy. If their participation is not to be perceived as 'tokenistic, pointless or a waste of time', volunteers 'need to feel, not only supported and valued, but also that their time commitments are meaningful' (Crawford 2003: 313). In the experience of youth offender panels, the efforts to draw on non-professional volunteers have not been enough. In fact, as discussed in further detail below, while delivering a theatrical production, youth offender panels have not experienced a real transference of responsibility from professionals to lay people. Other studies have also warned against the artificiality of community involvement in restorative justice initiatives (although usually *en passant* and whilst trying to make another point). For example, in her recent examination of 13 different restorative justice programmes in the USA (ranging from victim–offender mediation schemes to restorative conferencing), Greene (2013: 382) found that 'community participation is perfunctory, serving only to observe a conference between the two main parties (victim and offender)'.

This further suggests that the danger of falling into 'theatrical productions' may haunt other restorative justice programmes across the world.

Lay involvement and the role of professionals

As discussed in Chapters 5 and 6, the relationship that young people have with community panel members tends to be more formal (or, indeed, more 'professional') than the relationship they have with 'their' YOT workers. The experience of youth offender panels also reminds us that a 'layperson' may still be a professional – in fact, lay people may bring their own *professional* attitudes and biases to the process. Moreover, while it is often assumed that lay members of the community have better 'local intelligence' or 'personal knowledge' than professionals do, my interviews and observations suggest that YOT workers usually have better 'local knowledge' than community panel members. This, however, should not discourage the involvement of lay people in restorative justice processes: as argued in previous chapters, one cannot overlook the explicitly democratic values of lay participation (Dzur 2008). What the experience of youth offender panels suggests, though, is that we need to 'amend' our expectations for lay involvement, while *recognising the important role that remains to be played by professionals.* In fact, before being able to experience a genuine transference of responsibilities from professionals to lay people, we need to clarify the roles that professionals play vis-à-vis community members in the restorative process.

As Bauman (2001: 46–47) notes, in current times of 'liquid modernity':

> [...] nothing in the place stays the same for long, and nothing endures long enough to be fully taken in, to become familiar and to turn into the cosy, secure and comfortable envelope the community-hungry and home-thirsty selves have sought and hoped for. [...] Gone is the friendly postman, knocking on the door six days a week and addressing the inhabitants by their names [...]

What is more, as 'individuals gained access to media products, they were able to keep some distance from the symbolic content of face-to-face interaction and from the forms of authority which prevailed in the shared locales of everyday life' (Thompson 1996: 97). It follows that '[i]ncreasingly they gained access to what we may describe, in a loose fashion, as "non-local knowledge"' (Thompson 1996: 97). In fact, in times of 'late modernity', lay members of the community may well have more '*non*-local knowledge' than 'local knowledge'. In this context, it may well be the case – and the experience of youth offender panels provides evidence for this – that professionals have better 'local knowledge' than lay members of the community, *if for no other reason than because they ought to*. With nothing in the place staying the same for long, and in times of greater access to 'non-local knowledge', it is reasonable to expect that professionals who are trained, paid and have in their job description the responsibility to keep up to date on local issues, are more likely to know what is going on in a given 'community' at any one time than lay members of that very same community.

The idea that lay members of the community have better local knowledge also 'implies that lay participants are genuinely embedded in local interactions, interests, and normative orderings' (Crawford 2004: 697). This, in turn, implies that restorative justice programmes will be able to recruit a *representative* composition of lay volunteers, or a true 'blend of experiences'. Nevertheless, the experience of youth offender panels shows that, in practice, the recruited community members may represent a very limited section of the population living in that community, and thus have little in common with the offender and/or the victim and the lives they lead. In fact, professionals may have more in common with the offender and/or the victim, or may be better able to 'speak their language', than lay members of the community. Although I have not meant to be literal about the term 'language', this argument brings me back to the only panel meeting that I observed where the victim was present. In this case, 'mum' (the victim) was from Bangladesh and spoke little English. This was not a problem because the young person's *YOT worker* had a Bangladeshi family background and spoke Bengali! Indeed, in light of growing diversity in the workplace, it is reasonable to argue that professionals may well be more representative of the community than lay members of the community who have the time to volunteer. As Gill and Mawby (1990: 24) argue:

> [...] as accepted by proponents of voluntarism, volunteers tend to be drawn predominantly from the middle classes. There is then no reason to suppose that overall the helper-helped divide will be less, or its impact less stigmatic. Indeed, if employees in welfare agencies, as members of the semi-professions [...], consist of a disproportionate number of those from lower social-class backgrounds it might be that the divide is *greater* between volunteers and clients.

Restorative justice's appeals to community may have served the purpose of helping to dichotomise restorative and conventional criminal justice practice, as the emphasis placed on community involvement seems much greater in restorative justice discourses, but they have not helped to clarify the role that professionals play vis-à-vis community members in restorative justice processes. In fact, while increasing community participation has become a 'restorative justice mantra', restorative justice theorists largely ignore the role of professionals in restorative justice practice. It is important to note the irony that 'professionals have played a dominant part in initiating many restorative justice programs' (Olson and Dzur 2004: 139), as they have in enabling community participation in restorative justice experiments of all kinds (Bazemore 1998; Olson and Dzur 2003).

The truth is that 'restorative justice cannot get along without professionals' (Olson and Dzur 2004: 139). All restorative justice initiatives seem to have some kind of professional involvement – even discussions of the most genuinely community-based experiments with restorative justice, such as sentencing and peace-making circles, report crucial roles played by professionals (see, for example, Bazemore 1998; Fellegi and Szegó 2013; Weitekamp 2013). Indeed, distancing professionals from the process of restorative justice is neither feasible, nor is it necessary or desirable. Accordingly, I think, the commitment to lay participation does not entail a commitment to de-professionalisation. Quite the contrary, professionals may well play crucial roles in increasing and improving community involvement in restorative justice practice as they will normally be responsible for the recruitment, training, engagement and overall coordination of community members (Olson and Dzur 2003). In this context, the role of volunteer coordinators is crucial: 'organizing volunteers is a highly skilled task requiring expertise and specific training' (Gill and Mawby 1990: 116). The task of 'thinking' the involvement of the community cannot be an extra burden upon an already overloaded worker, as was often the case in the YOTs I visited.

Moreover, by balancing lay participation with a concern for individuals' rights, professionals may help restorative justice programmes to avoid some of the pitfalls of earlier experiments with informal justice (Abel 1982). For example, professional intervention in restorative justice practice may be key to stopping powerful parties from taking advantage of less powerful parties, or preventing personal prejudices from derailing restorative encounters (Olson and Dzur 2004). It may also help to control lay people's own professional attitudes and biases, by keeping them on track in their role as members of the community in a process aimed at restoration. As argued by Olson and Dzur (2003), reforming the criminal justice system towards restorative justice entails *reconstructing* (but not eliminating) professional roles – or indeed creating new 'restorative justice professionals' – in a way that professionals come to share authority and responsibility with lay members of the community. Professional expertise, we must remember, 'can be directed toward facilitating public participation and control' (Olson and Dzur 2004: 147). Hence, instead of dichotomising lay participation and professionalism, restorative justice programmes should reflect on the possibility of productive synergies between professionals and community members. Clearly, in youth offender panels this is not happening. On the contrary, youth offender panels have dichotomised the role of YOT workers and community members, based their working relations on discourses that do not reflect the reality (for example, on the idea that 'at the end of the day, it's up to the panel members to decide'), and as a result, they fall into a theatre production where volunteers copy and paste the ideas of YOT workers.

All in all, the restorative justice movement owes much to professionals. Instead of ignoring their roles, then, restorativists should reflect on how useful professionals may be in restorative justice programmes that are truly committed to lay participation. More research should be carried out to explore the question of what professional tasks are entailed in successfully facilitating greater community involvement in restorative justice programmes. In this vein, professionals may need to carry out completely new tasks that reflect the value of community participation – and here one could include the crucial tasks of 'getting community members to participate', 'attending to the quality of their participation', 'being concerned about whether participants are representative of the larger community', and so on (Olson and Dzur 2004: 161–162).

Rethinking the benefits to community

Restorativists generally promote the potential for restorative justice programmes to restore broken communities or to build (new) strong and peaceful communities (McCold and Wachtel 2003; Pranis 2003; Zehr 2002). Lurking behind such claims are the intertwined beliefs that processes of restorative justice allow for members of the community to interact and feel connected to one another, thereby becoming more aware of (and committed to) the common good, and consequently becoming more capable of resolving problems and conflicts in their own community. It is often argued that community involvement in restorative justice practices strengthens or reaffirms social bonds, which should increase community skills to develop communal responses in the aftermath of crime. The experience of youth offender panels, however, invites other programmes to rethink the benefits to community of its involvement in restorative justice initiatives.

As argued before, whilst communities may well be formed around a process of restorative justice, perhaps these will more often than not be 'aesthetic communities' (Bauman 2001). Indeed, in times of 'liquid modernity', where everything is so changeable and reversible, it is not difficult to imagine participants shaking hands at the end of a restorative justice meeting and then never meeting each other again; in fact, this is precisely how youth offender panels work. What is more, the experience from youth offender panels reminds us that in urban, 'late modern' contexts, distrust and risk do permeate social relations. As discussed in Chapter 5, some people even choose to serve as panel members in a neighbouring area/town/borough to reduce the chance of knowing the young offenders, and just as the evaluation of the pilot sites suggests, I have found that this was often explained in terms of concerns for personal safety and reprisals, or 'in terms of the inappropriateness of exerting power and authority over those with whom they have close social relationships' (Crawford 2004: 701). This may be reciprocal: young people and/or their parents may well choose not to come to panels where they know the 'panel people'; in fact, we should remember the case reported in Chapter 5 where a mother refused to attend a panel because she had understood that the two 'community members' would be people from her estate, who would end up knowing about her child's offending. She did not want that to happen.

As argued by Crawford (1997: 64), and as I have discussed before, the 'community-based rhetoric of current policy discourse speaks to, and echoes, a pre-modern age, of tradition, informality, homogeneity, and mutuality'. However, do we really want to revive traditional communities where members could not dissent from the dominant moral voices therein? Or can restorative justice live with the fact that its programmes may often only be able to create aesthetic communities – where there are no long-term commitments, but where offenders (and, it is hoped, victims) are truly heard (perhaps for the first time) and supported (throughout the duration of the process)? The world we now inhabit is a world:

> [...] where people choose their membership of this or that community; where people have multiple memberships of different communities; where people enter, exist and adapt their community to suit their needs; and where people construct and reconstruct their identities in response to an ever-changing social landscape.
>
> (Green 2014: 138)

That is, the world we now inhabit would seem one far more compatible with the idea of aesthetic communities than is the case with the romanticised image of community promoted by (most versions of) communitarianism. Earlier discussions about the importance of restorative justice programmes working out a modernised conception of community are again relevant here.

It should be noted, however, that this kind of 'on-the-spot' experience of restorative justice is more likely to occur in practices, such as youth offender panels, where the 'community of care' is *rarely included* (in fact, in the case of youth offender panels, one could argue, *nearly excluded*). Indeed, 'the restorative goals of building social capital, repairing relationships and increasing offender attachment to the community' are more likely to occur through the participation of neighbours, teachers, friends, relatives and other 'significant others' than through the sole involvement of 'strangers' (Boyes-Watson 2004: 691). In her analysis of the Vermont model, Boyes-Watson reached similar conclusions. She argues that boards should be cultivating two different types of volunteers: those who are recruited, trained and serve on a regular basis (just as community panel members in youth offender panels); and those who are invited to a specific meeting because they know the person directly involved in the case (that is, the 'community of care') (Boyes-Watson 2004: 691–92). Indeed, for her, the absence of the community of care 'hampers the capacity of boards to build long-term social bonds with offenders and to support victims over time'.

In this context, while operationalising community involvement, restorative justice programmes should not limit themselves to the involvement of lay members of the community helping to shape (and monitor) restorative plans; for all the reasons discussed above and in previous chapters (particularly in Chapter 2), the 'community of care' of both offender and victim *should* be included.[10]

Another lesson illustrated by the experience of youth offender panels is that instead of transforming the community at large, restorative justice programmes may be more readily beneficial to the internal community of volunteers. This, I would argue, is an important achievement in itself. Indeed, if we consider other, more conventional ways of involving the community in mainstream criminal justice practice – for example, through the participation of community members as silent jurors or as witnesses – in very few of them will community members leave the process feeling 'transformed'. In the context of youth offender panels, community panel members often reported that they enjoyed doing panels because they *learn* more about the underlying causes of youth offending, about the youth justice system and about their local area. Others have shared with me their plans to move on to paid work within the youth justice system – and their experience as community panel members will certainly help them in the pursuit of their career goals. Moreover, some of the retired community panel members felt that youth offender panels had taken them away from a life of sitting in the house, doing nothing. As Boyes-Watson (2004: 687–688) puts it, 'I believe it is important for citizens who do not commit crime to meet and get to know those who do, in order to understand their civic responsibilities in the prevention and reduction of future crime'. However, whether this has the actual benefit of transforming the 'whole' community, I am not sure, and the experience of youth offender panels does not provide any answer to this. The truth remains that 'social transformation and community empowerment through mediation [and, indeed, through any restorative justice programme] are difficult to assess' (Crawford 1997: 180).

The risk of giving restorative processes a 'justicy' flavour

> I still think we've got the referral order wrong. It seemed to me it was fundamentally flawed when the government introduced it. What they were really intended to do was to reproduce the model of the Scottish panel, which actually never went anywhere near a court at all but it was about identification that you're actually dealing with a child in need, and what you needed to do was to bring the family and the child into a support social care panel. But that's not anywhere near the court. But so we're sort of doing that, but by bouncing them into court, and so taking kids into court and then everybody knows they've come out with a

> referral order. So what is the point of it? And so we're giving it a '*justicy*' flavour and actually we're then wanting to engage in a restorative process. So for children and their families who are not familiar with all this, I think, we start off with them being thoroughly confused: they've been marched into court, they've been marched out again to go to a different place. And I think that's quite difficult for the panel then to engage with them, when there's a sort of an overarching, the court's got the control over this, but actually the panel is supposed to then have control of the order. So, I think the government gave us a really flawed bit of quick to work with. Having said that, it was a first serious attempt at community-based restorative justice.
>
> (YOT1, WORKER2, emphasis added)

Certainly, much of what has been said throughout this chapter relates very closely to the reality of a youth justice system – that of England and Wales – which, on the whole, is not driven by restorative justice principles. As argued in Chapter 3, referral orders and youth offender panels were an attempt at introducing elements of restorative justice into the heart of a youth justice system that was (and still is) heavily influenced by the 'populist punitiveness' (Bottoms 1995) and the 'managerialist pressures' or 'performance indicator culture' of our current times (Crawford and Newburn 2003; Earle and Newburn 2001; Matthews and Pitts 2001). On the one hand, in terms of its readiness to incarcerate children, for example, 'England now comprises one of the most punitive youth justice sites in the western world' (Goldson 2010: 170). On the other hand, youth justice practice in England and Wales is 'increasingly managerialized, target-driven, audit conscious and performance-indicator oriented' (Goldson 2010: 168) – all quite contrary to the informalising and deprofessionalising goals of restorative justice. Having said that, there are many non-restorative youth justice systems across the world seeking transformation in the light of restorative justice principles (O'Mahony and Doak 2009) – that is, seeking to introduce a restorative and community-based process within an otherwise punitive, formal and managerial youth justice system.

Accordingly, the quotation above illustrates one important lesson from the experience of youth offender panels: while trying to move 'from the margins to the mainstream' (London 2011), restorative justice programmes run the risk of giving a 'justicy' flavour to what should be an informal, community-driven process. That is, instead of challenging the 'managerialist pressures' on youth justice, and its obsessive tensions over whether to adopt notions of welfare or punishment, when introduced into the heart of a *non*-restorative youth justice system, restorative justice programmes may end up contaminated (and confused) by these very same non-restorative traits.

In this context, as my empirical data demonstrate, young people are not clear about the restorative goals of referral orders and youth offender panels, and have blurred views of the role of community panel members. This, as suggested by the above-quoted YOT worker, should come as no surprise: they have already been to the police and to court; they have already told their 'story' to the police and to a bench of members of the community (the magistrates); they have already been sentenced; and then they are sent to another place (the YOT), where they again have to meet with some (old, white, middle-class) 'members of the community', who will 'sentence' them to sign a 'contract'. What is more, there is nothing to prevent them from being on a referral order and, at the same time, for example, having to appear in court for another offence. Indeed, as if the mixed messages conveyed by the referral order process were not enough, young people are often experiencing court procedures and youth offender panel procedures at the same time. Within this remit of conflicting practical goals and discourses, the chances of them having a truly restorative experience, and of understanding the role of community panel members therein, are minimal.

While moving from the margins to the mainstream, restorative justice programmes also need to be aware of the risk of net widening (Roberts and Roach 2003). If restorative justice initiatives are introduced into the heart of the youth justice system only to deal with low-level crime – such as the many 'drunk and disorderly' cases that I have observed in youth offender panels – then all that we are doing, really, is bringing community members into a formal process, which is heavily controlled by professionals, to deal with problems that should not be dealt with anywhere near the youth justice system. It should be noted that net widening has been the experience in many past penal reforms (e.g. suspended sentence, parole, community corrections, etc.) in the UK and elsewhere. For example, in the UK, '[r]ather than diverting offenders away from prison, the suspended sentence was applied to those who would normally receive some other form of non-custodial sentence' (Green 2014: 49). In the USA:

> Benevolent penal reforms in particular have produced greater governmental ingress into the lives and communities of those being punished while swallowing an increasing number of people into the crime and punishment system(s).
>
> (Green 2014: 360)

In times when 'parents expect police or schools to control their children; neighbors expect police to prevent late night noise from people on their street; and citizens expect the courts to resolve disputes' (Clear and Karp 1999: 38), net widening entails more 'formal' social control. Within this conundrum, the state, then, is not rolling away; it is advancing. As Santos warned in his criticism of informal justice:

> Insofar as the state thereby manages to control actions and social relations that cannot be directly regulated by informal law, and insofar as the entire social environment of the dispute is integrated in its processing, to that extent the state is indeed expanding. *And it is expanding through a*

> *process that, on the surface, appears to be a process of retraction*. What appears as *de*legalization is actually *re*legalization. In other words, the state is expanding *in the form of civil society*, and that is why the dichotomy of state and civil society is no longer theoretically useful, if ever it was. And because the state expands in the form of civil society, social control may be exercised in the form of social participation, violence in the form of consensus, class domination in the form of community action. In other words, state power expands through a kind of indirect rule.
>
> (Santos 1982: 262, emphasis in the original)

This all is not to suggest that restorative justice programmes should remain at the margins of the youth justice system as a diversionary tactic – where, surely, it will be incapable of challenging the 'punitive apriorism' and the managerialist tendencies of formal responses to crime. However, it is to suggest that whilst embarking on the ambitious plan of moving to the mainstream, restorative justice programmes need to design a more coherent plan than that of referral orders, and one that is conscious of the risk of giving a 'justicy' flavour to an otherwise truly informal, community-based process. Moreover, as Greene (2013: 385) warns, 'restorative justice actors [and programmes] must steer clear of the errors of the past and commit to not expanding punishment and control'.

7.6 Concluding comments

> [Do you think referral orders are the most restorative orders in the YOT?] Overall I'd say it's the most restorative justice friendly.
>
> (YOT12, WORKER2, emphasis added)

In this chapter, I have been concerned with the question of what lessons can be learned from the English and Welsh experience of youth offender panels, with a view to establishing a more coherent framework for operationalising community involvement in restorative justice programmes. It was felt that a first step in drawing such lessons should be the analysis of the restorativeness of youth offender panels, particularly in what relates to the role of community panel members. In this vein, I have depicted a 'restorative justice *friendly*' process, where YOT workers and community panel members are familiar and repeat restorative justice discourses (such as the idea of giving a voice to the 'victimised community'), but where community panel members do not really play a significant role. I have then moved on to some more specific lessons around the danger of falling into 'theatrical productions', the relationship between lay involvement and the role of professionals, the need to rethink the benefits to community of its involvement in restorative justice programmes, and the risk of giving restorative justice processes a 'justicy' flavour. This, it must be highlighted, was not a rejection of community involvement. As Von

Hirsch (1998: 676) warns, what the restorative justice literature needs is 'not yet greater enthusiasm but more reflection'. This was an attempt at more reflection.

Notes

1 For an explanation about the Headway Project, see Chapter 5.
2 On this very topic, see Crawford and Burden 2005.
3 Greene (2013) quotes are reproduced with kind permission from Taylor & Francis.
4 Although some community panel members expressed in interviews with me that they would be willing to go beyond panel meetings to working with victims (see Chapter 6).
5 Bauman's concept of the 'aesthetic community' reminds me of Maffesoli's (1996) view of 'emotional communities'. As Delanty (2000: 124) writes, 'according to Maffesoli [...], the age of the masses is giving way to new social relationships and as a result we have entered the age of the "tribes". The idea of the tribe suggests for Maffesoli an "emotional community" which is defined by an affectual and aesthetic aura [...] Unlike the communities of the past, which were spatial and fixed, emotional community is unstable and open, a product of the fragmentation of the social and the disintegration of mass culture. People are increasingly finding themselves in temporary networks, or "tribes", organized around lifestyles and images'. As Maffesoli (1996: 76) himself puts it, 'in contrast to the stability induced by classic tribalism, neo-tribalism [or, indeed, the "emotional community"] is characterized by fluidity, occasional gatherings and dispersal'.
6 As argued by Iris Young (1990: 237), '[e]ven many of the most staunch proponents of decentralized community love to show visiting friends around the Boston or San Francisco or New York in or near which they live, climbing up towers to see the glitter of lights and sampling the fare at the best ethnic restaurants'.
7 This is one of the few YOTs where community panel members tend to follow the same case all the way through.
8 GCSE stands for 'General Certificate of Secondary Education'. The GCSE exams are taken by students aged 14–16, in secondary education in England and Wales, and they constitute an important step towards further education and employment.
9 Boyes-Watson (2004) quotes are reproduced with kind permission from the American Society of Criminology.
10 Of course, the involvement of one's community of care may have unintended side effects. For example, in his exploration of the use of restorative justice for hate crimes, Walters (2014: 190) warns against the fact that cultures of prejudice are nurtured within families, friendship circles and by neighbours, and that '[t]his will mean that many offenders' "community of care" will validate their negative views on race, religion, and sexual orientation (and other identities)'. Therefore, my intention here, it should be made clear, is not to paint a notion of 'community of care' in overly benevolent terms, but to point out how youth offender panels have side-lined the importance of involving the offender's community of care.

References

Abel, R.L. (1982) 'The Contradictions of Informal Justice', in R.L. Abel (ed.), *The Politics of Informal Justice*, New York: Academic Press.

Adler, J.R. and Mir, M. (2012) *Evaluation of The Forgiveness Project Within Prisons*, London: Forensic Psychological Services at Middlesex University.

Atkinson, J.M. (1982) 'Understanding Formality: The Categorization and Production of "Formal" Interaction', *British Journal of Sociology*, 33(1): 86–118.

Bauman, Z. (2001) *Community: Seeking Safety in an Insecure World*, Cambridge: Polity.

Bazemore, G. (1998) 'The "Community" in Community Justice: Issues, Themes, and Questions for the New Neighbourhood Sanctioning Models', in D. Karp (ed.), *Community Justice: An Emerging Field*, Lanham, MD: Rowman & Littlefield.

Bolívar, D. (2013) 'For Whom is Restorative Justice?', *Restorative Justice: An International Journal*, 1(2): 190–214.

Bottoms, A. (1995) 'The Philosophy and Politics of Punishment and Sentencing', in C. Clarkson and R. Morgan (eds), *The Politics of Sentencing Reform*, Oxford: Oxford University Press.

Boyes-Watson, C. (2004) 'The Value of Citizen Participation in Restorative/Community Justice: Lessons from Vermont', *Criminology & Public Policy*, 3(4): 687–692.

Clear, T.R. and Karp, D.R. (1999) *The Community Justice Ideal: Preventing Crime and Achieving Justice*, Boulder, CO: Westview Press.

Crawford, A. (1997) *The Local Governance of Crime: Appeals to Community and Partnerships*, Oxford: Oxford University Press.

Crawford, A. (2003) 'In the Hands of the Public?', in G. Johnstone (ed.), *A Restorative Justice Reader: Texts, Sources, Context*, Cullompton: Willan Publishing.

Crawford, A. (2004) 'Involving Lay People in Criminal Justice', *Criminology & Public Policy*, 3(4): 693–702.

Crawford, A. and Burden, T. (2005) *Integrating Victims in Restorative Youth Justice*, Bristol: The Policy Press.

Crawford, A. and Newburn, T. (2003) *Youth Offending and Restorative Justice: Implementing Reform in Youth Justice*, Cullompton: Willan Publishing.

Crow, G. (2002) 'Community Studies: Fifty Years of Theorization', *Sociological Research Online*, 7(3).

Cunneen, C. and Hoyle, C. (2010) *Debating Restorative Justice*, Oxford: Hart Publishing.

Delanty, G. (2000) *Modernity and Postmodernity*, London: SAGE Publications.

Dignan, J. (2005) *Understanding Victims and Restorative Justice*, Maidenhead: Open University Press.

Dzur, A.W. (2008) *Democratic Professionalism: Citizen Participation and the Reconstruction of Professional Ethics, Identity, and Practice*, University Park: Pennsylvania State University Press.

Earle, R. and Newburn, T. (2001) 'Creative Tensions? Young Offenders, Restorative Justice and the Introduction of Referral Orders', *Youth Justice*, 1(3): 3–13.

Etzioni, A. (1995) *The Spirit of Community: Rights, Responsibilities and the Communitarian Agenda*, London: Fontana.

Etzioni, A. (1996) *The New Golden Rule. Community and Morality in a Democratic Society*, New York: Basic Books.

Etzioni, A. (1998) *The Essential Communitarian Reader*, Lanham, MD: Rowman & Littlefield.

Fellegi, B. and Szegó, D. (2013) *Handbook for Facilitating Peacemaking Circles*. www.euforumrj.org/assets/upload/peacemaking_circle_handbook.pdf.

Fennell, G. (1997) 'Local Lives – Distant Ties: Researching Community under Globalized Conditions', in J. Eade (ed.), *Living the Global City: Globalization as a Local Process*, London: Routledge.

Forrest, R. (2009) 'Who Cares about Neighbourhoods?', *International Social Science Journal*, 59(191): 129–141.

Fox, K.J. (2012) 'Redeeming Communities: Restorative Offender Reentry in a Risk-Centric Society', *Victims & Offenders*, 7(1): 97–120.

Fox, K.J. (2014) 'Theorizing Community Integration as Desistance-Promotion', *Criminal Justice and Behavior*, 20(10): 1–13.

Frazer, E. and Lacey, N. (1993) *The Politics of Community: A Feminist Critique of the Liberal-Communitarian Debate*, London: Harvester Wheatsheaf.

Garland, D. (2001) *The Culture of Control: Crime and Social Order in Contemporary Society*, Oxford: Oxford University Press.

Gill, M. and Mawby, R. (1990) *Volunteers in the Criminal Justice System: A Comparative Study of Probation, Police, and Victim Support*, Milton Keynes: Open University Press.

Goldson, B. (2010) 'The Sleep of (Criminological) Reason: Knowledge-Policy Rupture and New Labour's Youth Justice Legacy', *Criminology and Criminal Justice*, 10(2): 155–178.

Gray, P. (2005) 'The Politics of Risk and Young Offenders' Experiences of Social Exclusion and Restorative Justice', *British Journal of Criminology*, 45(6): 938–957.

Gray, P., Moseley, J. and Browning, R. (2003) *An Evaluation of the Plymouth Restorative Justice Programme*, Plymouth: University of Plymouth.

Green, S. (2014) *Crime, Community and Morality*, Abingdon: Routledge.

Greene, D. (2013) 'Repeat Performance: Is Restorative Justice Another Good Reform Gone Bad?', *Contemporary Justice Review*, 16(3): 359–390.

Griffiths, C.T. and Hamilton, R. (1996) 'Sanctioning and Healing: Restorative Justice in Canadian Aboriginal Communities', in B. Galaway and J. Hudson (eds), *Restorative Justice: International Perspectives*, Monsey, NY: Criminal Justice Press.

Hirsch, H.N. (1986) 'The Threnody of Liberalism: Constitutional Liberty and the Renewal of Community', *Political Theory*, 12(3): 423–449.

Home Office (2002) *Referral Orders and Youth Offender Panels: Guidance for Courts, Youth Offending Teams and Youth Offender Panels*, London: Home Office/Lord Chancellor's Department/Youth Justice Board.

Hoyle, C. (2012) 'Victims, the Criminal Process, and Restorative Justice', in M. Maguire, R. Morgan and R. Reiner (eds), *The Oxford Handbook of Criminology*, Oxford: Oxford University Press.

Hoyle, C. and Young, R. (2002) 'Restorative Justice: Assessing the Prospects and Pitfalls', in M. McConville and G. Wilson (eds), *The Handbook of Criminal Justice Process*, Oxford: Oxford University Press.

Hoyle, C., Young, R. and Hill, R. (2002) *Proceed with Caution: An Evaluation of the Thames Valley Police Initiative in Restorative Cautioning*, York: Joseph Rowntree Foundation.

Hudson, B. (2003) 'Victims and Offenders', in A.V. Hirsch, J.V. Roberts, A.E. Bottoms, K. Roach and M. Schiff (eds), *Restorative Justice & Criminal Justice: Competing or Reconcilable Paradigms?* Oxford: Hart Publishing.

Hughes, G. (1996) 'Communitarianism and Law and Order', *Critical Social Policy*, 16 (49): 17–41.

Karp, D. and Drakulich, K. (2004) 'Minor Crime in a Quaint Setting: Practices, Outcomes, and Limits of Vermont Reparative Probation Boards', *Criminology & Public Policy*, 3(4): 655–686.

Kymlicka, W. (2002) *Contemporary Political Philosophy: An Introduction*, 2nd edn, Oxford: Oxford University Press.

London, R. (2011) *Crime, Punishment, and Restorative Justice: From the Margins to the Mainstream*, London: First Forum Press.

Maffesoli, M. (1996) *The Time of the Tribes: The Decline of Individualism in Mass Society*, London: SAGE Publications.

Matthews, R. and Pitts, J. (eds) (2001) *Crime, Disorder and Community Safety*, London: Routledge.

McCold, P. (2000) 'Toward a Holistic Vision of Restorative Juvenile Justice: A Reply to the Maximalist Model', *Contemporary Justice Review*, 3(4): 357–414.

McCold, P. and Wachtel, B. (2003) 'Community is Not a Place: A New Look at Community Justice', in G. Johnstone (ed.), *A Restorative Justice Reader*, Cullompton: Willan Publishing.

Nelken, D. (1985) 'Community Involvement in Crime Control', *Current Legal Problems*, 38: 239–267.

Newburn, T., Crawford, A., Earle, R., Goldie, S., Hale, C., Hallam, A., Masters, G., Netten, A., Saunders, R., Sharpe, K. and Uglow, S. (2002) *The Introduction of Referral Orders into the Youth Justice System: Final Report*, Home Office Research Study 242, London: Home Office.

O'Connell, M. and Hayes, H. (2012) 'Victims, Criminal Justice and Restorative Justice', in H. Hayes and T. Prenzler (eds), *An Introduction to Crime and Criminology*, Frenchs Forest: Pearson Australia.

O'Mahony, D. and Doak, J. (2009) 'Restorative Justice and Youth Justice: Bringing Theory and Practice Closer Together in Europe', in J. Junger-Tas and F. Dünkel (eds), *Reforming Juvenile Justice*, Dordrecht: Springer.

Olson, S.M. and Dzur, A.W. (2003) 'Reconstructing Professional Roles in Restorative Justice Programs', *Utah Law Review*, 57(1): 57–89.

Olson, S. and Dzur, A. (2004) 'Revisiting Informal Justice: Restorative Justice and Democratic Professionalism', *Law & Society Review*, 38(1): 139–176.

Pahl, R. (2000) *On Friendship*, Cambridge: Polity Press.

Pavlich, G. (2005) *Governing Paradoxes of Restorative Justice*, London: Glass House Press.

Pranis, K. (2003) *Peacemaking Circles: From Crime to Community*, St Paul, MN: Living Justice Press.

Quill, D. and Wynne, J. (1993) *Victim & Offender Mediation Handbook*, London: Save the Children.

Richards, K. (2014) 'A Promise and a Possibility: The Limitations of the Traditional Criminal Justice System as an Explanation for the Emergence of Restorative Justice', *Restorative Justice: An International Journal*, 2(2): 124–141.

Roberts, J.V. and Roach, K. (2003) 'Restorative Justice in Canada: From Sentencing Circles to Sentencing Principles', in A.V. Hirsch, J. Roberts, A.E. Bottoms, K. Roach and M. Schiff (eds), *Restorative Justice and Criminal Justice: Competing or Reconcilable Paradigms?* Oxford: Hart Publishing.

Santos, B.d.S. (1982) 'Law and Community: The Changing Nature of State Power in Later Capitalism', in R. Abel (ed.), *The Politics of Informal Justice*, New York: Academic Press.

Shearar, A. and Maxwell, G. (2012) 'Revolution, Decline, and Renewal: Restorative Youth Justice in New Zealand', in E. Zinsstag and I. Vanfraechem (eds),

Conferencing and Restorative Justice: International Practices and Perspectives, Oxford: Oxford University Press.

Sheldon, J.H. (1948) *The Social Medicine of Old Age*, Oxford: Oxford University Press.

Strang, H. (2002) *Repair or Revenge: Victims and Restorative Justice*, Oxford: Oxford University Press.

Strang, H. and Sherman, L.W. (2003) 'Repairing the Harm: Victims and Restorative Justice', *Utah Law Review*, 15(1): 15–42.

Taylor, M. (2011) 'Community Organising and the Big Society: Is Saul Alinsky Turning in his Grave?', *Voluntary Sector Review*, 2: 157–264.

Thompson, J.B. (1996) 'Tradition and Self in a Mediated World', in P. Heelas, S. Lash and P. Morris (eds), *Detraditionalization: Critical Reflections on Authority and Identity*, Oxford: Blackwell.

Von Hirsch, A. (1998) 'Penal Theories', in M. Tonry (ed.), *The Handbook of Crime & Punishment*, New York: Oxford University Press.

Walters, M.A. (2014) *Hate Crime and Restorative Justice: Exploring Causes, Repairing Harm*, Oxford: Oxford University Press.

Weitekamp, E.G.M. (2013) *Developing Peacemaking Circles in a European Context*. www.suggnome.be/pdf/onderzoek/PMC_final_report.pdf.

Wilcox, A. and Hoyle, C. (2002) *Final Report for the Youth Justice Board on the National Evaluation of Restorative Justice Projects*, Oxford: Centre for Criminology, University of Oxford.

Young, I.M. (1990) *Justice and the Politics of Difference*, Princeton, NJ: Princeton University Press.

Young, J. (1999) *The Exclusive Society*, London: SAGE Publications.

Zehr, H. (2002) *Fundamental Principles of Restorative Justice*, Intercourse, PA: Good Books.

Zinsstag, E. (2012) 'Conferencing: A Developing Practice of Restorative Justice', in E. Zinsstag and I. Vanfraechem (eds), *Conferencing and Restorative Justice: International Practices and Perspectives*, Oxford: Oxford University Press.

Conclusions

Motivated by the questions of *why* and *how* the community should be involved in restorative justice practices, the aim of this study was to advance our empirical and theoretical understanding of what 'community involvement' *means* and *what work it does* in restorative justice. For the empirical component of the book, I have used a case study approach to explore the *whys* and *hows* of community involvement in one selected practice of restorative justice: youth offender panels in England and Wales. The experience of youth offender panels, however, instead of providing a coherent framework for operationalising community involvement, suggests what *cannot* be expected from community participation in restorative justice programmes, and what *should be avoided* in realising community involvement. Said differently, this study advances our empirical and theoretical understanding of community in restorative justice's talks and practices, but it does so mainly by suggesting what 'community involvement' *does not* mean and what work it *does not do.*

Summarising the key findings[1]

Whilst making the case for greater public involvement in criminal justice, Crawford (2004: 697, emphasis added) argues that 'the punitive sentiments of public opinion may be the powerless expressions of *a largely impassive audience observing a drama in which they have no role nor for which do they exercise active responsibility over any outcomes*'. It is worth restating here that restorative justice aims to change this traditional way of doing justice by placing the decision of how to deal with a particular offence in the hands of those most directly affected by it: the victim, the offender and the community. That is, in restorative justice processes, instead of 'observing a drama in which they have no role nor for which do they exercise active responsibility over any outcomes', victims, offenders and the community all have an important role to play in putting right the wrongs caused by criminal offences. Indeed, victims should be given the opportunity to be acknowledged and to have a say in how they think their own case should be dealt with. Offenders should be empowered to face the consequences of their actions by making amends to victims and the community. The community should be empowered to help determine a plan of action through which repentant offenders are reaccepted into, rather than rejected by, the community. Indeed, 'for the harm caused by a particular crime to be fully restored not only must the offender accept responsibility; the victim's needs be met but also the community should embrace the offender back into civil society' (Green 2014: 65). In restorative justice processes, thus, the 'community' has at least three interrelated roles to play: 1 it should have a say in what reparation the offender should undergo to restore the victimised community; 2 as the victimised community, it should benefit from this reparation; and 3 it should be able to support the reintegration of offenders into the community as positive, contributing members.

The experience of youth offender panels, however, is a curious one: instead of 'observing a drama in which they have *no* role', community panel members *do have* a role, but *they play the role of 'actors' performing a 'script' that is written and directed by professionals.* Unsurprisingly, while playing their role, the community *still* resembles 'a largely impassive audience observing a drama for which they do not exercise active responsibility over any outcomes'. That is, they take part in the process of conflict resolution, but it is almost as if they did not – or, to put it differently, they 'participate' in the process, but are not truly 'involved'. Indeed, first and foremost, this study shows that community panel members *do not* have a real say in what reparation the offender should undergo, they *do not* clearly benefit from this reparation, and they *do not* support the reintegration of offenders into the community. Youth offender panels have fallen into what I have termed 'theatrical productions' (by 'theatrical' I mean 'rhetorical', or 'artificial'; I do not mean 'overly dramatic').

Apart from the argument that youth offender panels are based on an ill-conceived and inadequate notion of community, and all the criticisms that have been made of the communitarian agenda (see Chapter 7), one could argue that the danger of falling into theatrical productions has also to do with the often-discussed risk of restorative justice initiatives being co-opted by the traditional justice system. In fact, while formulating his abolitionist perspective on criminal justice, Hulsman (1991: 684) maintained that '[...] the cultural organization of criminal justice creates "fictitious individuals", and a "fictitious" interaction between them'. So what may be happening is youth offender panels may be replicating our conventional 'fictitious' (or 'theatrical') way of 'doing justice', and other restorative justice programmes should avoid doing the same.

Within this 'theatrical' context, the experience of youth offender panels suggests that the greater involvement of community members – or, indeed, their changing role from mere witnesses or juries to facilitators – *does not* help to fully incorporate community harm into criminal justice practice. The truth is that, in practice, community panel members rarely bring creative ideas on how these sorts of harms could be repaired by the offender. Quite the contrary, they tend to 'pick' from the YOT's 'dessert menu' – a 'one-size-fits-all' list of reparation programmes. What is more, contrary to Newburn *et al.* (2002), I have *not* found contracts drawing on community resources, and my respondents did not recall any examples of this happening. Indeed, this research shows that contracts tend to draw on YOT ideas *and* YOT resources. As such, and despite the involvement of community members, youth offender panels do *not* provide 'a restorative justice approach *within a community context*' (Ministry of Justice 2009: 7, emphasis added), as the *Guidance* indicates.

The English and Welsh experience also suggests that restorative justice advocates have placed unreasonably high expectations on the benefits of lay involvement, while in this study, none of the assumptions around *lay* involvement (discussed in more detail in Chapter 2) has been confirmed. For example, the experience of youth offender panels suggests that lay members of the community *do not* have better 'local knowledge' than professionals. In fact, my interviews and observations found that *YOT workers* have better 'local knowledge' than community panel members. This should come as no surprise: it is the job of youth workers to know what is available locally to support their 'clients' (i.e. the young people). What is more, one should bear in mind that:

> People do not live in one place for as long as they used to. Anonymity becomes characteristic of mobile urban communities; neighbors cease to be significant others, relatives become geographically separated, even school and church affiliations become more transient, not only because parishioners and students are moving more often, but the teachers and preachers are more mobile as well.
>
> (Braithwaite 1989: 86)

In addition, I have found that some people choose to serve as community panel members in a neighbouring area/town/borough explicitly *to reduce the chances of knowing the young offenders.* This, of course, also reduces the chances of them being 'locals', or possessing 'local knowledge'. Moreover, the experience of youth offender panels reminds us of how difficult it is to recruit and retain a diverse pool of volunteers – that is, one that is truly representative of the 'local' community. In all, one lesson from England and Wales is that restorative justice advocates need to lessen their expectations in relation to the benefits of lay involvement, while recognising the continuing important role of professionals in any restorative justice endeavour. Or, more broadly speaking, as Braithwaite and Strang (2001: 13) rather neatly put it, we should come to see the restorative justice agenda 'not as a choice between civil society and state justice, but as requiring us to seek the most productive synergies between the two'. Indeed, (re)thinking through the role of community in restorative justice programmes entails (re)thinking the role of the State in such processes.

The experience of youth offender panels also suggests that, alone, the involvement of lay members of the community *does not* help to strengthen social ties. On the one hand, in all but one case observed,[2] community panel members had never met the young offender or her 'appropriate person' before the panel meeting, so usually there are no 'social ties' to be strengthened. On the other hand, in only a few YOTs do community panel members tend to follow the same case all the way through: more often than not, the young people and community panel members meet only once during the referral order process. Besides, interviewees (YOT workers and community panel members) often expressed that they think it inappropriate for community panel members to maintain contact with the young people and their family after the process has finished. Indeed, another lesson from this study is that by involving lay members of the community who are *not* acquainted with the offender, restorative justice initiatives will probably only be able to build 'aesthetic communities', where the bonds between participants are to be experienced 'on the spot' and 'not taken home and consumed in the humdrum routine of day after day' (Bauman 2001: 72).

This, I have suggested, is not negative in itself: in times of 'liquid modernity', we enjoy urban life, among other things, because cities are places where people stand and sit together 'without becoming unified in a community of shared final ends' (Young 1990: 240). Indeed, 'Residents' associations; parents' associations; city-centre rate-payers; shopping-mall retailers; shareholders' meetings; women's groups: these are the kinds of collectivities which claim people's allegiances now, rather than [traditional] communities' (Hudson 1998: 251). In other words, '[w]hereas communities were once fixed, immutable and rigid, they are now chosen, changeable and fluid' (Green 2014: 138).

Restorative justice programmes need to accept such contemporary, urban contexts, *but without hindering the possibility for new relationships to emerge.* The challenge, I have argued, is not how to evoke the kind of community that featured in pre-modern societies – for all the reasons discussed before (particularly in Chapter 7), this would be both unfeasible and undesirable. The real challenge is how to make a meeting between strangers a meaningful experience. In this vein, and in the specific case of youth offender panels, community panel members should be encouraged to follow the same young person all the way through her referral order. In fact, I would argue that unless they have reasonable grounds for their absence (e.g. they are ill, or have stopped serving as a panel member in that area), community panel members *should commit* to being present at all meetings arranged for the case. We should remember that this study suggests that community panel members *prefer* to have the opportunity to follow the same case all the way through, and many volunteers expressed that they would like to be doing *more* panel meetings than they are currently doing (see Chapter 5 for more detail). In this context, it is reasonable to expect that they would commit to following the same case through with some enthusiasm. In addition, opportunities should be created for young people to stay in touch with 'their' community panel members, if they wish, after the referral order is finished – for example, through a mentoring project such as that mentioned in Chapter 7 (where young people will be able to meet with their community panel members, even after the process is finished, to work on CV writing and other practical skills).

Staying with the idea of restorative justice processes being able to build only 'aesthetic' communities, I have found that the involvement of lay members of the community in youth offender panels *does not* allow for the creation of informal support systems around offenders (and victims). Indeed, the experience of youth offender panels suggests that it is unrealistic to expect, for example, that community members participating in restorative justice encounters will be able to offer education and/or employment opportunities to youth at risk of further offending. On the one hand, in modern communities, 'reintegration may need to be a much more active and knowledge-driven process than when it was possible to rely on self-contained localities where everyone knew everyone and where to obtain necessary contacts' (Shapland *et al.* 2011: 136). Again, in this context, the continuing important role of professionals needs to be recognised. On the other hand, in times of 'liquid modernity', 'communities of care' are more likely to allow for the creation of informal support systems or safety nets for victims and offenders than people who are *not* acquainted with the victim or the offender. Indeed, youth offender panels should be involving more people *known to the offender* – for example, members of the young person's extended family, school teachers, friends and other people who appear capable of having a good influence on the offender. In fact, I would argue that another lesson from the English and Welsh experience is that instead of relying solely on lay members of the community, while aiming at greater community involvement, restorative justice processes should foster the involvement of the so-called 'community of care'. As has been highlighted in the previous chapter, this does not necessarily entail more *family* involvement, but can mean encouraging the involvement of *friends* – in fact, although the next section will discuss recommendations for future research, I can already state here that it would be interesting to see further research exploring the *role of friendship* in restorative justice.

All in all, as I have argued more extensively in Chapter 7, a key lesson from the experience of youth offender panels is that, while trying to evoke the kind of community that featured in pre-modern societies (or by ignoring the kind of community that features in contemporary, urban contexts), restorative justice programmes run the risk of paying lip service to genuine community involvement. Restorative justice programmes need to start from a more concrete and up-to-date notion of community, otherwise the tendency will be for them to run a 'play', like youth offender panels, where 'community representatives' will pretend to be taking the lead, but where there will be no real transference of responsibilities from professionals to the community. This, of course, is more easily said than done. One should bear in mind that restorative justice is very much about face-to-face encounters in times of 'postmodern cosmopolitanism', where 'our social identities and trajectories are apparently being increasingly shaped by the virtual and remote as opposed to the real and the proximate' (Forrest 2009: 129). This poses great challenges in terms of conceptualising an up-to-date notion of community. Nevertheless, what I have suggested is that a more concrete and up-to-date notion of community involves recognising, all at once: 1 the importance of place (particularly the importance of neighbourhoods); 2 the importance of family links, friendship and other social ties (or, as restorativists would put it, the importance of the 'community of care' of both offenders and victims); 3 and the importance of similar social traits and identities (or, indeed, of similar past experiences, such as that of ex-offenders or ex-drug addicts). As discussed in Chapter 6, the biggest problem related to the role of community in youth offender panels is that they *do not* explore (or develop) any of these three dimensions of community.

Reflection on the limitations of this study and recommendations for future research

One limitation of this study is associated with a natural bias in any research study: because of time and financial constraints, one needs to concentrate on certain aspects of the study. Indeed, there are many other aspects directly or indirectly related to the role of community in restorative justice that I would have liked to have explored, but was unable to. For example, it should be noted that youth offender panels theoretically endorse the vision of a 'Big Society', which became one of the coalition government's key policy programmes in the UK, and a guiding concept in debates about crime and its control (Cabinet Office 2010; Donoghue 2012; Downes and Morgan 2012; Evans 2011; Faulkner and Burnett 2012). A 'Big Society' would be a place 'where people do things for themselves rather than rely on government and public services' (Faulkner and Burnett 2012: 84); or, according to the Conservative manifesto (Conservative Party 2010: 39):

> [...] a society where people come together to solve problems and improve life for themselves and their communities. [It involves] redistributing the power from the state to society; from the centre to local communities; giving people the opportunity to take more control over their lives.

Indeed, when the coalition government was established, in 2010, one of the stated priorities was to 'strengthen civil society by increasing social action, devolving power to communities and opening up public services to a plurality of providers, including the voluntary and community sector' (Fujiwara *et al.* 2013: 3). Great emphasis has been placed on the need to 'foster and support a new culture of voluntarism, philanthropy, and social action'.[3] In fact, in 2011, the UK government published a 'Giving White Paper', 'with commitments to invest over £40 million in volunteering and social action over 2011 and 2012' (Fujiwara *et al.*, 2013: 3). However, as Clamp and Paterson (2011: 22) argue, '[t]he question remains as to both the ability of the coalition to create "big society" from the top-down and the desire of local people and organisations to take on responsibility for things that have traditionally been the domain of national government policy'. Although the 'Big Society' agenda runs quite independently of the national restorative justice agenda, the government's idea of 'giving power to the people' – and the critics' suspicion that the community may not be ready 'to take on responsibility for things that have traditionally been the domain of national government policy' – speaks to many of the same issues raised in this study. Indeed, although youth offender panels were introduced in 2002, nearly a decade before the coalition government was established, it would have been interesting to explore the possible impacts of current 'Big Society' discourses on the functioning of youth offender panels. The relationship between the government's 'Big Society' rhetoric and the involvement of lay volunteers in youth offender panels (and other restorative justice initiatives in the UK[4]), however, would comprise a book in itself. In fact, it would be interesting to see further research unravelling (for example, through elite interviews) the backstage of this relationship – or the prospects for this relationship in the years ahead. Also, if it is true that the 'Big Society' 'is consonant with a pre-existing broad desire to rethink the foundations of a justice system' (Clear 2012: 504), then there are many links to be explored between the logic of a 'Big Society' and the broader ambitions of restorative justice.

This is likely to have relevance beyond the UK context. Indeed, on the one hand, 'many of the policies advanced in the Big Society agenda have been implemented in other countries over the past two decades' (Szreter and Ishkanian 2012: 3; see also Gidron and Bar 2010). On the other hand, the 'Big Society' ideas (and slogan) are generating interest in other countries. This has become apparent, for example, in a recent report by the Australian Centre for Policy Development (CPD), entitled 'Big Society and Australia: How the UK Government is Dismantling the State and What it Means for Australia'.[5]

It is also important to restate my research 'end date': I left the field in June 2013 (although the vast majority of my data was collected by February 2013), and some important events, which may impact on the future of youth offender panels (and the role of community therein), occurred after I left the field. For example, in December 2013, a new Code of Practice for Victims of Crime came into force in the UK, giving victims the right to information about taking part in restorative justice schemes.[6] Also, a few weeks before that, in November 2013, the YJB announced that it plans to distribute around £2 million to the 158 YOTs across England and Wales, as part of a new 'Restorative Justice Development Grant'. According to the YJB's website:

> The development grant will enable YOTs to provide RJ Conference Facilitation (RJCF) training for all staff and advanced training for those

> staff who have already received RJCF training. The advanced-level training, accredited by the Restorative Justice Council, will enable YOTs to provide RJ services to victims of more complex cases, such as violent offences, or where there has been significant trauma.[7]

This grant would be issued in three parts over 2014 and 2015, and still in line with the YJB's website:

> In addition to the advanced RJ training, YOTs will be expected to ensure YOT managers and senior YOT practitioners are trained to utilise RJ practices in the day-to-day running of YOTs, and enable any new volunteer RJ panel members to receive the RJCF training.

As mentioned in the introductory chapter, this grant is part of a larger announcement by the Ministry of Justice that over the next couple of years, around £29 million will be made available for restorative justice. This means that the restorative justice activities in England and Wales, and youth offender panels in particular, may change drastically over the next two or three years. I hope this study helps to shed light upon what needs to be changed in youth offender panels to allow for more meaningful community involvement.

When I asked if she thought the involvement of community members was crucial to referral orders, one YOT worker replied: 'That's the wrong question. The process is the problem. [...] It's not that the panel members cannot contribute, it's that the process is wrong. In fact, *I would keep the community members, and dump the process*' (YOT4, WORKER2, emphasis added). This last sentence has since resonated with me. As argued in Chapter 7, the experience of youth offender panels shows that the introduction of restorative justice initiatives into the heart of a punitive system may jeopardise fundamental restorative values – and among them, that of genuine community involvement in (and ownership over) the process. There are many non-restorative youth justice systems across the world seeking transformation in the light of restorative justice principles, so the experience of youth offender panels will certainly be relevant to other initiatives which, like youth offender panels, may fall into the same mistakes and turn out to be only 'restorative justice *friendly*'. Nevertheless, one cannot ignore that much of what has been said here is deeply embedded in the English and Welsh context: in contemporary crime-control policies in the UK, the reality of the youth justice system in England and Wales, the specificities of the referral order process, and so on. Maybe this YOT worker is right; maybe we should 'keep the community panel members, and dump the referral order process'? Unfortunately, though, this study cannot categorically state that. Indeed, the problems associated with the role of community in restorative justice processes may be more complex than my empirical data convey.

For example, I have stated that the experience of youth offender panels suggests that lay members of the community *do not* have better local knowledge than professionals. This is true. However, maybe the problem is not so much the involvement of lay members of the community in times of 'liquid modernity' (and in urban contexts). Maybe the problem is indeed the referral orders process – how it has been conceived and designed. If youth offender panels were run *in* the community (for example, on the estate where the offender and the victim live), with the offender, the victim and their supporters always present (as a proper restorative meeting), and with local residents of that estate acting as facilitators, maybe these community members would have better local knowledge than professionals. I have not been able to test that, however. The point I want to make is that although I have criticised the referral order process as a whole, and even analysed its restorativeness (something that was not part of my initial plans), this study would also have benefited from a comparative perspective. That is, ideally, I would have liked to have *empirically* explored another restorative justice initiative – for example, a sentencing circle programme – to be able to compare it with youth offender panels. Of course, other researchers have already studied sentencing circles, and I have reflected upon their findings, but these studies tend to focus on the impact of these practices on reoffending, on offender/victim satisfaction and on the overall procedures involved (Pranis 2003, 2005; Stuart 1996, 2001). None of these studies was particularly focused on the role of community. Thus, future research might fruitfully concentrate on other restorative practices, with a focus on the role of community therein, and test, for example, if like youth offender panels they also fall into 'theatrical productions', if the professionals present appear to know more about the community than the community representatives, if people keep in touch after the process is finished, and so on. The hope is that this book will contribute to stimulating interest and research in the role of community in other restorative justice programmes.

Finally, in her recent analysis of the restorative justice movement in the USA, Greene (2013: 375) writes that when restorative activists were asked about future objectives their answers 'centered on expanding the volunteer base, raising more money, and increasing the volume and types of cases. The future was said to be about making more and bigger programs. There was no mention of any other tactics to foster or support movement development'. That is, 'their answers forecasted more of the same'. As Professor Carolyn Hoyle suggests in her kind Foreword, the arguments made within this book are an invitation for others to turn their critical lens upon their own restorative justice initiative and to question themselves: do we really need *more* of the *same*?

Notes

1 A part of this section was first published in F.F. Rosenblatt (2014), 'Community Involvement in Restorative Justice: Lessons from an English and Welsh Case Study

on Youth Offender Panels', *Restorative Justice: An International Journal*, 2(3): 280–301 (Hart Publishing, used by permission of Bloomsbury Publishing Plc).

2 The case, mentioned in Chapter 5, where a panel member ran judo classes attended by the young offender nearly 10 years before.

3 For details about the 'Big Society Agenda', see the transcript of David Cameron's Big Society launch speech in Liverpool, on 19 July 2010: www.gov.uk/government/speeches/big-society-speech.

4 For example, the 'Neighbourhood Resolution Panels' (NRPs), which, as youth offender panels, are supposed to 'involve restorative justice conferences arranged by volunteers' (Morgan 2012: 477; see also Ministry of Justice 2011).

5 The report can be downloaded from the CPD website at: cpd.org.au/wp-content/uploads/2012/05/cpd_big_society-FINAL-WEB-VERSION.pdf.

6 For details, see www.gov.uk/government/publications/the-code-of-practice-for-victims-of-crime.

7 For details, see www.gov.uk/government/news/victims-of-youth-crime-get-greater-access-to-restorative-justice.

References

Bauman, Z. (2001) *Community: Seeking Safety in an Insecure World*, Cambridge: Polity.

Braithwaite, J. (1989) *Crime, Shame, and Reintegration*, Cambridge: Cambridge University Press.

Braithwaite, J. and Strang, H. (2001) 'Introduction: Restorative Justice and Civil Society', in H. Strang and J. Braithwaite (eds), *Restorative Justice and Civil Society*, Cambridge: Cambridge University Press.

Cabinet Office (2010) *Building the Big Society*, London: Cabinet Office.

Clamp, K. and Paterson, C. (2011) 'Rebalancing Criminal Justice: Potentials and Pitfalls for Neighbourhood Justice Panels', *British Journal of Community Justice*, 9(1/2): 21–35.

Clear, T.R. (2012) 'The Big Society in the Context of a Changing Justice System', *Criminology and Criminal Justice*, 12(5): 500–505.

Conservative Party (2010) *Invitation to Join the Government of Britain: The Conservative Manifesto 2010*, London: Conservative Party.

Crawford, A. (2004) 'Involving Lay People in Criminal Justice', *Criminology & Public Policy*, 3(4): 693–702.

Donoghue, J.C. (2012) 'Anti-social Behaviour, Community Engagement and the Judicial Role in England and Wales', *British Journal of Criminology*, 52(3): 591–610.

Downes, D. and Morgan, R. (2012) 'Overtaking on the Left? The Politics of Law and Order in the "Big Society"', in M. Maguire, R. Morgan and R. Reiner (eds), *The Oxford Handbook of Criminology*, 5th edn, Oxford: Oxford University Press.

Evans, K. (2011) '"Big Society" in the UK: A Policy Review', *Children & Society*, 25 (2): 164–171.

Faulkner, D. and Burnett, R. (2012) *Where Next for Criminal Justice?*, Bristol: The Policy Press.

Forrest, R. (2009) 'Who Cares about Neighbourhoods?', *International Social Science Journal*, 59(191): 129–141.

Fujiwara, D., Oroyemi, P. and McKinnon, E. (2013) *Wellbeing and Civil Society: Estimating the Value of Volunteering Using Subjective Wellbeing Data*, London: Cabinet Office.

Gidron, B. and Bar, M. (2010) *Policy Initiatives Towards the Third Sector in International Perspective*, New York: Springer.

Green, S. (2014) *Crime, Community and Morality*, Abingdon: Routledge.

Greene, D. (2013) 'Repeat Performance: Is Restorative Justice Another Good Reform Gone Bad?', *Contemporary Justice Review*, 16(3): 359–390.

Hudson, B. (1998) 'Restorative Justice: The Challenge of Sexual and Racial Violence', *Journal of Law and Society*, 25(2): 237–256.

Hulsman, L. (1991) 'The Abolitionist Case: Alternative Crime Policies', *Israel Law Review*, 25(3–4): 681–709.

Ministry of Justice (2009) *Referral Order Guidance*, London: Ministry of Justice/ Department for Children, Schools and Families/Youth Justice Board.

Ministry of Justice (2011) *Testing Neighbourhood Resolution Panels: A Specification to Inform Expressions of Interest.*

Morgan, R. (2012) 'Crime and Justice in the "Big Society"', *Criminology and Criminal Justice*, 12(5): 463–481.

Newburn, T., Crawford, A., Earle, R., Goldie, S., Hale, C., Hallam, A., Masters, G., Netten, A., Saunders, R., Sharpe, K. and Uglow, S. (2002) *The Introduction of Referral Orders into the Youth Justice System: Final Report*, Home Office Research Study 242, London: Home Office.

Pranis, K. (2003) *Peacemaking Circles: From Crime to Community*, St Paul, MN: Living Justice Press.

Pranis, K. (2005) *The Little Book of Circle Processes*, Intercourse, PA: Good Books.

Shapland, J., Robinson, G. and Sorsby, A. (2011) *Restorative Justice in Practice: Evaluating what Works for Victims and Offenders*, New York: Routledge.

Stuart, B. (1996) 'Circle Sentencing: Turning Swords into Ploughshares', in B. Galaway and J. Hudson (eds), *Restorative Justice: International Perspectives*, Monsey, NY: Criminal Justice Press.

Stuart, B. (2001) 'Guiding Principles for Peacemaking Circles', in G. Bazemore and M. Schiff (eds), *Restorative Community Justice: Repairing Harm and Transforming Communities*, Cincinnati, OH: Anderson Publishing.

Szreter, S. and Ishkanian, A. (2012) 'Introduction: What is Big Society? Contemporary Social Policy in a Historical and Comparative Perspective', in A. Ishkanian and S. Szreter (eds), *The Big Society Debate: A New Agenda for Social Welfare?* Cheltenham: Edward Elgar Publishing.

Young, I.M. (1990) *Justice and the Politics of Difference*, Princeton, NJ: Princeton University Press.

Index

Abel, Richard L. 56, 170
abolitionism 8, 13, 14, 15, 20, 208
Aertsen, Ivo 79
Alper, Benedict S. 60
ASSET (Young Offender Assessment Profile) 95, 96, 97, 98, 109; AssetPlus 125
Atkinson, Paul 88
Australia 70, 180, 213

Bachman, Ronet 83, 84
Bartkowiak, Isabelle 52, 59
Bauman, Zygmunt 1, 184–5, 193, 202
Bazemore, Gordon 7–8, 20, 23
Biermann, Fiona 147
'Big Society' 212–13
Blair, Tony 79
Bolívar, Daniela 57, 188
Boyes-Watson, Carolyn 146, 165, 192, 197–8
Braithwaite, John 8, 22, 51, 209; regulatory pyramid 14; reintegrative shaming 25, 26, 46
Burden, Tom 78, 90, 178–9, 180

Canada 30; Canadian Restorative Justice Consortium 56
case study 2, 66, 74–8; community involvement 66, 77–8; criticism of the case study approach 74–5; empirical aims 78; England and Wales legal system 3; generalization 74–5, 83; young offender 15; youth offender panels in England and Wales 66, 74–7, 83, 207; *see also* methodology
Christie, Nils 15, 44; co-option of RJ (Restorative Justice) into the CJS (Criminal Justice System) 31; coercion 20; 'Conflicts as Property' 16–17, 26, 28, 42, 44; penal abolitionism 13, 31
CJS (Criminal Justice System): punishment-oriented mentality 26–7; restorative justice/CJS relationship 13–14, 19 (co-option of restorative justice into the CJS 9–10, 12, 31, 200, 208); youth offender panel, resemblance to a court room 105, 107, 117, 159, 186, 200
Clamp, Kerry 213
Clear, Todd R. 45, 58, 137–8, 139, 147, 161, 171
Code of Practice for Victims of Crime 213
coercion 12, 19–20
Coffey, Amanda 88
community 52; aesthetic community 184–5, 189, 196, 197, 202, 210, 211; community capacity 58; community justice 137, 147; definition 59–60, 137–8, 171; emotional community 202; *Gemeinschaft*/*Gesellschaft* distinction 60, 61; geography, interdependency and identity 137–8, 139, 189–91, 212; late modernity community 186–9, 193–4, 197, 210, 211, 212; romanticization of community 59, 61, 186, 187, 197; *see also* communitarianism
Community Boards Program, San Francisco 47
community involvement in modern criminal justice 1, 53; citizens as 'partners against crime' 1; community/CJS relationship 43–4; community involvement, limited research on 3; community ownership 156; meaningful community

participation 1, 53, 189, 190; 'non-restorative justice' movements/initiatives 53; types of community involvement 184; *see also* community participation in restorative justice; youth offender panel and community involvement
community of care 49, 128, 139, 189, 192; inclusion in youth offender panels 191, 197–8, 202, 211 (side effects of involvement of 202); offender's community of care 46–7, 191, 198, 202; power of 46–7; victim's community of care 46, 198; *see also* family; friendship
community panel member 106, 116, 123–4, 126, 128; conflict of interests 103, 154, 184; contribution of ideas and resources 129, 130, 134, 135, 152–3, 158, 196, 208–209; decision making 149–52, 196; distrust 106, 126, 196–7; ex-offenders 93, 145–7; following the same case 116, 153, 189, 202, 210; impartiality 103–105; lack of involvement with the young offender 103–105, 120–2, 153–4, 167–8, 184–5, 188–9, 210; over-used panel members 145, 167; participation in the referral order process 149–56, 201; period of service 124, 126; recruitment 92–5, 149, 190 (word of mouth 142–3); role 124–5, 128, 149, 151, 171, 208 (a theatrical production 124, 151, 172, 208); self-perception 130–4; short-comings 105, 118; students 93–5, 141, 143; training 72, 92, 95, 125, 128, 132, 168 (Foundation Programme 95, 125, 168; *Panel Matters* 87, 95, 107, 125; 'top-up' training session 168–9); under-utilisation of 154–6; waiting list 95, 143; YJB 95, 168; YOT 72, 92–5; *see also the entries below for* community panel member; lay volunteer; volunteering
community panel member, professionalisation of 55–6, 124, 125, 136, 166–71, 185; 'blended' YOT culture 165–6, 169–70; dangers of professionalisation 169, 170–1 (managerialism 170); de-professionalisation 17, 56, 58, 171, 185, 195, 199; professional background 160, 193, 195; 'We need to keep it professional' 167–9; *see also* community panel member
community panel member, representativeness 95, 104, 125, 128, 139, 140–9, 194; diversity and representativeness 141, 143–7, 169, 209; 'invisibility' of community panel members 147–9; minority ethnic group 95, 140, 141, 143, 149; 'mix and match' strategy 145, 155; socio-demographic profile of community panel members 140–3, 194; *see also* community panel member
community participation in restorative justice 41–65; community harm 42, 54–5, 132–3, 208; community/restorative justice as inseparable couple 61; empowerment 20–1, 43, 207–208; future research on 54–5, 59, 213, 215; ownership over the restorative justice process 43–4, 156–7, 183; referral order 77, 90–1, 100; roles to play 208; an under-researched topic 41; youth offender panel 77, 90; *see also the entries below for* community participation in restorative justice; community involvement in modern criminal justice; restorative justice; youth offender panel and community involvement
community participation in restorative justice, justification 1, 42–7, 53; community of care, power of 46–7; community should be able to solve its conflicts 43–4; conflicts belong to the community 42–3, 47; lay participation, benefits of 44–5, 55; *see also* community participation in restorative justice; restorative circle; restorative conference
community participation in restorative justice, unclear aspects of 52–9, 60; benefits of community involvement in restorative justice practices 43, 57, 60, 196; dangers of community involvement 57–9, 60 (power imbalance 58–9); lay involvement, benefits and shortcomings 55–6; meaningful community involvement 54–5; *see also* community participation in restorative justice
community participation in restorative justice, ways of 47–52; lay volunteers helping to shape/monitor restoration plans 47, 51–2; lay volunteers serving as mediators 47, 48; local residents helping to shape/monitor restoration

plans 47, 50–1; networks of victims/offenders helping to shape/monitor restoration plans 47, 49–50; *see also* community participation in restorative justice
community reparation 109, 178–9, 183–4; *Guidance* 109; hours and nature of reparation 109; 'local-*local* reparation' 113, 171; shortcomings 118–19; *see also* community service; reparation
community service 20, 53; as act of reparation 23–4, 41, 178
communitarianism 26, 44, 77, 79, 186–7; critiques of 187–8, 197; *see also* Etzioni, Amitai
Conservative–Liberal Democrat coalition government 69, 212–13
Conservative Party 212
corporatism 67
Crawford, Adam 76, 207; community 58, 59, 137, 197; community ownership 156; community reparation 178–9; lay involvement 158; referral order 73; victim participation 180, 181; youth justice system 68, 69, 70; youth offender panel 72, 76–7, 78, 144, 147, 163, 167
CRB (Criminal Records Bureau) check 122, 123
crime: an act that causes harm/criminal harm 23, 28, 30, 42, 180; an offence against the state 16, 26, 42; trivialisation of 12; *see also* restorative justice as response to crime
Crime and Courts Act 2013: 76
Crime and Disorder Act 1998: 68–71, 77; Action Plan Order 70, 78; Reparation Orders 70; restorative justice 68–70
Criminal Justice and Immigration Act 2008: 78–9; referral order 71
criminal justice professional: restorative circle 51; role in restorative justice 45, 47; role of professionals 193–6, 209–210, 211; scepticism on role of 45, 52; *see also* community panel member, professionalisation of; lay volunteer; YOT worker
critical criminology 26, 28–9
Crown Prosecution Service 97

Dandurand, Yvon 79
Delanty, Gerard 202
democracy: participatory democracy 1, 164
Denscombe, Martyn 31, 75, 77–8
distrust 106, 126, 196–7
domestic violence 11, 15
drug-related offence 119, 182; *see also* misuse of alcohol and other substances
Dzur, Albert W. 5, 24, 27, 29, 42, 43, 44–5, 160, 195, 196

Eglash, Albert 31
Erbe, Carsten 43, 44
Etzioni, Amitai 77, 171, 186–7
European Circle of Restorative Educators 11, 31
European Forum for Restorative Justice 11

family 21, 211; offender's family members and supporters 102–103, 139; parents 49, 52, 102, 139, 192; *see also* community of care
family group conference 49, 50, 52, 128; family structure diversity 191; youth offender contract 108
Fattah, Ezzat A. 8
Feeley, Malcolm 67
Feest, Johannes 13
Fellegi, Borbála 192
Fennell, Graham 190
Fitzpatrick, Peter 47
Fox, Kathryn J. 189
Frazer, Elizabeth 187–8
friendship 191–2, 211; *see also* community of care

Garland, David 1, 53
Gavrielides, Theo 13
genocide 6, 7, 13, 15
Gill, Martin 131, 142, 155, 162, 165, 194, 195
Goldson, Barry 68, 69–70, 199
Gray, Patricia 78, 178, 183
Green, Damian 3, 214
Green, Simon 53, 70, 77, 186, 187, 197, 200, 201, 208, 210
Greene, Dana 9–10, 182, 193, 201, 215
Griffiths, Curt T. 79
Guidance 73–4, 77, 92, 97, 98; 2002 *Guidance* 73, 77, 93, 122, 126; 2009 *Guidance* 73, 77, 122, 126; 2012 *Guidance* 73, 74, 77; community panel member 126; community reparation 109, 112; spent conviction 122; youth offender contract 108, 109, 114; *see also* referral order

Headway Project 99, 109, 112, 125–6, 179
health and safety issues 54, 92, 112, 152–3
Hillery, George A. 60
Hirsch, Harry N. 188
Hopkins, Belinda 8, 11
Hough, Mike 148
Hoyle, Carolyn x–xi, 30, 178, 180, 182–3, 215
Hudson, Barbara 28, 55, 210
Hughes, Gordon 186–7
Hulsman, Louk H.C. 208
human rights, violation of 7, 12, 15

incarceration, replaced by restorative justice 14
informal justice 195; criticism 56, 58–9, 200–201
International Institute for Restorative Practices 30, 31
International Network for Research on Restorative Justice 12

Jaccoud, Mylène 52, 59
Johnstone, Gerry: minimalist/maximalist continuum 7, 8, 11, 13

Karp, David R. 45, 137–8, 139, 147, 161, 171
King, Roy 60, 83
Kymlicka, Will 188

Lacey, Nicola 53, 187–8
lay volunteer 55; benefits of lay participation 44–5, 55; helping to shape/monitor restoration plans 47, 51–2; lay involvement and the role of professionals 193–6, 209–210, 211; meaning and value of lay involvement 158–62, 209 (local knowledge 55, 109, 160–1, 193–4, 209, 214–15); RJC Practitioner Quality Mark 56; serving as mediator 47, 48; shortcomings 55–6; transference of responsibility from professionals to lay people 192–3, 211; youth offender panel 77, 116, 123–4, 126, 128; *see also* community panel member; criminal justice professional; volunteering
Legal Aid, Sentencing and Punishment of Offenders Act 2012: 71
Liberal Democrat Party 56, 69
lip service 100, 146, 183, 187, 211
London, Ross 147

Maffesoli, Michel 202
managerialism 67–8, 170, 176, 199, 201
Maruna, Shadd 146
Mawby, Rob 131, 142, 155, 162, 165, 194, 195
McCold, Paul 9, 47, 49, 60, 79
Medawar, Peter Brian 60
mentoring 120, 146, 154, 157, 189, 211
methodology 83–9; confidentiality and anonymity 84, 86; contribution of the research 3, 78; data analysis 87–8 (grounded theory approach 88); data collection x–xi, 83, 84–6; documentary analysis 84, 87; future research 54–5, 59, 213, 215; interviewing xi, 83 (saturation 84–5; semi-structured interviews 84–6); limitations of the study 74–5, 212–15; non-participant observations 84, 86–7; observation of panel meetings 83; research sites 83–4; restorative justice, concept 15; triangulation 75, 84, 85; *see also* case study
Miers, David 28
Ministry of Justice 56, 214
misuse of alcohol and other substances 107, 109, 112, 114, 119; *see also* drug-related offence
Moulton, Abigail 147

NACRO (National Association for the Care and Resettlement of Offenders) 87; *A New Three Rs for Young Offenders* 70
Neighbourhood Watch 53
Nelken, David 184
Nelson, Lizzie 56, 76
New Labour 68–70, 77, 79, 186
new penology 67–8
New Zealand 26, 70, 90
Newburn, Tim 73, 180; victim participation 180, 181; youth justice system 68, 69, 70; youth offender panel 72, 142, 143, 147, 209
Nichols, Lawrence T. 60
NRPs (Neighbourhood Resolution Panels) 216

offender: community/community members in the views of the young offenders 134–7, 158–9; community of

care 46–7, 191, 198, 202 (family members and supporters 102–103, 139); community panel member/young offender lack of involvement 103–105, 120–2, 153–4, 167–8, 184–5, 188–9, 210; empowerment 20–1, 176, 207; label of 29–30; left out of the criminal justice process 29; rehabilitation 28; reintegration into the community 24, 28, 208; restorative justice 28–9; restorative justice and punishment 28; welfare of 107, 163, 169–70, 177, 181, 182; YOT worker, offender focused 169; YOT worker/young offender informal relationship 159, 164, 176–7, 193
Olson, Susan M. 5, 24, 27, 29, 42, 43, 44–5, 160, 195, 196

Pahl, Ray 191–2
Pali, Brunilda 13, 105
Paterson, Craig 213
Paul, Bettina 13
Pelikan, Christa 13, 105
Pitkin, Hanna Fenichel 144, 145
Powers of Criminal Courts (Sentencing) Act 2000: 71, 72
Pratt, John 67
punishment: CJS, punishment-oriented mentality 26–7; from punitive retribution to restoration 23, 26; populist punitiveness 68, 199; restorative justice as alternative to punishment 14, 28, 201; youth justice in England and Wales 67

reconciliation 24, 25
referral order 15; community involvement 77, 90–1, 100; a compulsory sentence 71; Criminal Justice and Immigration Act 2008: 71; criticism 74, 198–9, 214–15; description 71–2; discharge of 117–18; discretionary referral order 71; Home Office evaluation of the pilot areas 78; pilots and the national rollout of 73; referral order interview 95–7; repeated use of 71, 73, 74, 122, 123; restorative justice approach 3, 76, 119, 125, 199–200; Youth Justice and Criminal Evidence Act 1999: 71–2, 73; youth offender panel 72; *see also Guidance*; youth offender panel
rehabilitation 9, 28, 70, 178
reoffending: prevention of reoffending programme 109; reduction of, and restorative justice 25–6, 46; repeated referral order 71, 73, 74, 122, 123; youth offender contract 109
reparation: as aim of restorative justice 22–6, 30, 178; 'blanket-reparation' programme 178–9; from punitive retribution to restoration 23, 26; imposition of 24, 178; 'personalised' reparation 178; types of action 23, 70, 178 (community service 23–4, 41, 178; letter of explanation or apology 109, 111, 112, 156, 178, 183); victim 27; youth offender panel 177–9; *see also* community reparation
reparative board 51–2, 128
restorative circle 21–2, 46, 50–1, 52, 128, 190; criminal justice professional 51; *see also* community participation in restorative justice
restorative conference 21–2, 46, 55, 180; family group conference 49, 52; *see also* community participation in restorative justice
restorative justice: academy 5, 31; budget for 3, 213–14; campaign for 5–6; concept 6–7, 11, 12, 13, 15, 17, 30, 207; criticism 12, 54; fully restorative model 24–5, 184, 208; lack of explicit theoretical foundation 26; 'purist' model of 18, 22; restorative city/county 6, 30–1; restorative justice literature 1, 53–4 (referral orders and youth offender panels 76, 78); social transformation 5–6, 198; *see also the entries below for* restorative justice; community participation in restorative justice; youth offender panel
restorative justice, attributes 15–30, 196, 212; 'by-products' 24–5 (forgiveness 24, 25; reconciliation 24, 25; remorse 24, 25); cooperativeness and voluntariness 19–20, 21; deprofessionalisation 56, 58, 171, 185, 199; empowerment 20–1, 30, 176, 179, 207–208; inclusiveness 17–18, 30, 176; informality 18–19, 21, 30, 176; offender's reintegration into the community 24; a process and an outcome 17–18, 30, 178; reparation as aim of 22–6, 30, 178; restoring broken communities 184, 196; returning the conflict to those most affected by

crime 16–17; victim aware, not victim centred 26–30, 180; *see also* restorative justice
restorative justice and non-criminalisable matters 9–10; restorative practices/ restorative approaches 10; schools 6, 7, 8, 9, 10–11; *see also* restorative justice
restorative justice as response to crime 6–15, 30, 31; coercion 12, 19–20 (minimal coercion 19); confined to low-level crime 11–12; incarceration, replaced by restorative justice 14; minimalist/maximalist spectrum 7–9; reduction of reoffending 25–6, 46; referral order, restorative justice approach 3, 76, 119, 125, 199–200; restorative justice as alternative to punishment 14, 28, 201; restorative justice/CJS relationship 13–14, 19 (co-option of restorative justice into the CJS 9–10, 12, 31, 200, 208); restorative justice in most serious cases 12; truth commissions and peace committees 12–13; *see also* referral order; restorative justice; youth offender panel
restorative justice, lessons from the English and Welsh experience 185–201; benefits to community 196–8, 201; community of care, rarely included in youth offender panels 191, 197–8; danger of falling into 'theatrical productions' 186–93, 201 (autonomous volunteering 192–3; community as a 'place' 189–91; diversity of family structure 191; friendship 191–2; need of a modernised conception of community 186–9, 197); lay involvement and the role of professionals 193–6, 201, 209–210, 211; risk of giving restorative processes a 'justicy' flavour 198–201 (co-option of restorative justice into the CJS 200; net widening 200–201); *see also* restorative justice
RJC (Restorative Justice Council) 56, 76
RJCF (Restorative Justice Conference Facilitation) training 213–14
Roberts, Julian V. 148
Roche, Delcan 8–9
RSQM (Restorative Justice Quality Mark) 56

Santos, Boaventura de Sousa 59, 160, 200–201
Scaled Approach 97–8, 114
Schutt, Russell K. 83, 84
Scottish Children's Hearings system 90
sexual offences 11, 146
Sheldon, Joseph Harold 190
Simon, Jonathan 67
social control 12, 43, 58, 59, 186, 200, 201; benefits of informal over formal social control 45, 55
social transformation 25, 198
spent conviction 87, 122–3, 126
state 209; crime as an offence against the state 16, 26, 42; limitations to control crime 1, 52; net widening 200–201; responsibilisation strategy 53
Strang, Heather 11–12, 26, 51, 209
Straw, Jack 79
Sullivan, Dennis 15, 58
Szegó, Dóra 192

Tifft, Larry 15, 58
Tönnies, Ferdinand 60, 61
Tyler, Tom 18, 26

UNODC (United Nations Office on Drugs and Crime): *Handbook on Restorative Justice Programmes* 76, 79
USA (United States of America) 200; deinstitutionalisation of state mental hospitals 58; reparative board 51–2, 128; youth justice system 68

Van Ness, Daniel 79
Vermont Reparative Boards 51–2, 76, 146, 165, 197; CoSAs 189
victim 9; community involvement/victim participation tension 181; community of care 46, 198; empowerment 20–1, 179, 207; left out of the criminal justice process 26–7, 179; mass victimisation 6, 12; participation in the criminal justice process 28, 180–3 (attendance to restorative justice processes 180); re-victimisation/ secondary victimisation 11, 19, 179; restoration 27; restorative justice 27–8 (benefit to victim 28; victim aware, not victim centred 26–30, 180); victim awareness 111, 114, 156, 178, 180, 181, 183; victim restitution 20; victim safety 11; victim/victimhood 29–30 (a heavily politicised figure 29; a socially

constructed label 29); victims' rights 27; victims' rights movements 26, 27; victimisation 20; victimised community 132; youth offender panel attendee 102, 107, 126, 178, 179; youth offender panel, disregard for victims 179–83
victim–offender mediation programme 48, 49–50, 52, 104, 128
volunteering 72, 129, 131, 135, 162–6, 171; adults' views on voluntary status of community panel members 162–3; autonomous volunteering 192–3; under-utilisation of 154–5; unpaid volunteer 162–3, 166; unrepresentativeness of the general public 142, 194; value of 164–6, 192; volunteer coordinator 195; young people's views on community panel members' voluntary role 129, 163–4; *see also* community panel member; lay volunteer; volunteering, categories
volunteering, categories 131; agency-directed 131; career-directed 131, 143, 198; drift 131–2, 143; other-directed 131; religious-based 131; self-directed 131; *see also* volunteering
Von Hirsch, Andrew 201–202

Wachtel, Ted 30, 60
Walgrave, Lode 5, 9, 10, 11, 17, 20, 23, 31, 169; community 59–60; community and restorative justice 42, 55; formalization 19; minimalist end of restorative justice 7–8, 12, 31
Walters, Mark Austin 202
Weisberg, Robert 58, 59, 60
Weitekamp, Elmar G. M. 13, 14
welfare 67; offender's welfare 107, 163, 169–70, 177, 181, 182
White Paper: 'Giving White Paper' 212–13; *No More Excuses* 69, 70, 77, 120
Wilcox, Aidan 178
Willmott, Peter 171
Wincup, Emmma 60, 83, 87
Woolford, Andrew 29
Wright, Martin 8, 9, 12, 79

YCS (Youth Conferencing Service, Northern Ireland) 146
YJB (Youth Justice Board for England and Wales) 69–70, 213–14; Crime and Disorder Act 1998: 69; role 69; training programmes 95, 168
YJILS (Youth Justice Interactive Learning Space) 125
YOS (Youth Offending Service) 78, 111, 147, 148, 163
YOT (Youth Offending Team) 69–70, 87, 95, 168, 213, 214; Crime and Disorder Act 1998: 69; England and Wales 83–3, 88; generally unknown 148; *Guidance* 72; literature on 78; RJCF training 213–14; staff, lack of 118–19, 152; youth offender panel (recruitment and training 72, 92–5, 142–3, 149; YOT based 183); Youth Offending Service 78; *see also* YOT worker
YOT worker 102, 105, 143; advisory role 90, 92, 105, 124, 161; caseworker 105, 114, 115, 116, 118, 149–50; community/community members in the views of 129–30; ideas and resources 152, 196, 208–209; leading role 91, 92, 124, 150, 152, 153–4, 156–7, 208; local knowledge 55, 161, 193–4, 209, 214–15; offender focused 169; representativeness of the community 194; role of professionals 193–6, 209–210, 211; shortcomings 105, 118–19; YOT worker/young offender informal relationship 159, 164, 176–7, 193; youth offender contract 110, 112–13, 151–2, 156; *see also* criminal justice professional
Young, Iris 166, 202
Young, Richard 182–3
Youth Court 69, 70, 85
Youth Justice and Criminal Evidence Act 1999: 66, 71–4; referral order 71–2, 73; restorative justice 71; youth offender panel 71, 72–3
youth justice system 68, 69, 70; American-inspired policies 68; history of youth justice in England and Wales 67–8; restorative justice 66
youth offender contract 72–3, 90, 92, 97; announcement of 108; changes 117; community involvement 110, 112–13, 125, 128; compliance/non-compliance 115, 117; contract 'negotiations' 107–114, 176; *Guidance* 108, 109, 114; health and safety issues 92, 112, 152–3; main elements 109 (prevention of reoffending programme 109; reparation to the victim or community 109); panel report 96, 98–9, 124, 125, 149–

50, 156 (report/contract similarities 110, 111, 152, 176); reoffending 109; reparation element 119, 125; 'sign-off' letter/'certificate of completion' 120, 126; YOT worker 110, 112–13, 151–2, 156; young offender's involvement 108–109, 125, 149–52, 176

youth offender panel 90–127; case study: youth offender panels in England and Wales 66, 74–7, 83, 207; definition 72; hybridity 76–7, 104–105, 128; informality 107, 136, 171; literature on 78; purpose of 90; referral order 72; reparation 177–9; resemblance to a court room 105, 107, 117, 159, 186, 200; responsibility, reparation and reintegration principles 66, 72, 75, 178; restorative justice approach 75–7, 102, 115, 119, 125, 199–200, 209; role 90; a theatrical production 124, 151, 172, 187, 192–3, 208; venues for 100–102, 183 (community venue 100–102; YOT premises 101); Youth Justice and Criminal Evidence Act 1999: 71, 72–3; *see also the entries below for* youth offender panel; community panel member; youth offender contract

youth offender panel, assessment of restorativeness 175–85, 186, 201, 209; aiming at reparation 177–9, 183; community based 183–5; inclusiveness, informality and empowerment 175–7; victim awareness 179–83; *see also* youth offender panel

youth offender panel attendee 72, 77, 90, 102–106, 192; appropriate person 72, 96, 102, 192; offender's family members and supporters 102–103, 139; victim/representative of 102, 107, 126, 178, 179; *see also* youth offender panel

youth offender panel and community involvement 77, 90–1, 104–105, 129–71; artificiality of the role of community 91, 92, 125, 172, 182, 185, 192–3; case study 66, 77–8; community as 'a place' and community panel members as 'the public' 130, 134, 137–40, 189–91 (geography, interdependency and identity 137–9); community/community members in the views of YOT workers 129–30; community/community members in the views of the young offenders 134–7, 158–9; community involvement/victim participation tension 181; community of care 191, 197–8, 202, 211 (side effects of involvement of 202); community venue 100–102, 138; inadequate notion of community 186–8, 197, 208, 210, 211; passive conception of community involvement 156–7; rhetorical ownership 156–7, 183; victimised community 132; youth offender contract 110, 112–13, 125, 128; *see also* community involvement in modern criminal justice; community panel member; community panel member, representativeness; community participation in restorative justice; volunteering; youth offender panel

youth offender panel, process 95–123; breach panel meeting 114, 115, 117; continuity beyond the period of the contract 120–2, 184, 210, 211; contract 'negotiations' 107–114; final panel meeting 117–23; initial panel meeting 100–14; layout of the meeting 107; non-attendance dilemma 106, 119–20; pre-panel meeting 100; referral order discharge 117–18, 119, 125; referring the offender back to court 117, 118, 159, 177; 'restorative questions' 107, 125; review panel meeting 106, 114–17; spent conviction 122; victim-focused 107; young offender's involvement 108; young person's first meeting/referral order interview 95–7, 108; *see also* youth offender panel

youth offender panel report 96, 97–100, 115, 124; availability to community members 99–100, 115; Scaled Approach 97–8; youth offender contract 96, 98–9, 124, 125, 149–50, 156 (report/contract similarities 110, 111, 152, 176); *see also* youth offender panel

YRO (Youth Rehabilitation Order) 78–9; standard community sentence 79

Zedner, Lucia 53

Zehr, Howard 5, 23

Zwelethemba model 105

For Product Safety Concerns and Information please contact our EU representative GPSR@taylorandfrancis.com
Taylor & Francis Verlag GmbH, Kaufingerstraße 24, 80331 München, Germany

www.ingramcontent.com/pod-product-compliance
Ingram Content Group UK Ltd.
Pitfield, Milton Keynes, MK11 3LW, UK
UKHW011004180926
475701UK00004B/560
* 9 7 8 1 1 3 8 2 8 8 7 0 6 *